THE

HUDSON VALLEY

THE FIRST 250 MILLION YEARS

ALSO BY DAVID LEVINE

Life on the Rim
In the Land of Giants (with Tyrone "Muggsy" Bogues)
The Chicago Bulls: The Best Ever
Head-to-Head Football: Troy Aikman and Steve Young

THE
HUDSON VALLEY

THE FIRST 250 MILLION YEARS

A MOSTLY CHRONOLOGICAL AND OCCASIONALLY PERSONAL HISTORY

DAVID LEVINE

Globe
Pequot

Essex, Connecticut

To Kimberly and Grace
Always and all ways

Globe
Pequot

An imprint of Globe Pequot, the trade division of
The Rowman & Littlefield Publishing Group, Inc.
4501 Forbes Blvd., Ste. 200
Lanham, MD 20706
www.rowman.com

Distributed by NATIONAL BOOK NETWORK

British Library Cataloguing in Publication Information available

Library of Congress Cataloging-in-Publication Data available

ISBN 978-1-4930-4789-5 (hardback)
ISBN 978-1-4930-7316-0 (paperback)
ISBN 978-1-4930-4790-1 (e-book)

♾™ The paper used in this publication meets the minimum requirements of American National
Standard for Information Sciences—Permanence of Paper for Printed Library Materials, ANSI/
NISO Z39.48-1992

Contents

Contents

Introduction

I began writing for *Hudson Valley Magazine* in 2007; three years later, then editor Olivia Abel told me the magazine was starting a regular history column and asked if I would like to write it. I said yes, because, well, I am a freelancer and therefore must always say yes to every job that pays. Some yeses are better than others, of course, and this yes turned out to be one of my best.

The Hudson Valley is as historic a region as any in the United States. I didn't realize this when I started. I am not from the area originally. I knew it was a special place—I have lived in the Albany area for thirty-odd years (some of them very odd), and in our salad days, my wife, Kimberly, and I took frequent day trips and weekenders down the valley to visit the historic homes, eat at funky restaurants, and stay at cool, one-of-a-kind places like Mohonk Mountain House. But even with all that touristing, I had no idea what has been going on here for such a long, long time.

Over the past decade, I have learned. Beginning with that first assignment, about the nature writer John Burroughs, and continuing through the most recent article to make this book's deadline, about Alexander Hamilton's valley days, I have had the great pleasure of immersing myself in 250 million years of Hudson Valley history. From the dinosaurs that left their fossilized tracks here to the glaciers that carved its lakes and shaped its hills, from the First Peoples to first contact, from colonial rule to independence, from the slave trade to the Civil War, from the birth of a modern nation to the happy rise of craft beer and farm-to-table dining, the Hudson Valley has quite a story to tell.

Stories, in fact. All the stories here were first published in *Hudson Valley*, its sister publication *Westchester*, and the former Amtrak travel magazine *Arrive* between 2010 and 2019. Thanks are therefore due to the editors, past and present, of those magazines—Olivia Abel, Polly Sparling, Kate Walsh, Robert Schork, Amy Partridge, Leigh Flayton, and Jeff Ficker—and to all the others listed on those mastheads who helped polish these stories into their first published form. Some have been revised and edited for this book, but the bones were set by these skillful wordsmiths.

Thanks are also due—past due, really—to all the people who were interviewed for these stories. I am not a historian. They are. To every person I spoke with who works (or worked—some of these sources may no longer be at their ascribed posts) at a Hudson Valley town or county historical society, a historic home or museum, a library or college or institute, or simply as an obsessive, self-motivated history buff, thank you for doing the legwork that makes these stories stand up. My greatest hope is that I have told them accurately enough for you to forgive the small mistakes that I have surely made but only you will notice.

I also wish to thank my editor, Amy Lyons, copy editor extraordinaire Jennifer Kelland, production ringleader Kristen Mellitt, and everyone at Globe Pequot for agreeing to publish these stories in book form and producing this edition. More gratitude to the David Black Literary Agency, which has represented me since David and I met for drinks as young lions sometime during the second Reagan term and forged a handshake agreement that still holds, even though it has been twenty-five years since we last published anything together. "Once we dance, we always dance," David told me, and I am grateful to have him as a dance partner. On this particular pas-de-deux, his able associate, Matt Belford, cut in and led. Thank you, Matt.

Finally, I am thrilled to be able to dedicate a book to Kimberly—I told you I might someday—and my daughter, Grace. They have weathered the ups and downs of a freelance writer's life with nothing but love and support, and this is my small token of appreciation in return. To my girls.

Part 1:
Living in the Past

Jurassic Parkchester

Imagining Life in the Hudson Valley during the Age of the Dinosaurs

The midday sun, directly over the equatorial region of the great land mass Pangea, sears the warm and forbidding land. A creature leaves the herd and scurries across the edge of a marsh to find cover behind a fern. She waits, perched on three birdlike toes supporting her hind legs. She is not a bird, though; she is a lizard who stands about three feet tall at the hips but, leaning forward, spans nearly ten feet from nose to tail. She is looking to add to her forty-pound frame. She is looking for lunch.

Other beasts are grazing nearby, on the fruit and leaves of the cycads and other tropical plants that forest the region. But our creature wants meat. When a small, furry animal, rodent-ish but not rodent, pops out of its nest, she snaps it up in her long, powerful jaws, crunches it easily, and speeds off gracefully to rejoin the herd, leaving behind nothing but footprints in that marshy mud slowly drying under the deep sky, which is growing fantastically orange and red behind the setting afternoon sun.

More than 200 million years later, those very footprints—or at least some like them—will be found thousands of miles in latitude and longitude away, in an unexpected place, in a world unfathomably different from that in which they were left: Nyack Beach State Park, in Haverstraw, Rockland County, New York. These tracks and the relatively few other clues left in our geologic neighborhood from the Mesozoic Era tell us what the lower Hudson Valley was like during the age of the dinosaurs.

The first dinosaur fossils found in New York State, these footprints were discovered in 1972. Imprinted in slabs of rock that now belong to the New York State Museum in Albany, the footprints belong to a type of lizard known as a Grallator. Our beast was probably *Coelophysis*, a slender, bipedal carnivore that lived throughout the East Coast of what we call North America. It's also found in other parts of the world, because back then there was no North

America. There was no New York, no Hudson River, no Rockland County. There was only Pangea.

Triassic Tarrytown

Two hundred forty-eight million years is, when you think about it, unthinkable. As a species, we humans haven't made it anywhere close to 1 million years yet. The land on which we now live has drifted and changed, been uplifted, folded, submerged, frozen and melted countless times since the Mesozoic Era began those 248 million years ago. At the beginning of that time, called the Triassic period, the continents were all connected and stretched from pole to pole. Determined creatures could cover the entire land mass of Earth—and they did, which is why similar fossils are found in Nyack, Mongolia, and Australia.

Our region, though, is rather fossil-poor. Substrata of dirt and rocks from large portions of the Mesozoic simply don't exist in the lower Hudson Valley because of all that drifting, uplifting, folding, and submerging. Better records of our dinosaur past have been found in Connecticut and New Jersey and down the eastern seaboard, though, and scientists believe we can infer that, if those forms of life lived in Hartford or Newark or Baltimore, they likely lived in White Plains too.

If, back then, someone had put a GPS transponder at the future location of, say, the Westchester Mall, it would have pinged at about ten degrees north latitude, the same parallel as Costa Rica. We can't know what longitude, but it was probably somewhere in the middle of what is now the Atlantic Ocean, except there was no Atlantic Ocean, only Pangea and a great global ocean called Panthalassa. North America and Eurasia were mashed together, and that mashing had created enormous mountain ranges where they collided—what is now Connecticut, in fact, boasted peaks as high as Mount Everest, and the Ramapo Mountains were in fact legitimate mountains back then. That the highest point in Westchester today is 980 feet and that Connecticut is now known for its lovely, gentle, rolling hills shows what 200 million years of weathering can do.

The climate was much warmer, with no polar ice and higher sea levels. At the beginning of the era, life was limited. The Earth had just come out of the Permian Extinction, the largest mass extinction known. For unclear reasons, more than 90 percent of the planet's life forms vanished. It took much of the Triassic, which lasted about 50 million years, for life to return.

It was during this time that the continents began to pull apart; in our neck of the woods, that occurred somewhere along the New Jersey Turnpike.

Rift valleys ran all the way from Greenland to South America, and as North America pulled away, a rift formed that came to be called the Newark Basin. "The center was somewhere near the New Jersey–Pennsylvania border," says Paul Olsen, the man who found those dinosaur tracks at Nyack Beach, now the Storke Professor of Earth and Environmental Sciences at Columbia University. "There would have been a broad lake in Rockland-Westchester, running south to Maryland and Virginia. Westchester would probably have been on its eastern shore." As a basin, our land would periodically fill and drain. "It would have been a mud flat, with fringe vegetation, surrounded by islands," Olsen says.

Over the next 50,000 millennia, continental separation continued. The atmosphere contained carbon dioxide at concentrations two to three times as high as they are now. But that was just fine for the few small dinosaurs, other reptiles similar to crocodiles called *phytosaurs*, and, in Olsen's precise scientific phrasing, "many bizarre creatures" that came to inhabit the lands. Plants like cycads, conifers, and horsetail rushes grew abundantly, but there were no flowering plants—or bees or butterflies to pollinate them—just yet. Though no insect remains have been found near here, many that look very much like modern flies, beetles, bugs, and dragonflies have been found in North Carolina. Our earliest ancestors were here as well. These creatures, called *synapsids*, are also known as "mammal-like lizards," which means they are "not like anything we can compare [them] to," Carl Mehling, a senior scientific assistant in the Division of Paleontology at the American Museum of Natural History, says. "They were quadrupeds, but probably had no fur."

The skies were populated as well by creatures like *Icarosaurus*, a small lizard that could glide using "wings"—elongated ribs covered with skin and shaped like an airplane wing to create lift. (The only known *Icarosaurus* fossil skeleton was found in North Bergen, New Jersey.) The waters were home to lots of fishy creatures—"the most common were the coelacanths, related to gars, and others like sturgeons and clams," Olsen says. "But be careful. Croc-like *phytosaurs* would leap out of the water and grab you," he warns. They likely feasted on small, gopher- or shrew-like early mammals or on the larger dicynodont, "a Volkswagen-shaped mammal that was probably dumb as a brick," he says.

Jurassic Jefferson Valley

Another mass extinction about 206 million years ago killed off half of all land species, ended the Triassic period, and launched the Jurassic. The leading explanation for this, Olsen says, is massive explosions of lava from fissures in the Earth that buried about 11 million square kilometers. "We were covered in lava, from France to South America," he says, because the lands were still very close together. Carbon dioxide and sulfur gases were doubled, which likely was the real cause of the extinctions. The gas and smoke from these eruptions probably caused some spectacular sunsets, Olsen says. The Hudson Valley, along with the rest of planet Earth, was no place to be back then, unless you were a dinosaur.

"Mesozoic" means "middle animal," and for the next 150 million years or so, dinosaurs thrived. The climate was hot and dry at first, then warm and moist. More and bigger dinosaurs roamed the planet, and a few, like pterosaurs and archaeopteryxes, the first dinosaur-like birds, filled the skies. *Therapods*, fierce and superb hunters, seemed to like our location, as evidenced by the hundreds of footprints and trackways found in what is now Walter Kidde Park in Roseland, New Jersey, west of Newark, and in Rocky Hill, Connecticut, near Hartford, where they are now visible again, at Dinosaur State Park.

Most scientists think that the track makers there were similar in size and shape to *Dilophosaurus*, a twenty-foot long, half-ton beast, says Meg Enkler, environmental education coordinator at the park. "There was a large lake here, surrounded by mudflat—ideal conditions to preserve footprints—with high mountains to the east and west," she says. "We have mammal tracks from rodent-type creatures, ginkos, magnolias, different and unusual conifers, but no flowers yet."

The lake and others like it up and down our eastern shore were caused by the continued rifting of North America from Africa. "The rift basins just got bigger and bigger, would rupture, be covered with lava, then sink," Olsen says. "And the sea crept in." We were underwater for long periods. By the middle of the Jurassic the Atlantic Ocean began to take form, and by the end, 145 million years ago, it was hundreds of miles wide.

By now, we are up to about twenty-five degrees north latitude—where the Florida Keys currently bask. The Ramapos were still real mountains and may have produced rain, but otherwise the area was mostly arid. With more rifting during the Jurassic and greater intrusion of the ocean, and with the continental drift north through the subtropics, the landscape would have picked up a greater amount of conifer and fern forest, says Keith Landa, director of the Teaching, Learning, and Technology Center at State University of New York–Purchase College. "Shallow tropical seas in the region would have helped make a 'nicer' climate. On the other hand, the episodes of volcanic activity in the area due to the rifting would have resulted in periods of pretty nasty conditions." The lava flowing out of fissures extended throughout the length of the rift valleys, with the release of carbon dioxide, steam, sulfur dioxide, and other noxious gasses. "These episodes would have had a major impact on regional habitability," Landa says, and not in a good way. In Connecticut, three major episodes of volcanisms during the Mesozoic Era have been discovered.

Other creatures of the time discovered in our region include three prosauropod dinosaur skeletons from the Early Jurassic that were found in Manchester, Connecticut. These plant eaters, some of the largest dinosaurs of their day, were up to thirty feet long from tiny head to tail and could rise up on hind legs to munch on leaves and fruits thirteen feet above the ground.

Cretaceous Catskill

The third Mesozoic period, the Cretaceous, lasted from 146 million to 65 million years ago. This was the golden age of dinosaurs; nearly half of all the dinosaurs we know about lived during the last 15 million years of the Cretaceous period.

Pangea has broken into two large continents, and we are drifting toward our current global destination. The land is lower, and the seas are encroaching on the region of Westchester and Rockland. "Most of the time it's underwater or on the shoreline," Olsen says. No sediments from this period have been found in the area, but our neighbors give clues to what it was probably like.

In fact, the first nearly complete dinosaur skeleton in the world was found in Haddonfield, New Jersey, in the 1850s. Sediments from the Cretaceous period revealed a 75-million-year-old fossil of a *Hadrosaurus foulkii*, the first-known duck-billed dinosaur and the species that has since yielded the most plentiful dinosaur finds from this period on the East Coast. Hadrosaurs had long tails to balance the fronts of their bodies as they sped across the land at speeds of ten miles an hour up to—when being chased by a hungry adversary—perhaps thirty miles an hour. (In 1991, Hadrosaurus was named the official New Jersey state dinosaur.) Ellisdale, New Jersey, has also produced numerous late Cretaceous fossils, including specimens of giant dinosaurs like *Dryptosaurus*, a tyrannosaur six feet tall at the hip that may be a cousin of the fearsome T. rex; *Hypsibema*, which had about 1,000 small teeth, weighed up to four tons, and spanned thirty-plus feet from duck-billed head to tail; and even body-armored dinosaurs with clubs on their tails. Out in the growing ocean, giant marine lizards with long necks prowled the shores. "They looked like the Loch Ness monster," Mehling says. There were crocs off the coast of New Jersey that looked like they do today. "And," Olsen adds, "a giant turtle called *Archelon* lived around here, the largest sea turtle ever documented, sixteen feet wide from flipper to flipper."

During the 80 million years that the Cretaceous period lasted—longer than the time between its end and today—temperatures were higher than ever before or since, then cooled somewhat toward the end of the era. By about 65 million years ago, most of the continents were separated; India was drifting at sea, though Australia was still part of Antarctica, which was forested rather than frozen and well populated by the creatures of "middle life." While more volcanic eruptions were poisoning the atmosphere and making things difficult, all in all, life was good. Until it wasn't.

The End of an Era

The midday sun, low in the sky as the temperate land mass known as North America settles into winter, gently warms the subtropical landscape. A menagerie of strange beasts on the ground, in the water, and in the air live harmoniously, as they have for 180 million years.

A streak of light glows faintly in the firmament, then grows brighter, then impossibly bright. The creatures raise their scaly or thorny or furry or feathered heads in wonder. The streak arcs across the sky. Sonic booms shake the land. The streak disappears over the horizon. Then, the entire planet shudders and quakes and rends apart. Firestorms engulf the globe. Tsunamis flood every coast on Earth, including the northeastern coast of our continent, and drown everything for hundreds of miles inland. Acid rain burns the landscape, and layers of sediment containing iridium, a rare metal on Earth but common in meteorites, covers the ground from pole to pole. Darkness from this "impact winter" cloaks the globe, and within mere geologic moments, three-fourths of all life, including virtually every living thing over about

When Is a Dinosaur Not a Dinosaur?

About 450 million years ago, the "Hudson Valley" was part of a submerged continental shelf in the subtropical region of the Southern Hemisphere. Shifting land masses and sediment composed of sand, clay, and volcanic deposits called turbidity, left a pattern of wrinkled, flowing formations that have come to be known as "dinosaur skin outcroppings." These are found at, among other places, Coxsackie in Greene County. But dinosaurs didn't appear for another 300 million years, so don't be fooled. This skin is just interesting rock.

twenty pounds, becomes extinct. It is a very, very, very bad day. The Hudson Valley, along with the rest of planet Earth, was no place to be back then.

Unless you were a mammal.

Hudson Valley Critters Throughout the Ages

The dinosaurs and their peers roamed this land from about 230 million years ago to about 65 million years ago. As unimaginably long as those 160-plus million years may seem, they are just a fleeting moment in geological time. Using the familiar twenty-four-hour clock analogy, if the Earth's forming 4.6 billion years ago is considered midnight, the dinosaurs didn't appear until almost 11 p.m. and survived less than an hour. What else lived in what is now the Hudson Valley between the Earth's birth and the arrival of us human newbies, just a minute ago, at 11:59?

BD: Before dinosaurs. For the first 3.5 billion years, life on Earth was tiny and tenuous. From about 400 million to 300 million years ago, our land was underwater, drifting from somewhere near the South Pole north toward the equator. Invertebrates, such as trilobites (relatives of horseshoe crabs), brachiopods (early mollusks), cephalopods (ancestors of squids), tentaculites (conical, carrot-shaped organisms), and coral were abundant. And eurypterus, a giant sea scorpion that could grow up to four feet long and was one of the most fearsome predators in the sea before proto-sharks arrived on the scene, is New York's official state fossil.

Fossils of these long-gone creatures have been found at Thacher State Park in Albany County, along Route 209 from Kingston to Stroudsburg, Pennsylvania, and at Highland Mills.

AD: After dinosaurs. For 64 million years or so following the great extinction of the dinosaurs and much of life on Earth, the region was warm, moist, and conducive to the evolution of many of the plants and animals we see today. And more than a few we don't see any more. Creatures like mammoths, mastodons, giant beavers and sloths, musk oxen, and the giant short-faced bear roamed the land. Over the past 2 million years, though, periodic ice ages brought glaciers that covered the state and then retreated, each time recreating the landscape, carving rivers and lakes and mountains and killing off many of these animals. The mastodon, though, was probably still around when the earliest humans arrived here, about 13,000 years ago; the famous Cohoes Mastodon skeleton, found in 1866 near the Cohoes Falls, has been dated to about that time.

Ice Capades

Hudson Valley Journeys into the Past—the
Way, Way Past, That Is: The Ice Age

When you or I stand upon the great lawn at the Vanderbilt Mansion in Hyde Park, we picture ourselves living the grand lifestyle of fin de siècle Hudson Valley aristocracy, of opulent balls and market-rigging business dealings all held amid the stunning landscape of the river and mountains under Frederic Church skies.

When Johanna and Robert Titus stand on that same lawn, they picture something a bit different. In their mind's eye, they are knee-deep in water, at the edge of a vast lake that stretches from the middle of the eastern Hudson Valley counties to the middle of the western counties and from somewhere near Glens Falls all the way to the Atlantic Ocean (which was about one hundred miles farther south than it is now). Far to their north, a glacier thousands of feet high that once covered the continent from the middle of Long Island, west through Cleveland, Chicago, and Omaha to the Dakotas, Montana, and the Great Northwest, is in the process of melting its way back to the Arctic.

The Tituses, you see, are standing at the Vanderbilt Mansion circa 15,000 years BP (the geological notation for "before present"). Robert has a PhD in geology and teaches in the geology department of Hartwick College. Johanna, who calls herself "a geologist by marriage," has a master's in molecular biology and teaches at State University of New York–Dutchess. You may know them as columnists for *Kaatskill Life*, the *Woodstock Times*, and other newspapers. They recently published a delightful book called *The Hudson Valley in the Ice Age: A Geographical History and Tour* (2012). Part popular science, part travelogue, it is that rare science book that is both challenging and entertaining. Readers learn about arcane geological formations like moraines, alluvial fans, and rock drumlins. Better yet, they learn where to find the remnants of those formations through first-person hikes and drive-bys at dozens of easily accessible spots up and down the valley. Consider them postcards from the Ice Age.

I asked the Tituses to pick, as a sampler platter, a handful of their favorite spots to get interested parties started on their own geological time travel. Once you do, our beautiful valley will never look quite the same again.

1. The floor of glacial Lake Albany. That's what the above-mentioned vast lake is known as, and the site of the Vanderbilt estate is just one of many places where you can imagine the soft, flat lake bottom. "Get used to the idea that anytime you see flat landscapes, you may well be literally on the floor of the lake," Robert says. The New York State Thruway south of Kingston, for instance, was built on such a flat stretch of land, which is the result of deposits left behind as mud on the floor of the lake. "Flat isn't all that interesting, until you realize you are at the bottom of a lake," he says.

2. North Lake. The area's many lakes and rivers are all remnants of the Hudson Valley glacier, which preceded and then was overridden by the greater Laurentide Ice Sheet that covered all of the northern reaches of North America. As the ice advanced, it left scratches in the rock, called striations. One of the best places to find these is along the eastern shore of North Lake. "Look at the bedrock at the edge of the water, and you'll see the footprints of glaciers," Robert says.

3. The Kaaterskill Clove. When deltas, like the one the Vanderbilt Mansion sits on, are carved into gorges by rivers, they are called cloven deltas or cloves. The Kaaterskill Clove, on which Palenville now sits and which contains Kaaterskill Falls and the Red Chasm, is such a clove, cutting through what's known as an alluvial fan. Streams from the retreating glacier all headed into this delta in a fan-shaped formation and cut through the rock, sand, and clay to create the landscape. Johanna recommends that you stop at Red Chasm. "This is a really scenic spot, many use it to swim, and you can really see how the waters from the melting ice carved the canyon," she says.

What's most important about this site, the Tituses say, is that this landscape carved by melting glaciers became the touchstone of the Hudson River School of Art. "Thomas Cole painted his first paintings there, and they figure so importantly in the cultural history of the Hudson Valley," Robert says. "And that all comes out of the Ice Age."

4. The Mansions. The big houses built on the eastern edge of the river, including the Vanderbilt Mansion and Franklin Delano Roosevelt's Springwood, are all positioned on ice age deposits at the bottom of glacial Lake Albany. Hyde Park rests on one of the biggest deltas of Lake Albany, and the mansions sit on the crest of that delta. "The aristocracy didn't know it, but 150 years ago they were following the path of the glaciers," Robert says.

They also didn't know that one day their houses might slip toward the river valley. The houses are not built on bedrock; they sit on soft sediments like clay. Whenever you hear of a home damaged by a landslide, usually after a heavy rain, it's the result of land like this sliding down the slope of the pre-historic lakebed. "The sediments are very prone to landslides," Robert says. "We have met people who lost homes that slid downhill, and we have visited homes to evaluate their threat of slides and had to tell them they were threat-ened. It is a present danger anywhere in the valley these deposits exist."

The Tituses say they have seen evidence of the bigger mansions install-ing new drainage systems to shore up the Ice Age grounds on which they sit. "But there is no way to know when a landslide might happen," he says. "It could be 1,000 years, or 10,000 years, or in March if we get a lot of rain." He doubts the latter, though. "The land has been there 15,000 years, so I don't think there is an immediate threat."

5. The Pine Bush. These days, the Pine Bush Preserve in Albany County is a foliage-covered plot of hilly, sandy soil. Just after the glaciers retreated, though, it was a full-blown desert, not unlike something you'd see in *Law-rence of Arabia*. "All that was missing were camels," Robert says.

The sand was blown in from what is now Schenectady County, which then was one of Lake Albany's biggest deltas, fed by the Mohawk River. As the lake retreated, the sandy deposits that were its bottom were blown by the west winds and dropped here, forming the dunes and swales that have since been overgrown. "Stand on top of the dunes and imagine what the area looked like 12,000 years ago," he suggests.

There are dozens more spots to pick up the Ice Age trail. The Gunks reveal, along their upper edges, erratic carvings left by the passage of ice. Olana, the de facto home of the Hudson River School of Art, sits on the top of a rock drumlin, a hill shaped like an inverted spoon bowl that is a signature of glacial advance. "Each location has its own chapter, so we suggest you pack the book up and go see what we saw," Robert says, "because it is an autobi-ography of our great adventures." Adventures that can take you to the dawn of your own homeland.

The People of the Waters
That Are Never Still

Who Discovered the Hudson Valley? Meet
the People Who Met Henry Hudson

A great many people traveled from the north and west. For years they moved across the land, leaving settlements in rich river valleys as others moved on. Reaching the eastern edge of the country, some of these people settled the river later named the Delaware. Others moved north and settled in the valley of the river where the waters, like those of their original homeland, were never still. They named this river Mahicannituck and called themselves the Muhheconneok, the People of the Waters That Are Never Still.

This is the origin story, as told by an early-1700s Mohican historian named Hendrick Aupaumut, of the people who truly discovered America, including the river valley in which we now live and they, for the most part, do not. The river and valley's name were usurped by a man named Henry Hudson, a member of an invasive species from the east that, in the comparative blink of an eye, nearly ended a story that stretches back perhaps 13,000 years.

Today, about 1,500 men, women, and children, most of whom live in Wisconsin, trace their ancestry back to this great people who traveled from the north and west as the ice-age glaciers receded and humans first populated our land. That the descendants of these original settlers are doing well, after four hundred years of disease, degradation, and dislocation, is good to know. It is still better to know their story in full, to appreciate their history and honor their pride of place as the first people of the Hudson Valley.

"It Was a Rich Life"
Two distinct but closely related nations inhabited the Hudson Valley at the time of European contact. The Mohicans (or Mahicans) lived in the northern

valley, approximately from present-day Kingston up to Lake Champlain, west to the Schoharie Valley, and east into Massachusetts, Connecticut, and Vermont. The Lenape (sometimes Lenni-Lenapi, meaning, roughly, "the real or original people"), first populated the Delaware River Valley, particularly around Minisink ("at the place of the islands") where New York, New Jersey, and Pennsylvania meet. They are also called Delaware Indians, and the nation eventually comprised clans that lived in an area they called the Lenapehoking, their territory in what is now eastern Pennsylvania, New Jersey, eastern Delaware, and the lower Hudson Valley. The northeastern clans who moved into our region spoke a Lenape dialect known as Munsee and are thus also known as the Munsee Indians. It was the Munsee who were waiting on shore when Giovanni da Verrazano "discovered" his narrows in 1524 and when Hudson "discovered" his river in 1609 and who famously sold Manhattan to Peter Stuyvesant in 1626.

Though the Mohicans and Munsee were distinct, their languages were similar enough to allow communication (both are part of the larger Algonquian language group that covers much of northeastern North America), and their relations were mostly peaceful. They knew they were relatives and assisted each other when in danger of attack to their west, from the Mohawk/Iroquois, and to their east, from the Mohegans, who despite the similar sounding name were a competitor nation. But these were temporary alliances; the tribes never formed a larger confederacy like the Haudenosaunee (Iroquois) Confederacy in central New York State.

Their daily lives were similar too. In the approximately 1,000 years before European contact, known as the Late Woodland Period, the native peoples lived in small clans or villages of perhaps ten to a hundred or so family members. The full number of native peoples living in the valley is hard to estimate, but the total Lenape population of all the villages from Delaware Bay to Esopus Creek was probably around 10,000 in 1600.

They were migratory, moving from area to area to follow the hunt and hunker down for winter. They typically lived in clearings they slashed and burned in the thick forest along creeks and rivers, usually on terraces above the floodplain, in places that still bear their names: Wappinger ("the people of the east lands" or, possibly, "white-face opossum"), Esopus ("the small river"), and Manhattan (perhaps "hilly island," perhaps "place of timber," perhaps presciently, but not likely, "island where we became drunk").

In present-day Westchester County, the native presence goes back at least 7,000 years. The oldest oyster shell middens on the North Atlantic coast were uncovered by archeologists on Croton Point; Croton, in fact, is named for the Indian sachem Kenoten ("wild wind"). The Wiechquaesgeck, another clan, occupied the western reaches of the county, centered around Dobbs Ferry. In the 1600s, the Kitchawanks, members of the Wappinger family, built and lived in a large, fortified village on the high flat at the neck of Croton Point, one of the most ancient and imposing fortresses south of the Hudson Highlands. They called their fortress Navish. (A marsh, which the natives called Senasqua, separates Croton Point from Croton Neck; you can find a plaque there at the spot where the Dutch signed a peace treaty with the Kitchawanks.)

"The Native Americans who lived in the Hudson Valley just before and at the time of European Contact were agriculturalists," says Joseph Diamond, a professor of archaeology at the State University of New York (SUNY)–New Paltz. "They grew corn, beans, and various species of squash as well as gathering plant foods such as hickory, nuts, butternuts, walnuts, acorns, and chestnuts, and various berries to supplement their diet."

Corn, beans, and squash, in fact, were so central to native diets that the crops were known by the Iroquois as the "three sisters." That interdependence required rather advanced horticultural skills. "There is a conception that the Algonquians were not sophisticated farmers like the Iroquois. I think that is not the case," says Dr. John P. Hart, director of the Research and Collections Division at the New York State Museum in Albany. "To grow successfully you have to understand how crops respond to soils, water and rainfall, any type of unusual weather. When growing the three crops together, you have to understand how they interact with one another. If you have, say, one hundred acres, that's a lot of plants, so you have to understand what you are doing to have a successful harvest. And they had no plows, no metal tools, it was all hand labor, and they were very successful at it."

They were also meat eaters, hunting bear, elk, white-tailed deer, rabbits, squirrels, turkey, river otter, raccoons, and woodchucks, as well as various waterfowl. "Archaeological sites in the Hudson Valley have also produced evidence of fishing for most freshwater species, and during the spring they caught sturgeon, striped bass, shad, and herring and probably dried, smoked, or roasted them," Diamond says. Oyster beds found near the riverbanks provided abundant nourishment as well. In the spring, the natives tapped maple trees for syrup and sugar. After a hunt or harvest, the meat, vegetables, and berries were dried, the fish was smoked, and the bounty was stored in pits dug deep in the ground and lined with grass or bark. "They were producing enough food for large surpluses in case of crop failure for any reason," Hart says.

What's in a Name?

Tracing the original meaning of native words to current usage is an inexact science; however, here are some possible-slash-probable derivations of familiar Hudson Valley places.
Ashokan: people walking in the water
Chappaqua: mountain laurel
Kisco: mud
Mahopac: that which is a lot of water
Mamaroneck: striped stream
Mohonk: place of bears
Ossining: place of stones
Poughkeepsie: reed-covered bridge by the small water place
Ramapo: under the rock
Tappan: rolling stream

Source: Robert S. Grumet, *Manhattan to Minisink: American Indian Place Names in Greater New York and Vicinity.*

They lived in several different kinds of houses, which the Lenape called wik-wams (and the interlopers bastardized into wigwams), made of bent saplings covered with animal hides or tree bark, with a hole in the roof to vent smoke from fire pits. The homes could be circular, square, or oval, and some were rectangular longhouses. "One of the longest in the Hudson Valley is 110 feet by 29 feet," Diamond says. Several families from the same clan might live in a longhouse, each family getting its own section.

While the men traveled to hunt, fish, or fight, the women were generally in charge of the home, raising the children and tending the gardens. But they were hardly subservient. "Contrary to American 'squaw' stereotypes of Native American women, the Lenape female had recognized authority roles within the family and the village community, comparing favorably in position to women in European society of the day," Laurence M. Hauptman, professor emeritus at SUNY New Paltz, writes in *The Native Americans: A History of the First Residents of New Paltz and Environs.*

Winter was domestic time. They carved containers and utensils, made or repaired their hunting, trapping, and fishing gear, fashioned new baskets and pottery, and made clothing, which they decorated with porcupine quills, shells, and other "natural gifts."

"Winter was also the time of teaching," according to Dorothy Davids, author of *A Brief History of the Mohican Nation, Stockbridge-Munsee Band.* The storytellers passed on tales of "how life came to be, how the earth was created, how the people learned to sing, the story of the drums and rattles, and what the stars could teach them." They also learned how to live with their extended families peacefully, with respect and shared responsibility.

Ceremony was central to their existence. They had a ceremony whenever something needed "paying attention to," Davids writes, such as the planting of the corn, beans, and squash and the harvest. "They practiced several kinds of burial," Diamond says, "including secondary burial, which is a common form of mortuary treatment around the world that involves a second ceremony several months to a year later."

In all, the native peoples of the Hudson Valley at the time of European contact were more than just eking out a living, more than just surviving. "They were living complex lives, like we do," Hart says. As Dorothy Davids writes, "It was a rich life."

"Civilized"—and Its Discontents

It was the people of this impressive and ancient civilization that one of Henry Hudson's men, upon meeting the natives in Westchester, condescendingly called "well proportioned," stating, "Their limbs are properly formed, and they are sprightly and active."

European conquest quickly took sad care of that. Disease, specifically smallpox, measles, diphtheria, and scarlet fever, against which the native people had no immunity, wiped out hundreds of thousands—sometimes, entire villages perished at once. Colonization took out the rest. By 1639, the Dutch West India Company, under the colony's director, Willem Kieft, had begun a landgrab in present-day Westchester and the Bronx. The natives, who believed the land was theirs by grace of their gods, realized too late that their deals with the Dutch were sales, not rentals.

Wars soon erupted. In 1643, what became known as Kieft's War decimated the Wappinger. The Dutch, aligned with the Mohawk nation, wiped out about half the Wappinger population of 3,000 in two years. The notorious British Indian raider John Underhill devastated an Indian village near present-day Bedford in 1644. The Peach Tree War of 1655 left another sixty or so Wappinger dead, and their confederation broke apart. Many survivors left the area to live with neighboring tribes in western Massachusetts.

Things were little better under British rule. The Munsee and Mohicans stopped living their traditional lives and making their traditional items, as the English endeavored to "civilize" all the native people. "The vast lands, which the Mohicans had used for gardens, hunting and fishing, began to have boundary lines and fences when shared with non-Indians," Davids writes. Between 1680 and 1708, much of the Munsee land around present-day Bedford was sold to the British, the deeds signed by an Indian leader named Katonah.

When the Munsee joined forces with the Continental Army during the Revolutionary War, many of them were killed—including their powerful sachem Daniel Nimham—at the infamous Battle of Kingsbridge in 1778. By the turn of the nineteenth century, there were virtually no natives left in Westchester County.

The rest of the valley suffered similar fates. The two Esopus Wars, in 1659 and 1663, were brutal and bloody affairs that devastated the Esopus, who dispersed to live with their Minisink brethren to the west. Many surviving Mohicans, meanwhile, also relocated to western Massachusetts with the remaining Wappinger. They were converted to Christianity by missionary John Sergeant, who started a mission in 1738 in the area he named Stockbridge. "Some native people, noting that the Europeans seemed to be prospering in this new land, felt that perhaps their God was more powerful and agreed to be missionized," Davids writes.

After the war, the Stockbridge-Mohican Indians and other tribes moved to western New York near Oneida Lake, then moved again to Indiana to live with their relatives, the Miami and Delaware Indians, and then again in the 1830s to inhospitable land in Wisconsin.

And that was that. The Mahicannituck was the Hudson River. The Muhheconneok and Munsee were gone, replaced by the Europeans. A civilization dating back to the time of the mastodons had been nearly eradicated, and its few survivors were forced to live thousands of miles from their ancestral home, all in the span of about two hundred years.

Many Trails, Leading Back Home

"Most people think we are all dead and gone," says Bonney Hartley, who is most certainly not dead and gone. Neither are roughly 1,500 of her fellow citizens of the federally recognized Stockbridge-Munsee Mohican nation, about half of whom live on the reservation in Wisconsin. Hartley, in her position as tribal historic preservation officer for the nation, is hard at work advocating for her people from her office in Troy.

The nation set up this office, on the campus of the Sage Colleges, to increase its presence in the Hudson Valley. Hartley collaborates with state and federal authorities whenever land development may encroach on ancient tribal lands. If native artifacts may be disturbed, "we work on trying to avoid it and not disturb the site," she says. "If that is not possible we work on mitigation. The sites are irreplaceable. They may seem like just stones or pieces of pottery, but to us these are extremely precious." She also consults on museum exhibits, conducts public outreach, and, perhaps most importantly, strives to preserve burial grounds, the nation's most sacred sites.

The nation, though long removed from the Hudson Valley, has maintained an ongoing relationship with its ancient homeland. Bus trips pull into the area regularly to visit important sites—the exact locations of which they prefer to keep unknown for fear of poaching and vandalism. Without being too specific, Sherry White, tribal historic preservation manager, names the towns of Pine Plains, Lansingburg, Schaghticoke, White Plains, Poughkeepsie, New Paltz, Papscanee Island, Schodack Island, Schuyler Flats, Bethlehem, Peebles Island, and Coeymans as destinations, but she adds that "from Manhattan to Vermont it is pretty hard to put a shovel in the ground without hitting a site of some sort—fishing camp, hunting camp, burial ground, habitation site." Members of the nation are always moved when they return to the valley. "I have been on a bus trip, and it is really amazing," Hartley says. "When you pull into the area, a hush falls over the bus. Everyone feels the connection. It is a beautiful thing to see."

Hartley says that, in general, the nation is healthy. A casino has brought economic opportunity, and a health center keeps the population well. Young people who once had to leave to find work are now able to stay. "We have a thriving tribe with continued leadership that has existed since time immemorial," she says. "We have come a long ways from the devastation that occurred after contact, marked by the 'Symbol of Many Trails.' We are so far from our homeland, first forced to Stockbridge, then multiple times west, and onto the worst land in Wisconsin. After all that, it is really a remarkable story of resiliency that we even exist at all. A lot of people could learn from our tribe. We want people to know."

To Learn More

Much of the information in this chapter comes from the collected works of Robert S. Grumet, widely acknowledged as the foremost scholar of Native American history in New York State and the northeastern United States. A quick Google or local library search will direct you to his many books on the subject, including *The Munsee Indians: A History*; *First Manhattans: A History of the Indians of Greater New York*; and *Manhattan to Minisink: American Indian Place Names in Greater New York and Vicinity*.

The Stockbridge-Munsee Mohican nation's website is mohican-nsn.gov.

Part 2:
Colonization

Black, Like Us

In the Hudson Valley, as in the Rest of the Country, African American History Is Everyone's History

The story we like to tell ourselves of what was to become the United States of America typically features two main characters: the native peoples who had lived on these lands for centuries and the Europeans who took those lands from them. But this drama includes a third group of cast members whose role is at best downplayed and at worst ignored: Africans and their descendants.

In 1613, just four years after Henry Hudson's crew sailed up the river that would bear his name and seven years before the Pilgrims arrived in Plymouth, a mixed-race man named Juan Rodrigues (or some spelling variant near that) left Hispaniola for the New World, set up shop in and around Manhattan Island, traded with the natives for a time, squabbled with the Dutch—who called him a "black rascal"—and then disappeared from the public record as the first African to set foot in the Hudson Valley.

In 1626, just ten years after the establishment of New Amsterdam, the Dutch West India Company shipped eleven African male slaves—whom they labeled "proud and treacherous"—into the colony, with women brought in two years later. Some slaves were moved to Fort Orange, the outpost that became Albany. As land patents divvied up the valley, every patent holder whose name still graces the region stocked his farm with slaves. In 1664, when the Dutch handed the keys to the new kingdom to the British, about eight hundred Africans and their children inhabited the valley, only about seventy-five of them considered free.

The British increased slave importation, and by the early 1700s New York State had more slaves than anywhere else in the colonies, more than the Deep South, more than Boston, more than the Virginia plantations. "The two biggest slave markets in the country before the American Revolution were in New York City and Albany," says Dr. A. J. Williams-Myers, a retired professor of black studies at the State University of New York (SUNY)–New

Paltz. By 1790, the first federal census counted more than 19,000 enslaved New Yorkers; Georgia had 12,000. "New York was not a society *with* slaves, it was a *slave society*, dependent on enslaved Africans," Williams-Myers says.

As New Yorkers, we like to think we differed from southerners regarding slavery. We were different only in that, numerically speaking at least, we were worse. Any history of African descendants in the Hudson Valley must first come to grips with this fact. From the earliest moments of European contact, African Americans have been among the valley's *dramatis personae*. "Africans have been portrayed as in the shadow of history, when actually they were center stage," Williams-Myers says. "Where European people went, Africans went with them, shoulder to shoulder with their enslavers."

The Oppressed as Oppressors

As the Hudson Valley economy transitioned during the seventeenth century from the fur trade to farming, Africans helped make the region the most prosperous in the New World. Hudson Valley farms helped feed Great Britain, its newest colonies, and its holdings in the Caribbean, and Africans did much of the work. A 1733 painting titled *Van Bergen Overmantel*, by artist John Heaten, depicts the Marten Van Bergen farm near the Greene County town of Leeds. Historic Hudson Valley writes on its website that "no other single artifact offers more information about life in colonial New York. Here African, Native American, and European people populate the landscape." Dr. Myra Young Armstead, the Lyford Paterson Edwards and Helen Gray Edwards Professor of Historical Studies at Bard College, calls this painting "a good picture of what was going on and why the Hudson Valley was a big area of slavery."

Even those who came here because of oppression became oppressors. The French Huguenot founders of New Paltz purchased the first of their many slaves in Kingston in 1674, a hypocrisy not lost on a Huguenot descendant. "My ancestors fled France for religious and political freedom. Before leaving France, they saw their own families tortured, enslaved, and killed. Yet these emigrants came to the New World and, for their own personal gain, forced other human beings to labor against their will," Mary Etta Schneider, board chair of Historic Huguenot Street (HHS), said this summer. "For this I am ashamed."

Schneider was speaking in advance of a September 2016 event, in which HHS welcomed Joseph McGill, founder of the Slave Dwelling Project. McGill travels the country, inviting community members to spend the night with him in historic slave dwellings to bring awareness of their existence, history, and need for preservation. More of these are in the North than most people know. "The history I learned in school was junk," McGill says. "Slave dwellings are part of the history of this nation. They are hidden in plain sight." Huguenot slaves were likely locked in at night so they couldn't escape, Schneider says, and spending a night where they did gives contemporary overnighters "a sense of what it must have felt like to [not] have any control over your life." Addressing another myth, that northern slave owners were "better" than southern ones, McGill says bluntly, "There were no great slave owners. When you assign a degree of severity, you start with bad."

Long before Nat Turner, slaves in New York were rebelling against their owners. In 1712, twenty-three slaves killed nine whites in New York City, and rumors both real and unproved of slaves plotting revolts from the city to Albany kept tensions high throughout the eighteenth century. In 1794, three slaves—including two girls of twelve and fourteen—were hanged for setting a fire that burned much of downtown Albany; two were hanged from "the Hanging Elm Tree," at the northwest corner of State and Pearl Streets (planted in front of the house of young Philip Livingston), the third on Pinkster Hill, site of the current capitol. "Slaves and owners were on constant war footing," Williams-Myers says. "The Hanging Tree in Albany shows you the use of fear to keep Africans in their place."

Revolutionaries and Warriors

And yet slaves helped their masters win independence. "You cannot discount Africans' input in the Revolutionary War," Williams-Myers says. Though they often were sent to battle in place of their owners, under the assumption that they would be freed after the war, they fought bravely and well. "They are never pictured ... but they were there on the battlefield," he says. Slaves held positions along the Hudson River as General Henry Clinton made his way up from New York City and fought at the battles in Saratoga, along the Mohawk River, and throughout the region. "African warriors were one of the colonies' secret weapons," he says. "They were significant in winning the war."

After the war, slaves weren't freed right away, but Federalists like John Jay and Alexander Hamilton founded the New York Manumission Society in 1785 to promote abolition. Emancipation happened in fits and starts and was fully realized when the last New York slaves were freed on July 4, 1827. It was the largest emancipation in North America before the Civil War.

The Hudson Valley, to a large extent, welcomed freed African Americans. During this gradual emancipation, Quaker groups offered land—usually rocky, undesirable land, to be clear—to help freed slaves, and self-sustaining black communities sprang up in Rockland (Skunk Hollow, near the New

Jersey border), Westchester (The Hills in Harrison and another community near Bedford), Dutchess (near Hyde Park, Beekman, and Millbrook), Ulster (Eagles Nest, west of Hurley), and all the other river counties. Though legally emancipated, blacks weren't entirely free yet, and the valley, like the rest of the state, was in no way free of racism. Laws limited blacks' rights to vote, to travel with whites on public transportation, to attend school, and more. "You could argue that the earliest 'Jim Crow' laws actually appeared in the North, not the South," says Dr. Oscar Williams, chair of the Department of Africana Studies at SUNY Albany.

The opening of the Erie Canal in 1815 precipitated the slow and steady migration from upstate farms to river cities for employment. "Cities like Newburgh and Poughkeepsie offered jobs to blacks, while there was bigger movement to New York City or Albany, the nodes of the valley," Armstead says. Black institutional and social life took hold in these cities. Rhinebeck, for example, had a vibrant neighborhood of black artisans on Oak Street. African American Revolutionary War veteran Andrew Frazier and his family, who are buried in the "potter's field" section of Rhinebeck Cemetery, owned land in the town of Milan. In Kingston, the African Methodist Episcopal Zion Church on Franklin Street, the oldest African American church in Ulster County, owns the Mount Zion African American Burial Ground on South

Can't We All Get Along? Yes—at Pinkster

Every spring, the city of Albany still celebrates Pinkster as a way to honor the city's Dutch roots. This ancient religious and social holiday, though, survived long after the Dutch were replaced by the English—thanks to African American slaves, for whom Pinkster became the most important holiday in the year.

At Pinkster, slave owners allowed their slaves time to reunite with friends and family members, some of whom lived far away, to celebrate, play games, dance to African music, trade goods, and of course drink. By the early 1800s Pinkster was considered an African American holiday, with big celebrations in New York City and on Albany's Pinkster Hill, now occupied by the state capitol.

During the 1700s, slave owners grew more fearful of slave rebellions, and Pinkster was outlawed in the 1820s. It took 150 years before the holiday was revived in Albany and at places like Phillipsburg Manor in Sleepy Hollow. Today, Pinkster is recognized as the oldest African American holiday in the United States.

Wall Street. The cemetery holds the remains of members of the US Colored Infantry's 20th Regiment, which fought in the Civil War. An extension of the Mount Zion cemetery on South Pine Street is "one of the earliest, and potentially largest slave cemeteries known in the northeast," according to an anthropologist who conducted an archeological survey for the city of Kingston in 1993. The Rye African American Cemetery, inside the Greenwood Union Cemetery, was established in 1860 as a burial place for blacks. It is on the National Register of Historic Places and is the final resting spot for African American Civil War veterans and the descendants of many slaves from Rye.

As the Civil War approached, the Hudson Valley was a hotbed of abolition. So-called colored conventions, movements held by freed slaves to oppose slavery and push for rights for free blacks, were held all over the country, including in Poughkeepsie, Armstead says. The Underground Railroad had important station stops along the river, such as the Beecher House in Peekskill and the Stephen and Harriet Myers House in Albany. Sojourner Truth started on her march to freedom as Isabella Baumfree, a slave born on an estate near what is now Ripton, sold to a family in New Paltz. In Troy, an African American named Henry Highland Garnett was Malcolm X before Malcolm X. Garnett led a radical movement from his position as the first pastor of the Liberty Street Negro Presbyterian Church. First working with abolition leaders like William Lloyd Garrison and Frederick Douglass, he gave a famous speech in 1843 at the National Negro Convention, a "Call to Rebellion," encouraging slaves to rise up in open revolt. His position was opposed.

Past, Prologue

After the Civil War, blacks continued to move from local farms to industrial centers and to the North in the "Great Migration." New York City was a major destination, and in time blacks also moved into the suburbs, exurbs, and growing river cities of the valley. Freedom did not mean integration, however. As just one example, in the 1920s, land in the Nepperhan neighborhood of Yonkers, now known as Runyon Heights, was sold to blacks because whites didn't want it and it was naturally separated from white communities.

Work, as always, continued to be the magnet drawing African Americans north, and the valley had one of the world's most powerful magnets: IBM. After World War II, "IBM was really important, ahead of its time, a global force that recruited from black colleges and universities," Armstead says. By the late 1950s and the 1960s, black professionals populated the area. "That generation is dying or dead now, but they became the first black heads of organizations, the first black teachers," she says.

Setting a Precedent for Integration

In the 1930s, a newly minted lawyer named Thurgood Marshall joined the National Association for the Advancement of Colored People. Marshall and his team of lawyers wanted to end school segregation nationally. To do that, they knew they needed to establish local precedents, and in 1943 they set one at the Hillburn Main School in Rockland County.

Hillburn Main School, known as the "white school," was modern; the Brook School, the "colored school," was unheated, unplumbed, and poorly lighted, with lousy recreational facilities. Marshall's team tried to enroll a black child named Allen Morgan at Hilburn; when he was, as expected, denied, black parents withheld their children from the Brook School to protest the separate and unequal elementary school system. It only took a month for the New York State commissioner of education to close the Brook School and order that all forty-nine children be admitted to Hilburn.

Famed actress Helen Hayes, a Nyack resident, said at the time, "I am sure that the white people in Hillburn will have faith in democracy and . . . meet the situation with tolerance and understanding. Their audience today is as wide as the world."

Sadly, that worldwide audience saw every white family but one pull its children from Hillburn and send them to school in nearby Suffern or Tuxedo. But they were on the wrong side of history. Marshall used the Hillburn case in winning the landmark 1954 *Brown v. Board of Education* case declaring school segregation unconstitutional. The renamed Hillburn Elementary School closed in 1967, the same year Marshall became the first African American nominated to the US Supreme Court.

African American history over the last half century is a story of progress and regression, of course, both nationally and here in the valley. The current political climate is restive. The struggle has been ongoing for more than 400 years now, ever since Juan Rodrigues stepped ashore and began battling the Dutch. The story has evolved, but it hasn't ended. As William Faulkner wrote, "The past is never dead. It's not even past."

The Wars at Home

The Esopus Wars in Ulster County Pitted Native Americans against the Dutch More Than 350 Years Ago

The "Indian Wars," that ignominious history of colonial and American devastation of the native peoples of North America, effectively ended in 1890 at the Battle of Wounded Knee, in South Dakota, though smaller battles were fought as late as the 1920s. The wars started almost as soon as Europeans began their hegemony in the early decades of the seventeenth century, with the Jamestown Massacre of 1622 in Virginia and the Pequot War of the 1630s in New England. These wars are now deeply ingrained in the American psyche, having inspired some of the best literature, art, and film ever to come out of this country, and they helped form perhaps the singular American identity in the minds of much of the world. Yet one of the earliest and most dramatic of the Indian Wars has been mostly forgotten: the Esopus Wars that took place in Ulster County in the 1660s.

The biggest battle between the Munsee Esopus tribe of the Lenape Indian nation and the colonists from the Netherlands took place in 1663, making 2013 the 350th anniversary of a conflict that took dozens of lives, destroyed valuable property, claimed hostages on both sides, and nearly wiped out an entire tribe. The wars marked the ultimate and literal release of the bad blood that began as soon as the Dutch tried to gain a foothold in the New World.

Two New-World Wars

In 1614, just five years after Henry Hudson sailed up the river that the Lanape called the Mahicannituck —the river that flows two ways—the Dutch tried to establish a trading post near what is now Kingston. The Lenape, who had never seen nonnatives before and thought of themselves as the only people on Earth, would have none of it and drove them off the land. The same happened in 1652. In 1658 the persistent Dutch finally succeeded in building a stockade and a village, which they called Wiltwijck. Tensions only escalated.

"'Clash of cultures' is an outdated term, but the fact is, the Indians were confronted with a culture that was vastly more sophisticated," says Marc B. Fried, author of *The Early History of Kingston and Ulster County*. "It was a stone-age society that didn't even have the wheel or wagons. And by the time of the settlement, all the Lenape Indian tribes had been decimated by disease. Their population was declining and they were becoming dependent on guns, iron, copper, and so many things that they were trading for. With all these changes they were demoralized, as anyone would be."

They were also upended by alcohol, which the Dutch were trading to them against direct orders from the New Netherlands leadership. The natives had no experience with alcohol and started to abuse it, according to Fried.

The Dutch were guilty of racism—they viewed the natives as "heathens and lacking in hygiene," Fried says—and conflict burst into war in September 1659. Some natives, who had been working the fields for the Dutch, were paid in brandy. They got a bit rowdy, and one fired a musket in celebration. A Dutch mob attacked their village, and in retaliation perhaps five hundred Esopus returned to Wiltwijck and killed livestock, destroyed crops, burned buildings, and laid siege to the village. This first war didn't end until July 1660, when the Dutch, now reinforced with men and weapons, struck a truce with the Lenape.

The Dutch then made unreasonable landgrabs, Fried says, and also enslaved some natives and shipped them to Curaçao to work on Dutch sugar plantations. The Dutch thought all was quiet on their western front, but by 1663 the natives had had enough. They planned a bloody ambush that came to be known as the Esopus Massacre.

The tribe called for a meeting out in the open, as was its custom, to discuss things with the Dutch, who met them around 11 a.m. on June 7. The Dutch left the stockade gates open. Shortly thereafter, Dutch citizens from the nearby settlement of Niew Dorp (now Hurley) rode into Wiltwijck to report that Niew Dorp had just been attacked, and a band of Esopus were destroying the village and taking prisoners. As Dutch captain Martin Kregier reported, "The Indians here in this village immediately fired a shot and made a general attack on our village from the rear, murdering our people in their houses with their axes and tomahawks and firing on them with guns and pistols; they seized whatever women and children they could catch and carried them prisoners outside the gates, plundered the houses and set the village on fire."

Twelve men, four women, and two children were killed inside the stockade. Another ten women and children were kidnapped. Twelve homes had burned. In Niew Dorp, three men were killed, and eight women and twenty-six children were taken prisoner. That entire village was burned to the ground.

This began the Second Esopus War, which rocked the whole of the colony and may have encouraged the Dutch to hand it over to the British just one year later.

War Spreads West

The Esopus and their hostages retreated, guerrilla style, into the woods. The two sides courted allies. The Lenape enlisted a delegation from the Kaatskill tribe and sent them to Fort Orange (now Albany) to warn the Dutch to stay put. The Dutch ignored the threat and sent reinforcements upriver from New Amsterdam; unable to find their adversaries, they collaborated with a Mohawk contingent that led them on their search.

Throughout the summer, the two sides played cat and mouse. In late July, Indian scouts found an Esopus fortress in what is now either Wawarsing or Kerhonkson. Kregier and his small army destroyed the site and burned the fields and food. The Esopus retreated and hid again, but in September the Dutch found their new redoubt and killed several natives, including the Esopus chief, Papequanaehen, effectively ending the war. A few of the white captives were still missing but were tracked down living with other tribes. Most reported having been treated well, and some had grown fond of their captors. "There were two children who had become caregivers for an elderly woman, and they stayed with her for some time," Fried says.

Their nation destroyed, the Esopus signed a peace treaty. And the future of the Hudson Valley was established. The Dutch, now leery of all the native tribes, also grew increasingly preoccupied with the English interlopers and ceded their territory in 1664. "The wars may have weakened the Dutch, and you could even argue that without the war the Dutch may have put up a fight against the English, though that is purely speculative," Fried says. "Instead they gave it up without a shot being fired."

The war also gave white people their first glimpse of the interior regions of the Hudson Valley. One of the captives was perhaps the first to spend time in the Shawangunk Mountains. Her description of the region is said to have inspired the Duzine, the twelve Huguenot families who bought property in what became New Paltz in the 1670s. By that time, all the Esopus were gone from the area. What few remained had crossed the Shawangunks and joined the Mohawk tribe. Their descendants now live on the Stockbridge-Munsee reservation in Wisconsin.

Although there was general accord between the British and the natives, skirmishes still broke out between them. And in 1781, during the Revolutionary War, a group of Iroquois joined a band of Loyalists to attack and burn the hamlet of Wawarsing, killing eleven people. After that, though, the Indian Wars moved steadily west. The white empire expanded and overpowered the native tribes from the Hudson Valley all the way to the Pacific Ocean.

Let My People Come

The Hudson Valley Boasts the Oldest Standing Jewish Dwelling in the United States

Every spring, Jews around the world celebrate Passover, commemorating Moses's leading his people out of bondage in Egypt more than 3,000 years ago. It took his tribe forty years to find the Promised Land—but it then took them another three millennia to find the Hudson Valley. Wouldn't you know, the Jewish man who discovered this promised land was also named Moses. Sort of.

His full name was Luis Moises Gomez, and he was a Sephardic Jew who was a successful merchant and trader in New York City when, in 1716, he purchased 1,200 of what would eventually grow to about 3,000 acres of untamed wilderness in what is now Newburgh. There he built a fieldstone blockhouse to serve as his trading headquarters in the mid-Hudson region. Now known as the Gomez Mill House, it is the oldest standing Jewish dwelling in North America and the oldest historic house in Orange County.

Gomez was far from the first Jew to come to the New World—indeed, Jews may have even helped discover America, as there are unconfirmed reports that at least one Jew sailed with Columbus. It is certain that Jews predate the Puritans. Luis de Carabajal y Cueva, a Spanish Jewish conquistador (now there's a Mel Brooks screenplay begging to be written), rode into what is now Texas in 1570. In 1584 and 1585 a Jew named Joachim Gaunse (or Gans or Ganz) sailed onto and then off Roanoke Island, North Carolina, which was Great Britain's first, but ultimately unsuccessful, colony.

Jews had greater success with the Dutch, who were more interested in business acumen than religious beliefs. Many Jews fleeing the Spanish Inquisition in the seventeenth century ended up in the Netherlands and helped the Dutch set up shop in their New Amsterdam colony. When the British took over in 1664, they allowed the Jews to stay, and more began to come over in search of opportunity. One of them was Luis Gomez.

"The Onions Are Beginning to Smell"

The first permanent Jewish settlement in North America was established in 1654, when twenty-three Spanish/Portuguese Jews, refugees from the Inquisition, arrived in New Amsterdam from Brazil. Without resources of their own, they were supported by Jews working with the Dutch West India Company in Amsterdam. Within four years, one of the group's leaders, Asser Levy, owned real estate as far north as Albany, and by 1678 another, Jacob de Lucena, was trading in Kingston.

Gomez's family was still back in the Old World. He was born in Iberia in 1654, where his father was an adviser to King Philip IV of Spain. The elder Gomez had a deal with the king, says Ruth K. Abrahams, executive director of the Gomez Foundation for Mill House. "If the Inquisition got too hot, Philip would give him warning," she says. "The code was, 'The onions are beginning to smell.'" When the onions did indeed begin to smell, the Gomez family fled, first to France, then to England.

Luis Gomez followed his father into business and eventually traveled to Barbados and Jamaica. His first wife died during this time, and he remarried; he had five sons in all. In the late 1690s, already a successful member of the bustling Atlantic Basin trade in sugar, cocoa, and spices, he ventured to New York. (There is no evidence he was involved in the concurrent slave trade, Abrahams says, though his son Mordecai may have been.) The first documentation of him in New York dates from 1703. More importantly, in 1705 he purchased an Act of Denization from Queen Anne of England. This act afforded him the right to do business, own property, and live freely within the colonies without pledging his allegiance to the Church of England. (The Mill House contains the original document; "The language in it is remarkable," Abrahams says.)

Sensing a business opportunity, he purchased land on the Hudson Highlands in 1716, where existing Native American trails converged, to set up a trading post on what was then the wild frontier. He built a single-story fieldstone blockhouse where he and his sons oversaw their trading operations in fur, limestone, and milled timber. Though they never lived there permanently, future owners, including American Revolutionary patriot and Orange County civic leader Wolvert Ecker, nineteenth-century conservationist William Henry Armstrong, arts and crafts artisan and paper historian Dard Hunter, and twentieth-century social activist Martha Gruening, all did, building upon the original house and creating a three-hundred-year, religiously diverse historic legacy.

But its roots are unquestionably Jewish. Gomez was not only a business-man. In 1727 he was the financial leader behind the construction of the Mill Street Synagogue in lower Manhattan, the first synagogue of Shearith Israel, America's oldest Jewish congregation. He served as the first president of the congregation, which totaled three hundred to four hundred families at that time, Abrahams says. "His children and grandchildren also became presidents of the Congregation," she says. "His descendants remained important in the community through the early nineteenth century."

The New Exodus

Gomez died in 1740, still a Jewish pioneer in the New World. Jews comprised fewer than 2,000 of the total population of about 2.5 million colonial Americans at the time of the American Revolution. Most were still in the city, with a few settled on Long Island and in Westchester. After the War of 1812, as it became easier to travel thanks to steam ships and the Erie Canal, Jews joined gentiles in populating the hinterlands and formed communities in the bigger cities, from Albany to Buffalo. A wave of German Jewish immigration in the 1830s and 1840s saw Jewish communities forming in Newburgh, Poughkeepsie, Kingston, Hudson, and Troy, as well as farther north and west. Reform Judaism was partially begun in Albany in 1846, when Rabbi Isaac M. Wise, its driving force, allowed mixed, then-called family seating, in synagogues and other reforms.

By 1860 there were twenty congregations in the state; by 1877, fifty-three. In 1880, an estimated 60,000 to 80,000 Jews lived in New York State. With the massive eastern European immigration over the next few decades, the number reached 1,835,500 by 1928. A few fortunate Jews escaped the tenement squalor of the Lower East Side to form congregations in towns such as Haverstraw (1896), Ossining (1891), Peekskill (1894), New Rochelle (1880s), Liberty (1880s), Spring Valley (1901), Yonkers (1860s), Mamaroneck (1890), Suffern (1880s), and Tarrytown (1887). At the outbreak of World War II, 90 percent of the state's 2.2 million Jews still lived in the city, but after the war they joined everyone else in the mass suburban exodus to Nassau, Suffolk, and Westchester counties and beyond.

That's when Gomez's house was first recognized for its historic significance. It was bought in 1947 by Mildred and Jeffrey Starin, thanks to a GI Bill loan. The Starin family lived there for fifty years, and Mildred Starin, a renowned Hudson Valley preservationist, restored the buildings and got the property listed on the National Register in 1973. She also established the

New York City–based Gomez Foundation in 1979, which now owns the house and operates it as a museum.

That, as Luis Gomez and all the Jews who have followed him into the valley over the past three hundred years would say, is a *mitzvah*.

Cheaper by the Duzine

Some of the Valley's Earliest European Settlers,
the Huguenots, Arrived in New Paltz Not Long
after the Pilgrims Landed at Plymouth Rock

The Puritans get all the press, but they were hardly the only group to settle the New World in the seventeenth century. The Dutch and Spanish also receive a lesser share of deserved credit, but one group of pilgrims often gets overlooked: the French-speaking Calvinist Protestants from France and Belgium who fled persecution in Europe and established a colony right here in the Hudson Valley just fifty-seven years after Plymouth Plantation. They were called Huguenots and Walloons (though the latter name is less well known than the former), and while their more famous peers are celebrated in historic recreations of their colonial lives, they left behind in New Paltz what has been recognized as the oldest authentic street in America with intact late-seventeenth-century stone houses, now museums.

The key word here is "authentic." "I'm not dissing Colonial Williamsburg or Sturbridge or Plymouth, but they are not authentic," says Tracy Doolittle McNally, executive director of Historic Huguenot Street (HHS). "They are reproductions. What is so amazing about this place is that we really are the preeminent museum of family history." By this she means that for 350 years, before becoming part of a protected living museum, the houses in this National Historic Landmark District were owned by the same families, who lived in them for generations. "There is no place in the United States like it," she says. "It is really quite amazing."

Like the Puritans, the Calvinists (both Huguenots and Walloons) fled religious persecution. A group of twelve families, known as the Duzine, left an area then called the Spanish Netherlands, which included parts of present-day France and Belgium, and purchased 40,000 acres of land from the Esopus Indians on the west side of the Hudson River. The contract, with purchase price, which included domestic supplies, farming tools, clothing, blankets, wine, horses, tobacco, and gunpowder, was signed by five Esopus chiefs, and the deed, signed by twenty-one Esopus braves, secured the patent grant given by Governor Edmund Andros on September 29, 1677. (The original contract, deed, and patent grant are held at the Huguenot Historical Society Museum.) Note that this occurred five years before William Penn negotiated his treaty with the Native Americans to found Pennsylvania.

In 1678, the Duzine—from the Bevier, Crispell, Deyo, DuBois, Freer, Hasbrouck, and LeFevre families—settled the area, which they named Die Pfalz (New Paltz) in honor of Pfalz-am-Rhein, the German state where they had found refuge from Louis XIV. Their village was set up like a commune; the Duzine owned the land in common and shared their products and labor. The heads of the twelve families held power over the community in various governmental forms until 1826.

They first built simple wood houses, which they replaced in the 1700s with the stone dwellings along what is now known as Huguenot Street. Seven of these houses, built from 1705 to 1799 by succeeding generations of the settlers, survive. They are all built of field stone, laid in clay and straw and jointed with lime and sand, with chimneys constructed of locally made "thin bricks." The 1722 Jean Hasbrouck House features one of only three existing original jamb-less fireplaces in America. The 1799 Ezekiel-Elting House mimics the Jean Hasbrouck House but adds a brick facade and symmetrical window pattern in the then popular Federal style. The Bevier-Elting House represents pure Dutch urban architecture, with its original gable end with side-porch passageway. Other houses are similar in design, though their orientations were later changed. The Deyo House originally followed the same Dutch plan but was extensively modernized in 1894, the year that the Huguenot Historical Society was founded by the Duzine's descendants to prevent future changes to their historic town.

Today, all the houses stand in their original locations and display architectural features, furnishings, clothing, textiles, and other collections that depict the lives of the occupants. Outbuildings also remain on-site, as do a reconstructed 1717 French church and original burial ground. The 1705 fort serves as the site's visitor and exhibition center.

Upkeep is of course a primary concern of the HHS, and last summer the 1721 Abe Hasbrouck House, which had been closed for restoration, reopened. "It was restored to interpret life at the time from women's point of view," says Doolittle McNally, herself a descendant of the Deyo family. "The house held seven children, with four slaves living in the basement, all in this

What Is a Huguenot?

Huguenot. It's fun to say, hard to spell, and mysterious in origin. According to the National Huguenot Society, the word may be a combination of Flemish and German and describes Protestants who met to study the Bible in secret; they were called *Huis Genooten*, meaning "house fellows."

Other possible etymologies, found in the *Encyclopedia Britannica*, suggest that Huguenot is an old French word "common in 14th- and 15th-century charters. As the Protestants called the Catholics *papistes*, so the Catholics called the protestants Huguenots. The Protestants at Tours used to assemble by night near the gate of King Hugo, whom the people regarded as a spirit. A monk, therefore, in a sermon declared that the Lutherans ought to be called Huguenots, as kinsmen of King Hugo, inasmuch as they would only go out at night as he did. This nickname became popular from 1560 onwards, and for a long time the French Protestants were always known by it."

Another explanation says the word is derived from the German word *Eidgenosen*. "The origin of the name is uncertain, but it appears to have come from the word *aignos*, derived from the German *Eidgenosen* (confederates bound together by oath), which used to describe, between 1520 and 1524, the patriots of Geneva hostile to the duke of Savoy. The spelling Huguenot may have been influenced by the personal name Hugues; a leader of the Geneva movement was one Besancon Hugues (d. 1532)."

Source: National Huguenot Society.

small house in the years leading up to the American Revolution. We now present the life of a large family in small quarters."

And that, as well as the architecture they left behind, is part of the Huguenots' lasting significance to early America. "This culturally diverse group of settlers who built this community—including Dutch, French, English, Native Americans, and slaves—that's what the country became," Doolittle McNally says. "They were the precursor, the frontier of the diversity of America. They didn't know they were making the American story when they left their country of origin and settled here, but that is their legacy."

Poor No More

The "Poor Palatines" Who Settled in Columbia County Three Hundred Years Ago Have Left a Rich and Proud Legacy

You don't have to be smarter than a fifth grader to know that this country's first European settlers were the Dutch, Spanish, and English. But another country soon followed these pioneers and, in the end, sent more people here than any of the others.

That country is Germany. It's true. Ask your fifth grader.

Or ask just about anyone in Germantown, Columbia County. More than three hundred years ago, Germantown saw the arrival of the largest group of Hudson Valley settlers in colonial times: farmers from the Palatinate region of southwest Germany, who settled here in October 1710.

A little history: Through much of the seventeenth and early eighteenth centuries, the German Palatinate region was fraught with war, famine, and devastation. Refugees were known as "the poor Palatines."

About 13,000 poor Palatines fled to Holland and then to England between May and November 1709, but the British government failed to integrate them successfully. So they transported nearly 3,000 refugees in ten ships to New York in 1710. About 850 families settled in the Hudson River Valley, primarily in what are now Germantown and Saugerties. Many of them first were assigned to work camps along the Hudson River to pay off their passage.

"The area around Germantown was known as East Camp then," says Nadine Rumke, a ninth-generation descendant of the Palatines, who cochaired Germantown's 300th Anniversary Committee. Rumke's ancestors were the Hovers (then called Haber), and her family tree takes up ten square feet of wall space.

Germantown grew from four hamlets established by her ancestors and those of many residents still living in southern Columbia County. Those family names, including Rifenburgh (originally Reiffenberg), Clum (formerly

Klumm), Fingar, Coons (from Kuhn), and many others, still fill the local phone book—if there still is a phone book—and adorn many street signs.

Indeed, Helen Coons Henderson, who lived to be 105, grew up on land that had been in the family for generations. She remembered her father, James Snyder Coons, telling stories of the early Palatine settlers' struggles to survive. "There are stories of them eating grass in 1712!" said Henderson, who assisted Columbia County historian Mary Howell with research and also helped the 300th Anniversary Committee. Henderson's grandmother was a Snyder, another Palatine family, originally called Schneider. These two families still celebrate Thanksgiving together, Palatine style, with fresh pork and root vegetables cooked according to one-hundred-year-old recipes.

The Oblong

How a Border Dispute Opened the
Door for the Pawling Quakers

There aren't many Quakers in Quaker Hill anymore. But in the late seventeenth and eighteenth centuries, this hamlet in the town of Pawling was one of the most thriving Quaker communities in the country. It would be romantic to think the early settlers came to this area because of some great spiritual awakening or metaphysical yearning. But what drew them here was far more prosaic—real estate. It's still a pretty good story, though.

Back in the early 1700s, the colonies of New York and Connecticut were arguing about the exact location of their shared border. The surveys were inaccurate, and the colonies' land allocations were often in dispute. The issue was finally settled in 1731. Connecticut got the weird "panhandle" that juts into the southeast corner of New York. In return, New York was awarded an equivalent amount of land, two miles wide by sixty miles long, running along its eastern edge all the way up to Massachusetts. This patch of land was called the Oblong, a much cooler word than rectangle or parallelogram but basically the same thing.

The Oblong was unsettled wilderness at the time. But it was special wilderness for one particular reason. It really was wild. No one owned it. It was not included in any of the original Dutch patents, and therefore it immediately became the first New World land in a long time to go on the open market.

One of the first to get in on the action was a surveyor named Nathan Birdsall, a Quaker who had visited the area in 1728. "At the time the road ended at Danbury, so he had to cut through the forest to find it," says Robert P. Reilly, Pawling's historian. When the land became available for purchase, Birdsall sent word to other Quaker communities in Long Island, Rhode Island, and Massachusetts, and a few hardy souls bought five-hundred-acre plots around what they quickly christened Quaker Hill. "It was kind of a land rush," says Reilly.

Making—and Ignoring—History

The early homesteaders cleared the land, built roads and homes, and farmed the fertile soil, and by 1740 there were forty to fifty families, enough Friends of sufficient means to request permission from the Quaker meeting in Purchase to establish a meeting of their own and to build a meetinghouse. The Oblong Friends Meeting House, as it came to be known, was finished in 1742. But the influx of Quakers and their progeny wasn't, and over the next twenty years the community had outgrown it. "By 1760 it was overpopulated," says James Mandracchia, the librarian at Akin Free Library and Oblong Friends Meeting House. "Each family had ten to fourteen kids, and some of them were already moving out to settle other towns in New York and Vermont."

In 1763 the community petitioned the Quaker regional office to build a new brick building forty-five feet long and thirty-five feet wide but were told instead to construct "a framed house of timber, the dimensions to be 45 feet long, 40 feet wide and 15 feet stud to admit of galleries." The new meetinghouse was completed in 1764, just north of the original site, where it still stands more than 250 years later. And three years after that, the community did something else that will last even longer. It abolished slavery.

In the 1760s the Oblong Friends stopped doing business with slaveholders—substituting locally produced maple sugar for slave-trade cane sugar, for example—and at the annual meeting of 1767 discussed whether it was "consistent with the Christian spirit to hold a person in slavery at all." It took nine years to resolve the question, but in 1776 the community decided that meetings would not accept financial contributions or receive services from any Friends holding slaves. "I love the brutally logical way they decided," Reilly says. "They reasoned that god's spirit is in every human, and you can't enslave god, so slavery is inconsistent." According to records, the last slave owned by a member of Oblong was freed in 1777—almost one hundred years before the Emancipation Proclamation.

The Oblong Friends also used that logic to abstain from the French and Indian and Revolutionary Wars. Reilly says they were the "first conscientious objectors," but even if they refused to go to war, the war for independence nevertheless came to them. With some of General George Washington's soldiers encamped nearby during the fall and winter of 1778–1779, the Continental Army commandeered the meetinghouse and used it as a hospital for soldiers injured at Purgatory Hill. Some of the soldiers who perished are buried south of the meetinghouse. The Quakers, true to their pacifist beliefs, would not go into the house or help in the war effort, and they never mentioned these events in their meeting minutes. When the army left, they went back to their meetings as if nothing had happened.

The End Is Nigh

The war couldn't break the Quakers. They did that to themselves. In 1828 the Friends were rocked by a national religious schism that split the community into the conservative Orthodox and progressive Hicksite Societies of Friends. At Quaker Hill, the Hicksites used the meetinghouse, while the Orthodox members built their own meetinghouse in 1831, in what is now a private home.

While internal combustion started the Quakers' decline, steam combustion sped it down the tracks. On December 31, 1848, the New York and Harlem Railroad reached Pawling. The area rapidly transformed from a quiet religious community into a hot spot for wealthy vacationers from the city. Two popular resorts, the Dutcher House and the Mizzentop Hotel (the latter marketed as the "Closest World Class Country and Mountain Resort to New York City") led to an increase in temporary and permanent non-Quaker residents.

Further, as the Industrial Revolution took hold, the agrarian Quakers found themselves losing membership and influence. In 1885, the Hicksite Meeting was "laid down," in the vernacular, and the Orthodox Meeting petered out about a decade later; at the same time, in 1895, a nondenominational Sunday school became Christ Church. The reformation was complete.

Where did the Quakers go? Reilly has a theory. "They abolished slavery one hundred years before Lincoln. They were conscientious objectors two hundred years before Vietnam. They believed in women's rights long before the suffragettes. I think they may be gone because they developed interstellar travel—they were so far ahead of their time." Who's to say he's wrong?

The Quakers who remain on earth still hold a yearly meeting at the Oblong, which has been owned by the Historical Society of Quaker Hill and Vicinity since 1936.

And though there aren't many Quakers in Quaker Hill anymore, the spirit of the Friends remains strong in Pawling. "The Akin Hall Association, organized in 1880 as an association of people concerned with religion, charity, and benevolence, still exists," Mandracchia says. Reilly adds, "Pawling has always been a very giving community. People here do not go for want. During World War II the school became a hospital, and people opened their homes to the wounded and their families. That has continued even through

Hurricane Sandy. I have family that lost their home due to a generator fire, and the outpouring of help to this family is just phenomenal."

Friends in need, friends indeed—whether Quaker Friends or not.

Part 3:
Independence

Hamilton Slept Here. And Here. Here Too

Hamilton: An American Musical Made Its First Appearance at a Capital Region Theater in August 2019, but Hamilton the Founding Father Had a Deep and Meaningful History with the Hudson Valley

Alexander Hamilton is most often associated with three places: the Caribbean, where he was born and orphaned; New York City, where he spent most of his professional and political life; and Weehawken, New Jersey, where he was mortally wounded at the famously pistoled hand of Aaron Burr. Missing from that GPS-inspired biography, however, is another place that defined Hamilton as much as the others—the Hudson Valley.

From White Plains, where he fought alongside George Washington, to Albany, where he was wed, his children were baptized, and he was venerated in an enormously influential eulogy, to numerous spots in between, Hamilton spent a great deal of time all over the valley.

"What a huge part it played in his life, his family," says Nicole Scholet, president of the Alexander Hamilton Awareness Society. "He is so associated with New York City, but in every period of his life the Hudson Valley played a major role. When you look at how much time he spent in the valley, it's a really important story."

"Hamilton Is a Gone Man"

It's a story that began in October 1776, as Washington's troops fled Manhattan into what is now Westchester County. Hamilton, then a captain, tried to inspire what Ron Chernow, in his musical-inspiring biography *Alexander Hamilton,* called a "slovenly, dejected bunch," firing from the high ground of Chatterton's Hill as the Red Coats splashed across the Bronx River. He wasn't there long, though, and the even more dejected bunch retreated farther, to New Jersey.

Hamilton made his first visit to the city that would become his second home, Albany, in 1777. Washington sent him there to ask General Horatio Gates to borrow some troops. Hamilton covered sixty miles a day for five days on horseback, "riding like a man possessed," Chernow writes. He got to Albany on November 5, but despite his already keen powers of persuasion, the twenty-five-year-old Hamilton failed to convince Gates. "I used every argument in my power to convince him of the propriety of the measure, but he was inflexible.... I found myself infinitely embarrassed and was at a loss how to act," Hamilton wrote. It was not a total loss, however; he met and fell head over spurs for twenty-two-year-old Eliza Schuyler. ("Hamilton is a gone man," a colleague wrote.) On his return to Philadelphia, Hamilton wrote letters to Washington mentioning stops in Fishkill, New Windsor, Poughkeepsie, and Peekskill, where he nearly died of a high fever and spent weeks recovering.

By the summer of 1778, Washington and Hamilton, now aide-de-camp—essentially, chief of staff—returned to White Plains and made their headquarters at the Jacob Purdy House, where they spent the next seven weeks. In 1779, Washington and Hamilton set up headquarters at the Thomas Ellison House, in New Windsor, to which they returned several times over the next few years. While there, Hamilton helped plan the taking of Stony Point on July 15, a critical battle in the war. They stayed at the captured fort the following two nights.

Hamilton also spent considerable time at the Van Wyck Homestead, the Dutch colonial house on Route 9 in Fishkill that served as headquarters for the Fishkill supply depot. This important strategic military center was one of three major encampments for the Continental Army, along with Morristown, New Jersey, and Valley Forge, Pennsylvania. Hamilton, Washington, the Marquis de Lafayette, and John Jay all made their way to the homestead frequently.

The Man behind West Point

A Revolutionary Zelig, Hamilton had a way of being at interesting places at interesting times. In September 1780, he was at West Point for a meeting with General Benedict Arnold. When Arnold was handed a note, he grew agitated and fled the scene; later that day, Hamilton and Washington learned that the note told Arnold that his coconspirator, British major John Andre, had been captured with the military plans Arnold had tried to sell him stashed in his boot.

Hamilton was involved in the search for our most notorious traitor, and the incident helped spur his belief that West Point should become a permanent stronghold. Indeed, he as much as anyone pushed for the establishment of a national military academy there, going so far as to design the curriculum and budget for professors' salaries. As secretary of the treasury, he authorized the purchase of the land, for $11,085, in 1790. "West Point was very important for him," Scholet says. "He really cared about making that location something." He eventually convinced those against the idea, including Thomas Jefferson, to change their minds. Jefferson, as president, signed the legislation establishing the academy in 1802—"and now he gets credit for it," Scholet says, with a hint of lingering bitterness befitting a captain of Hamilton awareness.

Fresh from the Arnold debacle, Hamilton rode to Albany in November to get married. At the time, Chernow writes, Albany was "a rough-hewn town of four thousand inhabitants, about one-tenth of them slaves." The Schuylers lived in a mansion south of the city that they called "the Pastures," which then overlooked the bucolic Hudson River from a high bluff (and today overlooks the opposite-of-bucolic I-787 and the industrial Port of Albany). The Hamiltons were married in one of the mansion's parlors on December 14, 1780, and stayed through the holidays. "With fairy-tale suddenness, the orphaned Hamilton had annexed a gigantic and prosperous clan," Chernow writes. Family was as important to Hamilton as nation-building, and his Albany home is as integral to his story as his work. "These are national figures, but this is a family that experienced birth, death and squabbles," says Diane Shewchuk, curator at the Albany Institute of History & Art.

Then it was back to work. In January 1781 the couple headed to Washington's headquarters at the Ellison House in New Windsor, and in mid-April they rented their first home, a house on DePeyster's Point, also known then as Fishkill Hook, in Beacon. It was directly opposite Washington's quarters, and Hamilton shuttled back and forth across the river in a small boat. While awaiting his next military assignment, Hamilton was out and about, debating politics at local taverns and writing extensively. In August, he got his orders: to Virginia, for the Siege of Yorktown.

Nation-Building, from the Hudson Valley

After the war, Hamilton became perhaps the most powerful lawyer in New York City but frequently traveled up the valley to visit the in-laws and to conduct business from his Albany office. "He spent quite a lot of time [at the Pastures]," says Molly Belmont, director of marketing for Discover Albany.

"He studied for the bar exam in the law library at Schuyler Mansion. His marriage and baptism records are still at First Church," on North Pearl Street. He probably wrote three of the Federalist Papers there, says Heidi Hill, historic site manager for Crailo and Schuyler Mansion State Historic Sites.

But those who know Hamilton only from the musical don't know the entire story—for instance, about the slaves that he helped the Schuylers buy and sell. Hill and other historians are pretty OK with these and other lapses in the play's veracity. "We don't feel the musical has to be an accurate portrayal of history," Hill says. "People can come here [to Schuyler Mansion] and hear a fuller story." She and her staff are expecting the play's fans to do just that, adding to the doubling in yearly attendance since *Hamilton: An American Musical* opened in 2015.

During this time, Hamilton helped shaped the new government, writing many of the papers critical of the Articles of Confederation, including his first essay, "Federalist No. 1," while on a sloop traveling up- or downriver in October 1787. Not content with just writing, he almost singlehandedly lobbied the New York delegation to ratify the new US Constitution in July 1788 in Poughkeepsie. Most of the delegates were against it, but over six weeks of intense debate at the Dutchess County courthouse, Hamilton spoke passionately and long—often for hours on end—and finally turned enough votes to approve the document and make New York the eleventh state.

Life was good for the Hamiltons until a fateful dinner at the home of Judge John Tayler on State Street in Albany. At that dinner, Hamilton and others said some nasty things—"despicable opinion" in the words of an eyewitness—about Aaron Burr, Jefferson's vice president, who was running for governor of New York. A guest at the dinner wrote about the comments in a letter, which somehow ended up being published in the *New-York Evening Post*. Burr challenged Hamilton to an "affair of honor," as duels were called. On the History Channel's list of all-time legendary duels, this one takes the top spot.

Hamilton was buried at Trinity Church in Manhattan, but back in Albany's Dutch Reformed Church on North Pearl Street, mourners filled the pews to hear Hamilton's friend, Reverend Eliphalet Nott from Albany's Presbyterian Church, give a rousing and powerful eulogy denouncing dueling. Called "one of the most influential funeral sermons in American history," it helped lead to a law that required state officials to take an antidueling oath.

Alexander Hamilton lost the duel but, unlike Burr, maintained his honor and, indeed, earned everlasting glory—not to mention a hit play, starring him. And the Hudson Valley's Hamiltonian tourist attractions have been welcoming bigger crowds of history and theater nerds ever since.

Point Well Taken

The Small Battle of Stony Point Had Big Consequences in the War for Independence

If you were to rank Revolutionary War battles in order of importance, this one wouldn't make the top ten. As a historical reference point, its name is irrelevant in comparison to Lexington and Concord, Bunker Hill, Saratoga, and Yorktown. The fight took less than half an hour, and the winners abandoned the ground they had taken just two days later. Still, the Battle of Stony Point, just south of West Point, was a critical victory for the nascent nation's Continental Army.

As with most things, context is key. The battle took place on July 16, 1779. The war had been going on for four long years. George Washington's army had won very few battles but had managed to play the British army to a virtual stalemate. That didn't sit well with the Crown, and Henry Clinton, commander in chief of the British forces in America, wanted to force the issue to its, in his view, logical conclusion. He would goad Washington into what military parlance of the time called "general and decisive action," says Michael Sheehan, historical interpreter at the Stony Point Battlefield. "In other words, 'Let's beat him and be done with this,'" Sheehan says.

In May 1779, a British force of about 8,000 men, under Lieutenant Colonel Henry Johnson, captured Fort Lafayette on the eastern bank of the Hudson and built fortifications at Stony Point, an arrowhead-shaped peninsula on the western bank. These spots were chosen because they were near a strategically narrow point in the river where the Kings Ferry crossed, making it key to controlling passage into the Hudson Highlands and West Point. The Brits were armed with heavy artillery, a Royal Navy gunboat was moved in to add more protection, and an armed sloop, the *Vulture*, set anchor nearby. Stony Point, not a fort in the true sense of the term, was defended not by stone walls but by redoubts of cannons fronted by felled trees with sharpened points, called abatis. The terrain was rocky and steep, and the swampy riverbed made approach even more difficult. Washington saw all this from his encampment at nearby Buckberg Mountain. Typical eighteenth-century military tactics involving straight-line approaches seemed hopeless. But he had—forgive the pun—a revolutionary plan.

The Navy Seals of the Day

Rather than attack frontally, Washington and his field commander, Brigadier General Anthony Wayne, decided on a stealth approach. They called in the Corps of Light Infantry, formed only one month earlier. This was the army's most seasoned and best-trained unit—"they were the Navy Seals of the day," says Sheehan. On July 15 Wayne and about 1,300 troops began an eight-hour march from Sandy Beach, just north of Fort Montgomery, to Spring-steel's farm just west of Stony Point.

Arriving there near midnight, Wayne divided his force into three columns. Two of them moved down to the river, north and south of the fort, taking advantage of low tide to gain a beachhead. These troops were ordered to carry unloaded muskets, so a misfire would not alert the enemy, and to use only fixed bayonets in the attack. When they were in position, the third column began firing muskets as a diversion to draw the attention of the 564 British soldiers. The two riverside columns then crept up the hill. A group of volunteers, called the "forlorn hope" in recognition of their dangerous mission, were first in, charged with breaking the abatis with picks and axes. The troops crossed the defenses and stormed the fort. It was a bloody fight. Wayne lost fifteen killed and eighty-three wounded—including himself, hit in the head by a spent musket ball but not seriously injured. The British suffered at least twenty deaths and seventy-four wounded. But it was also quick, and by 2 a.m. on July 16, Wayne sent a letter to Washington reporting the fort captured.

The Continental Army was fortunate—bad weather had forced the two guard ships downriver. But it was also brilliantly marshaled. Never before had such guerrilla tactics been used so successfully. Washington visited the battle site the next day and commended his troops for succeeding in such a difficult assignment.

And the day after that, he took his army, and a lot of British weaponry and supplies, and fled.

Freedom Fighters

Washington never intended to hold the point because he knew he didn't have enough men to defend the inevitable large-scale response the Brits were sure to make. The British moved back in but stayed only a few more months before turning their attentions toward the southern front. Stony Point turned out to be the final battle in the northern colonies.

So what's the big deal? For one, the battle was in our front yard. More importantly, it was a turning point in several ways. The tactics that Washington deployed were "experimental," Sheehan says. "These troops were trained to fight outside of linear formation and to go where needed. Warfare had never been done like this before by the Americans. It proved that the painful training done in previous years was solid, and proved that this was an effective fighting force."

After a long time fighting with little or nothing to show for it, the Continental Army earned itself and the nation an enormous emotional lift by so easily embarrassing the mighty British army, which no longer could take the ragtag army lightly. An entire British company, about five hundred men, was taken prisoner, and the fifteen captured cannons and additional booty were worth "in the low millions" in today's money, Sheehan says. "For an army with nothing, this was a huge boost." Congress agreed. Of the eleven medals in total that were awarded during the war, three went to soldiers at Stony Point. One of them was Wayne, who went on to win other stirring, against-all-odds battles, which earned him the lasting nickname "Mad" Anthony.

The victory also helped Ben Franklin convince King Louis XVI that the Americans had staying power and that the French should continue to support the Revolution. But perhaps the true lasting value of the battle, despite its seeming second-rate status in the pantheon of Revolutionary War battles, is best summed up in the letter that Mad Anthony Wayne scribbled, semiconsciously, to be dispatched to General Washington. It reads, in its entirety, "Dear General, the fort and garrison with Colonel Johnson are ours. Our officers and men behaved like men who are determined to be free."

The Great Chain

How Blocking River Passage Helped Win the War

From the earliest moments of the War for Independence, each side knew that the key to victory was the Hudson River. Boston was the hotbed of the Revolution, and most of General George Washington's nascent Continental Army came from the Northeast. The river separated the New England states from the rest of the country. If the British took control of the Hudson, the head would be cut off from the body, and both sides knew what would follow.

In 1776, the British had seized New York City, held on to Canada, and had a water route just about the entire way between the two. Blocking British ships became paramount. But American fortifications in the valley were not sufficient. General Washington needed a great idea. He got it from an English-born patriot named Thomas Machin.

Machin knew water. He had been an apprentice canal builder in England, and as a captain in an artillery company, he was called by Washington to help defend the river at the Hudson Highlands. The river was narrow there, and since ancient times armies had placed sharpened logs, scuttled ships, and other debris in a narrows to block passage. But here the river was too deep. Machin had his a-ha moment: Why not forge a large iron chain and float it across the river, anchoring it to both shores?

Some kind of chain or boom system had been in the original concept to block the Hudson as part of a fortification system, says Colonel James M. Johnson (Ret.), the Frank T. Bumpus Chair in Hudson River Valley History, military historian of the Hudson River Valley, and executive director of the Hudson River Valley Institute at Marist College. "Gen. James Clinton and Christopher Tappen [the brother of Clinton's wife] recommended them in their report of June 1775. They also mentioned the possibility of using 'four or five booms chained together on one side of the river, ready to be drawn across,' as a means of blocking navigation," he says. Their report recommended West Point, "as it is not only the narrowest part of the said river, but best situated, on account of the high hills contiguous to it, as well on the west and east side of the river which cover those parts; so that without a strong easterly wind, or the tide, no vessel can pass it; and the tide on said part of the river is generally so reverse, that a vessel is usually thrown on one side of the river or the other, by means whereof such vessel lay fair and exposed" to the men and guns lying in wait on shore.

They tried a chain at Fort Montgomery first in 1777. When British general Henry Clinton sailed upriver to support General John Burgoyne at Saratoga in the fall of 1777, the chain stopped him—sort of. Clinton recognized the chain was too much of an obstacle, but the troops on shore were not. Clinton's men disembarked, overpowered the American guards, removed the chain, and sailed upriver, burning Kingston for good measure.

West Point then was not what West Point is now. It was a somewhat shabby redoubt, one of many up and down the river that failed to halt the enemy. But the chain had succeeded. "The lesson was not that the chain was not a good idea, it was that the fortifications weren't strong enough," says Lieutenant Colonel Sean Sculley, assistant professor of history and chief of the American Division at the US Military Academy at West Point. When Burgoyne was defeated at Saratoga and the British retreated to New York City, Washington ordered an even bigger chain in 1778. It was built of iron mined in New Jersey and other areas, Sculley says, and smelted in secret forges (see sidebar). The links were brought by wagon to New Windsor, assembled in chains of ten links, and floated on rafts to West Point. "Machin was in charge," Sculley says. "He was the expert."

Meanwhile, Polish-born engineer Tadeusz Kościuszko was charged with building West Point—"not to fire on ships but to defend the chain from assaults by land," Sculley says. "They had learned from what Henry Clinton had done, so they built the fortification on high ground to defend it."

Each link weighed more than one hundred pounds, and the finished chain weighed sixty-five tons. It floated on wood rafts, with a wood boom south of the chain to prevent ships from trying to ram it. It could be disconnected in the center to allow friendly traffic through and was taken out in the fall so ice didn't break it, then replaced in spring.

And it worked. "It protected the Hudson Valley from the kinds of raids Clinton routinely practiced on the Connecticut shore during the war," Sculley says. "The significance of that is hard to overestimate." Johnson adds, "By blocking the Hudson River to British ships, the Great Chain was the center of gravity or long pole in the tent for Fortress West Point." Indeed, the British deemed the Great Chain so critical to victory that they were willing to

Forged in Secret

Where was the Great Chain forged? That has been a mystery since the Revolution—but is a mystery no longer. Donald "Doc" Bayne, president of the Friends of Sterling Forest, found evidence of the forge in Sterling Forest and is now working with the state to turn it into a historic site.

At the time of the war, the forge was a secret; the British had enacted laws prohibiting the colonists from making iron for their own purposes, Bayne says. He has found and tagged more than fifty artifacts, including chunks of iron called "skulls," from nine of the seventeen forge fires that the Continental Army had contracted for with Peter Townsend, who owned the Sterling Iron Works. "I have been studying the area for nine years," he says.

Bayne is trying to raise funds for an extensive archeological dig and in the future hopes to create a tour from the forge to West Point, showcasing the journey of the Great Chain. "Once the dig is done, the state said they want to make this a National Historic Site," he says.

pay a malcontent American general named Benedict Arnold to deliver the plans to West Point so they could circumvent it. "It was so important to Clinton he paid Arnold 20,000 pounds and gave him a generalship even though he failed and the plan was foiled," Sculley says. "That was a lot of money to give and he failed to deliver what he promised."

Two hundred and forty years later, the Great Chain is a nearly forgotten bit of history, and that's a shame, Sculley says. "I have an aunt in New Jersey, where the iron came from, and they are very proud of the part they had in forging the chain," he says. "Kids in school there learn about it." At West Point's Trophy Point, the remaining thirteen links, a swivel, and a clevis of the Great Chain are symbols of early West Point and the Hudson River, which John Adams knew as the North River and called the "key to the whole continent." "Militarily, the Great Chain proved that deterrence works because, as a part of Fortress West Point, it appeared strong enough with its supporting fortifications to dissuade the British from attacking it," Johnson says. As such, the chain deserves a more prominent place in the history of the American road—or perhaps better said, river—to independence.

Foreign Legions

The Young Europeans Who Joined the Fight for American Freedom

Their names are well known to anyone who remembers seventh-grade social studies—or drives over the bridges or past the monuments dedicated in their honor. But the reasons we know the unpronounceable names of Tadeusz Kościuszko and the Marquis de Lafayette might need a little refresher. How and why could a twenty-something Pole and a French teenager become so important to the American War of Independence against Great Britain?

Kos and Effect

Tadeusz (anglicized to Thaddeus) Kościuszko (1746–1817) was born in the Polish-Lithuanian Commonwealth, now Belarus. He was educated at Poland's military academy, the Corps of Cadets, and later studied art in France. He was also a revolutionary at heart, and when he learned of the uprising in the British colonies, he set sail for the New World in October 1776 and joined the war effort as a colonel of engineers in the Continental Army.

His first job was building fortifications in Philadelphia, along the Delaware River. The next spring, he joined the Northern Army and recommended adding fortifications to Fort Ticonderoga. His commander ignored him; the British army soon thereafter took the fort without much trouble. Kościuszko, ordered to slow the Brits' pursuit of escaping colonials, blocked their progress by cutting trees, damming streams, and destroying roads and bridges.

He then selected a strong position near Saratoga and built defenses that were instrumental in winning the Battle of Saratoga, the first major victory for the colonies in the war. Kościuszko's defenses earned high praise from General Horatio Gates, who later told his friend Dr. Benjamin Rush, "The great tacticians of the campaign were hills and forests, which a young Polish engineer was skillful enough to select for my encampment."

In March 1778 Kościuszko was assigned to West Point. He worked for the next two years strengthening the fort. Much of his legend was built there—a legend that Paul Ackermann, museum specialist with the US Military Academy Museum, thinks is "extremely overrated." Ackermann says Kościuszko essentially learned on the job but was not a highly skilled engineer. "His work in Saratoga is quite worthy of praise, as is his allegiance to the cause, to Gates and to America," Ackermann says. "His work was real and very valuable. But what he did at West Point laid the groundwork for the middle phase of development, which is important but not how West Point reached its final extent of defenses."

According to Ackermann, Kościuszko's work was "adequate but poorly thought out," and one redoubt was overdesigned and later amended. It was during this time that West Point was commanded by Benedict Arnold. "[Kościuszko's] allegiance was with Gates, not with Arnold, and he doesn't want to work for Arnold," says Ackermann. "To be polite, he tries to abandon his job and quit." George Washington assigned him to the Southern Army in 1780.

The third and final phase of West Point's design was completed by his successor. "His window at West Point is shorter than what most people think," Ackermann says. In the South, though, he aided the Continental Army through campaigns in the Carolinas as an engineer and a fighter. (He was stabbed in the buttocks by a bayonet in one battle.) At the end of the war, he was among the troops that reoccupied Charleston after the British left. He even set off a fireworks display there in 1783 to celebrate the signing of the Treaty of Paris. He left the army as a brigadier general and returned to his homeland—where he became an even bigger hero.

He fought in his country's wars against Russia and Prussia, and in 1794, as commander of the Polish National Armed Forces, he led a fight known as the Kościuszko Uprising (which was defeated). He was imprisoned and later pardoned, immigrated to the United States for a time, and eventually returned to Europe and settled in Switzerland, where he died.

His accomplishments here, if not quite heroic, as Ackermann believes (though others would dispute), were still commendable, especially considering his age and nationality. "Kościuszko worship, in my estimation, is a bit overplayed," Ackermann says. "The thinking is that he came here making decrees, whereas I think he learned along the way. He made mistakes. But he was loyal and followed through. He did make great contributions in all theaters of the Revolutionary War."

Noblesse Oblige

With a name like Marie Joseph Paul Yves Roche Gilbert du Motier, the Marquis de Lafayette (1757–1834) clearly had blue blood running through his veins. He could have sat in his château drinking fine French wine his whole life. Instead, he supported revolutions against his own class on two continents and became known as "the hero of two worlds."

He was born into a noble military family in Chavaniac, France, and his parents and grandmother had all died by the time he was thirteen, leaving him a large inheritance. He joined the French army at fourteen and got married at fifteen to a fourteen-year-old of similar nobility. Clearly, he was a young man in a hurry, and at age nineteen he set sail for the arising United States of America to join the fight.

According to the website marquisdelafayette.net, "In person Lafayette was tall and powerfully built, with broad shoulders, deep chest, and a tendency toward corpulence. His features were large and strongly marked. He had much dignity of manner, and was ordinarily quiet and self-possessed." He was commissioned a major general and was shot in the leg in his first fight, the Battle of Brandywine, while directing a retreat. General George Washington took a liking to the teenage rebel and asked doctors to take good care of Lafayette. The fondness was mutual and lasted throughout their lifetimes. "They had more like a father-son kind of relationship, which you don't see with Kościuszko," Ackermann says. "Washington had more of a business relationship with Kościuszko and a more personal relationship with Lafayette."

Once he had recovered from his wound, Lafayette's imprint was felt nearly everywhere during the war. In 1778, he escaped British capture at Barren Hill—now called Lafayette Hill. He served in Albany, debating strongly against a proposed invasion of Canada. He led the Continental attack at Monmouth Courthouse and served in the Battle of Rhode Island. He also played diplomat, returning to France to lobby King Louis XVI for the support that helped the colonials win the war. (Before he got there, though, he fell ill and spent several weeks in Fishkill recovering.) He returned to fight in 1780 and led the forces that held off the British until the American and French armies were well positioned to win the Battle of Yorktown and, effectively, independence.

"Washington had great pride in Lafayette," Ackermann says. "For Washington to give him command showed great trust and confidence. He commanded a valuable elite force in the Continental Army, considered the Special Forces of its day. He was a critical element of Washington's army."

At twenty-four, with one world-class rebellion under his belt, he returned to France to help in another. He rejoined the French army and worked with another new American friend, Thomas Jefferson, the American ambassador to France, to establish trade relations. When the French Revolution broke out in 1789, he sided with the underclass and helped draft the Declaration of the Rights of Man and of the Citizen. But as a nobleman, he was ordered arrested and fled. Caught by Austrian troops, he spent more than five years in prison. After Napoleon Bonaparte ordered his release in 1797, he lay low but returned to government after Bonaparte was deposed. He served as a member of the French parliament for most of the rest of his life.

He was not forgotten in the United States, and in 1824 President James Monroe invited him back as the nation's guest. He visited all twenty-four states, including a triumphal ride up the Hudson River from New York to Albany. "Most of the leaders of the war had already died, and here was a hero of the Revolution who was still alive," Ackermann says. "He was the living embodiment of the Revolution."

He died in 1834, leaving behind two daughters and a son named George Washington. He is buried in Paris, covered in part with soil from Bunker Hill, befitting his position as a hero of two worlds.

And Then There's Von Steuben

Another foreign-born supporter also helped win American independence. Friedrich Wilhelm August Heinrich Ferdinand Steuben, which morphed from his birth name, Friedrich Wilhelm Ludolf Gerhard Augustin von Steuben— names were *names* back then—was born in Prussia in 1730 but earned eternal fame as a major general of the Continental Army. He was a low-level aristocrat but a true military man and helped teach the motley army how to drill, how to plan, and how to fight.

In fact, he wrote *Regulations for the Order and Discipline of the Troops of the United States,* which became the standard drill manual of the US Army until the War of 1812. He served with Washington at Valley Forge and with General Nathanael Greene in Yorktown, and he was Washington's chief of staff in the final years of the war, even though his English was poor. (He reportedly often yelled to his translator, "Over here! Swear at him for me!")

Known here as Baron Von Steuben, he also sat on the court-martial of John Andre, the British officer who plotted with Benedict Arnold. Given American citizenship by the Pennsylvania legislature in 1784 (and by New York in 1786), he lived after the war in Manhattan and New Jersey before settling near Rome, New York, on land given to him for his military service. He died in 1794 and is buried at what is now the Steuben Memorial Historic Site in Steuben, New York—one of scores of towns, counties, bridges, boats, festival days, buildings, football fields, and whatnot named in his honor.

Spy versus Spy

Was Benedict Arnold a Traitor or a Hero?

Lieutenant Colonel Sherman L. Fleek (Ret.), command historian at the US Military Academy at West Point, has three books on his nightstand at the moment: *A Hero and a Spy, Patriot and Traitor,* and *Misunderstood Hero.* These seemingly contradictory and problematic epithets all apply to the same person—a person who in the view of the American public for the past 230 years is hardly contradictory or problematic at all. In fact, you could joke that if you looked up the word "traitor" in the dictionary, you'd find his picture: Benedict Arnold.

How can the words "hero," "patriot," and "misunderstood" describe this poster boy for treason? That's what Fleek is hoping to learn more about. "I have been here three years, long enough to know the history of West Point generally, but now I know what types of things I don't know," he says. "To know the history in depth, you have to start from the beginning, and that's the Revolution." And no one personifies the glory, the ignominy, the tragedy, and the confusion of that time better than Benedict Arnold.

Arnold's Army

The basic biography is well known. The Arnolds were one of the first families of the New World. William Arnold, born in England in 1587, came to Providence in 1636 as one of the fifty-four proprietors in the first settlement of Rhode Island. His son Benedict was governor of the colony for much of the 1660s and 1670s, and his grandson Benedict was a member of the assembly. The next Benedict—that's the third Benedict, if you're scoring at home—moved to Connecticut, where he was a prosperous businessman and political leader. His first son, Benedict, died in infancy. But his second son, Benedict, our Benedict, was born in Norwich on January 14, 1741.

Our Benedict Arnold has been described as romantic, adventurous, proud, sensitive, impulsive, brave, strong, handsome, good, and evil. All these traits truly began to come into play when, during his teens, several of his siblings died and his father fell into alcoholism and lost much of the family fortune. At sixteen he enlisted in the Connecticut militia to fight the French invasion at Lake George. He lasted about thirteen days and then left, probably as a deserter, though that's unproven. He marched back to Norwich, where he built his own business empire—druggist, bookseller, landowner—got married, and had three sons. Yes, the first son was named Benedict.

He was also a captain in the militia, and when the Revolutionary War broke out in 1775, he jumped in. He was instrumental in two early triumphs, the capture of Fort Ticonderoga and the attack on Quebec, for which his bravery and injury—he was shot in the leg—earned him not only a promotion to brigadier general but also the support of boldface-name generals Horatio Gates, William Schuyler, and the commander in chief, George Washington. But he also earned the enmity of others, including many in Congress, for his disputatious nature and his constant need for power, recognition, fame, and compensation. One of his rivals, in fact, posted a handbill that read, "Money is this man's God, and to get enough of it he would sacrifice his country."

That would come later, though. First, he nearly sacrificed himself to save his fledgling country.

From Hero to Turncoat

Feeling slighted because he was passed over for promotion to major general, he took part in the Battle of Ridgefield, near Philadelphia, and was wounded in the leg for the second time. That earned him his promotion, but he still felt abused because he had lost his seniority and was considered junior to the other major generals. He attempted to resign his commission, but Washington wouldn't allow it.

Arnold was posted up the Hudson River and became a hero of the two battles of Saratoga. But not without pissing more people off. Fighting his superiors (he was removed from the first battle by General Gates) and disobeying orders (Gates again), he led reckless but successful attacks against the British, which helped lead to their surrender ten days later and the first substantive victory by the Continental Army in the war.

Arnold was shot in the leg, again, and severely wounded. He later said he would have been better off had he been hit in the chest. And Fleek agrees. "If that ball had hit his heart instead of his leg, he would have gone down as a great patriot leader like Ethan Allan or Nathan Hale," he says. But it didn't, and he didn't.

After Saratoga, Congress restored his seniority, but Arnold interpreted this as sympathy for his injury rather than recognition of his achievements or redemption of his wronged reputation. Pouting, he soon returned to Philadelphia, where he tried to capitalize on his wounds and his heroism by making a lot of money. "He was a privateer," Colonel Fleek says. He also became even angrier about his treatment and less optimistic about the Revolution. In Philadelphia he fell in with British sympathizers and courted Peggy Shippen, the eighteen-year-old daughter of a Loyalist judge, whom he married in 1778. (Arnold's first wife had died in 1775 while he was at Ticonderoga.) Arnold's dismay with the Revolution was out in the open, and the British knew he might be willing to turn.

Peggy Shippen Arnold, by all accounts a lovely young lady, had previously caught the eye of a British major named John Andre. Andre was a spy. And through a series of intermediaries, Arnold and Andre began to correspond through letters, in secret, sometimes using code and invisible ink, often using Peggy Arnold as a runner. By 1779, Arnold had switched sides. He provided information on troop and supply locations (while haggling over money). He also let the Brits know of his impending appointment, by Washington himself, as commander of West Point. This was the key. "If there was a critical piece of terrain in the colonies that would possibly determine the outcome of the war, it would be the Hudson River Valley and West Point," says Colonel Fleek. "He who controlled the Hudson would probably win the war." Arnold's price for turning it over to the British: 20,000 pounds sterling. British general Henry Clinton's answer: Deal.

While in command of West Point, which he took on August 3, 1780, Arnold resided at the well-known Robinson House, across the river in what is now Garrison. The Robinsons were Loyalists who had lost their estate to the Continental Army. Arnold chose to stay there, against orders, because it allowed him an easy escape should he need to flee (see sidebar).

He immediately began to plot West Point's turnover. The famous iron "chain across the Hudson," meant to block British ships, was left in disrepair. He kept troop levels and supplies at West Point deliberately low. In September 1780, he gave Andre the plans for West Point. The next day, Andre was captured near Tarrytown by three Westchester patriots; the plans were in his boot. The following morning, September 24, 1780, Arnold learned that Andre had been caught and that their plans were on their way to General Washington. Arnold fled, leaving his wife and son in the lurch.

Andre was hanged on October 2 in Tappan. Arnold served in the British army for the remainder of the war, including leading several devastating attacks against the colonies, but the British never fully trusted him. (Andre, meanwhile, is still celebrated as a true English patriot.) Following the war, Arnold and his family, since reunited, moved between England and Canada, where he made more money and more enemies; historians have called his life

Whither Arnold?

Want to walk in the boots of a traitor? Simply head to the shoreline near Philipstown, just south of the Garrison Metro-North station. There you'll find the path that America's most notorious turncoat, Benedict Arnold, took to flee capture. You'll also find a gazebo, historical information, and some terrific views of the river and West Point.

Two separate entrances lead to the trail. From route 9D in Garrison, turn down Glenclyffe Road at the sign for the Garrison Institute. There is a small parking lot above the entrance to the trail that leads to the overlook where Arnold left. Also, down Lower Station Road, just before the entrance to the Metro-North station parking lot, there are two stone pillars that lead into the Arden Point trail, which also leads to the gazebo and overlook.

Besides the path, there are many memorials to Benedict Arnold. But sometimes you have to use your imagination to see them. Like Voldemort, Benedict Arnold was for a long time "he who shall not be named."

On the Saratoga battlefield within Saratoga National Historical Park, you'll find the Boot Monument, depicting an injured leg and inscribed, "In memory of the most brilliant soldier of the Continental army, who was desperately wounded on this spot . . . winning for his countrymen the decisive battle of the American Revolution, and for himself the rank of Major General." Guess who.

And the victory monument at the Saratoga Park has four niches, three of which are occupied by statues of Generals Gates, Schuyler, and Daniel Morgan. The fourth niche is empty. Guess who.

On the grounds of the US Military Academy at West Point, in the Old Cadet Chapel built in 1836, prominent plaques commemorate all the major generals, by name, who served in the Revolution. One plaque, however, is tucked away by itself, up high near the balcony in the back. It says only, "Major general . . . born 1740." Guess who. "The builders couldn't deny the fact that there was another guy, but his name was so odious they wouldn't recognize it," says Fleek.

There are also markers that do bear his name, in Massachusetts and Maine and along the western bank of Lake Champlain. Perhaps most ignominious of all, a plaque on the house where Arnold lived in central London calls him an "American Patriot."

after the war one of "controversy, resentment and legal entanglements," and he even fought a bloodless duel. In 1801, his health declined, possibly due to his many serious leg injuries, and he died on June 14 at age sixty. He was buried in London. Many years later, his remains were mistakenly relocated to an unmarked mass grave.

Who's the Patriot?

Arnold was immediately and thoroughly vilified in the new United States. Benjamin Franklin wrote that "Judas sold only one man, Arnold three millions." His name was effectively stricken from early military histories (see sidebar).

And yet, "he was a great commander and a visionary," Fleek says. His work at Ticonderoga and Quebec, including long marches through the Maine wilderness, were marvels of military ingenuity, Fleek contends, and his bravery at Saratoga helped turn the tide of the war in the colonies' favor. "He was a smart guy, very motivated, full of initiative—all the traits of a solid commander," Fleek continues. "But I wouldn't want him as my brother-in-law. His transformation was not political or ideological, it was more personal in nature. He always wanted credit, and he allowed himself to be won over because he felt he was insulted and neglected.

"But here's the dichotomy," Fleek continues. "Who really were the traitors in this war? The true rebels in the middle of an act of sedition were the colonialists, not the British. The winners get to choose the terms, so we call ourselves patriots now. But who really were the patriots, and who were the traitors?"

Best. Clinton. Ever.

*It's Not Hillary or DeWitt—George Clinton
Belongs in the Pantheon of Founding Fathers*

One of these things is not like the others: George Washington, Thomas Jefferson, Alexander Hamilton, George Clinton. Can you name which one?

Right—but for the wrong reason.

They are all Founding Fathers of the United States of America. They all have cities and counties and roads and schools and bridges named after them. The only real difference is that you know lots about the first three, but the fourth typically elicits a collective "George *who?*" (Or, in another context of course, "Dr. Funkenstein!")

Clinton—raised in the Hudson Valley, first and longest-serving governor of New York State, fourth vice president of the United States, and a political linchpin in the earliest days of the republic—should be as well-known and celebrated as his peers. He was *all that* in his day, but history has tended to treat him as a footnote. If the Founding Fathers are the Beatles, George Clinton is Pete Best.

But make no mistake, there would be no USA—at least not as we now know it—and New York would not be the Empire State without Clinton's military, political, and business savvy. "He was a dominant figure throughout the 1770s and 1780s," says his biographer, John Kaminski, director of the Center for the Study of the American Constitution at the University of Wisconsin–Madison. So why doesn't his face grace our currency today?

New York State of Mind

George Clinton was born in Little Britain in 1739 to an English family that actually emigrated from Ireland. Little is known of his early years, but at the outbreak of the last French and Indian War, he joined the British army and was commissioned a lieutenant. As a civilian he read the law and served in a number of capacities in Ulster County, including as Ulster County clerk,

63

a position he held for fifty-three years. He was also elected to the provincial assembly and joined the restive leaders who were beginning to oppose British rule.

At the outbreak of the War of Independence in 1775, he was a brigadier general of the militia and a member of the New York Provincial Congress, where he was a mid–Hudson Valley leader of the Revolution. Once independence was declared, he was elected the first governor of New York State in 1777. He was also assigned by General Washington to command the defense of Fort Montgomery, one of the first and most important forts built to fend off the British. "This was a critical time in the battle for control of New York State," Kaminski says. "He took over command there, though in essence both he and Washington thought it was a death sentence. Washington never forgot his assistance, and though he became estranged from many friends who were anti-Federalists [as Clinton was], that was not the case with Clinton." And vice versa. Clinton even named two of his children George and Martha. "They were very much alike," Kaminski says. "If you look at the attributes that made Washington great, many of those same attributes apply to Clinton."

Clinton was governor from 1777 to 1795, left politics for a few years, then served in the state assembly in 1800 and 1801 and was reelected governor from 1801 to 1804. According to the New York State Museum, "He led what became a government on the run that first began meeting in Albany in 1781." After the war, the legislature met in a number of locations; in 1797, Albany became the de facto state capital. During that time, Clinton secured New York's strength with his business acumen.

"George Clinton created the Empire State in the mid-1780s," according to Kaminski. The state became prosperous in large part because of tariffs he levied at the Port of New York, which supplied half to three-fourths of the state's revenue, he says. Clinton also subsidized farming and other industries, furthering growth and development. "Almost all the economic policies advocated by Hamilton on a national level were already implemented at the state level by Clinton," Kaminski says.

That state-level success led Clinton to fear the Federalist bent of other Founding Fathers. "Clinton, like many others, had his misgivings about the Constitution," he says. "New York felt put-upon by its neighbors and Congress. He felt threatened." Threats included losing the western part of the state to Massachusetts, which had put in a claim for the land under the Articles of Confederation, and losing the northeastern part to the Green Mountain Boys of Vermont. New York was doing well and didn't want a strong federal government interfering.

And yet, Clinton became one of the most important backers of the Constitution, which was critical if the new nation were to survive.

Nation-Building

Clinton was initially so against the Constitution that he called for a second constitutional convention to start the drafting process over. New York was the only state to do that, Kaminski says, and holding a second convention would be "opening Pandora's box. Who knows what would have happened."

The state was also critical for geographic reasons. Both New York and Virginia had misgivings about the Constitution; if they failed to ratify, the nation would have been split in thirds—New England, the mid-Atlantic states, and the southern states all cut off from one another. "That is just what the British wanted," Kaminski says. Clinton's call for a second convention essentially died, but the threat of it and other anti-Federalist agitation led to the compromise that saved the day: the Bill of Rights. "Clinton was the spur that egged James Madison on to get the Bill of Rights passed," he says. After that, "Clinton raises the green flag and says it is all right to vote for this."

Clinton and Washington were so close that Clinton "stood" for president in 1789—the term used for running back then, as "running" for office was considered gauche—hoping to come in second and become the vice president. "Washington would have loved him as his vice president," Kaminski says. But the Federalists had the power, and he lost. He returned to Albany, but in 1805 he was elected vice president, serving under both Jefferson and Madison, until his death, while in office, on April 20, 1812. The vice president had even less power then; "the VP was not considered an executive, he was the president of the Senate, where he presided every day," says Kaminski. That's an important role, but one with little sway on governance. Clinton's most important action, Kaminski says, was casting the deciding vote against rechartering the First Bank of the United States in 1810. As Clinton was now an old man, his hope of moving into the presidency, as all the previous and many subsequent veeps did, never came to pass.

That's probably one reason he fails to appear on our money or in our middle school American history quizzes. Another reason, says Kaminski, is fire. "Historians write about people they know about, so having documents helps. Many of the Founding Fathers kept their papers, which were published in the nineteenth and twentieth centuries. But that is not so with Clinton." When the British burned Kingston, all his papers about his early life were destroyed. And in 1911, a fire at the New York State Library incinerated fifty boxes of his records. "Without those other papers, that cuts off access to historians."

Despite that, Kaminski learned enough to write the life story of this enigmatic but important New Yorker. "His command of Fort Montgomery shows the patriotism and courage he had," he says. "Even though he may have been on the opposite political side, he was still admired for what he did. It's impossible not to consider him a Founding Father."

Heavy Metal

*Sterling Forest Was Once the Center of the
Valley's Rich Iron-Ore Industry*

As a nonhistorian writing a history column, I am continually amazed and amused by the Hudson Valley's varied and colorful past. Not long ago I learned that we were once the Violet Capital of the World, growing and shipping fashion's most popular petal to all parts of the globe in the late nineteenth and early twentieth centuries (see page 170 for that story). And now I find that this forgotten, delicate industry was preceded by an equally forgotten but much more masculine one.

To me, Iron City meant only the Pittsburgh-brewed beer. The Iron Range was an area in northern Minnesota that produced hard-nosed hockey players. Turns out that both are relative latecomers, newbies, tyros. If you want to know about American ironworks, you need only look downstate.

Black Rock

Edward Lenik, an archeologist in Wayne, New Jersey, who literally wrote the book on the area's iron history (it's called *Iron Mine Trails: A History and Hiker's Guide to the Historic Iron Mines of the New Jersey and New York Highlands*, but sadly it's out of print), says that when the English settled northern New Jersey and southern New York around the 1730s, they began looking for gold and silver. There wasn't any, but a man named Cornelius Board met some Native Americans who said they knew about some "black rock" in the area. "They showed him outcrops of this rock, which he recognized as iron ore," Lenik says.

It was actually a mineral called magnetite, an iron oxide. With the area's abundant virgin timber and water supply, Board knew he could forge it into iron. So, in 1736, according to records at the New York State Library, Board and a partner named Timothy Ward bought 150 acres of land and formed the Sterling Forge and Furnace Company (soon to be called the Sterling Iron and Railway Company). They built a bloomery, a kind of furnace for smelting iron ore, and a forge. Four years later, Board sold out to Ward, and over the years others gained partial ownership.

The company, and others that formed after it, explored and dug dozens of mines in the region. "There are at least twenty known mines within Bear Mountain State Park," Lenik says. "Some were successful, some were not. Some were just exploratory pits, which you can find hiking." Bigger mines, such as the Pine Swamp and Hogancamp mines in Harriman State Park, are favorites of hikers today, he says. (The Pine Swamp mine was owned and operated by the famous Parrott brothers, Robert and Peter, and their ore was used to make the Parrott rifle that helped win the Civil War for the Union army.)

Along with Sterling, there were two other large mining operations, Lenik says. One, in Ringwood, New Jersey, operated until 1930. The other was the O'Neil mine in Orange County. All three were full-fledged mining complexes. "The companies built villages, and the miners, first the English and later Germans, Irish, and Italians, lived there." "Workers were paid eighty-one cents a day at O'Neil in 1870, and you could feed a family on that."

Another famous mine, on the other side of the river, was the Tilly Foster Mine in Brewster. Foster's land was bought after her death by the Harvey Iron and Steel Company. The mine opened in 1853 and hired large numbers of immigrants, who were often known by numbers because the owners couldn't pronounce their names. This mine was most prosperous in the 1870s, when it was the largest open mine pit in the world, employed three hundred miners, and produced 7,000 tons of ore per month. But a mine collapse in 1895 that killed thirteen miners—many of them recorded in the *New York Times* by their numbers—effectively ended its operations, and it was flooded by a reservoir.

Sterling Reputation

The Sterling Company was probably the biggest in the area, though. It built its first furnace in 1751 and another forge a year later. Sterling got into the ship anchor business in 1753, and the business took off in the 1760s, producing such goods as pig and bar iron; cart, wagon, and chair spindles; teakettles, skillets, and pots; and lots of anchors.

Around this time a man named Peter Townsend gained partnership in the company, and under his family's leadership, Sterling bustled during the American Revolution, manufacturing arms and ammunition for Washington's

Continental Army and supplying anchors for navy warships. The mine also made one item in particular that may have saved the uprising.

In February 1778 the army contracted with Townsend to make an iron chain that was to be placed clear across the Hudson River at West Point and block British ships from attacking New York from the north. Townsend's chain, as it came to be known, was laid in place on April 30, 1778—and the British never even tried to cross it.

In 1783 Peter Townsend died, but the ironworks remained in his family's possession. The Sterling Ironworks were granted rights of incorporation by the New York State Legislature on April 1, 1814, and shortly thereafter, Peter Townsend II built a cannon foundry on the site. The first cannons were produced in 1817, but records show that the foundry proved unprofitable and the federal government probably took over.

Records from 1817 to 1825 are scant, but it is thought that legal or financial trouble hampered the ironworks. It stayed in business from the 1830s through the 1850s. In 1864 the Townsends sold the business to the Sterling Iron and Railway Company, which had been formed to assume control of the ironworks. In 1867 a separate company, the Sterling Mountain Railway Company, was established to manage the railroad.

From the post–Civil War period until 1890, there is a gap in the Sterling records, and not much is known about the ironworks during this time. However, by the turn of the century the business was failing. The depression of 1892 to 1896 had something to do with that, but a bigger concern, one that eventually ended the iron industry here, was the discovery in 1866 of a vast deposit of iron ore called the Mesabi Range. Located in northern Minnesota—an area still known as the Iron Range—this deposit was not only more extensive than the eastern range but far more easily accessible. Most of the iron was close to the surface and could be extracted in shallow open pits rather than in deep mines. Shipping on the Great Lakes also made transportation easier, so the economics of the industry shifted seismically. Except for a brief flurry of activity during World War I, the Sterling Mine declined and, in 1923, closed for good.

Take a Hike

Though the forge fires have long since cooled and the buildings deteriorated, remnants of the mining industry still dot the landscape. Many are accessible on nature hikes, and the man to follow on one of these hikes is Doc Bayne.

Now retired from his post as historian at Sterling Forest State Park, he still volunteers for the Friends of Lake Forest and leads tours of the park.

One of his favorites is the mine hike, which he holds about once a month during hiking season.

"We follow the Lakeville Iron Trail, walk past the furnaces, stop by the Wildcat Mine and point out the old buildings—well, their foundations, anyway," Bayne says. He possesses a wealth of knowledge on the subject and has in fact written a book, *Vanishing Iron Works of the Ramapos*, as well as created a video presentation on Townsend's chain titled *The Chain That Saved America*.

"Sterling Forest has such a gift of iron history," he says.

Secret Agent Man

America's First Spy, a Cobbler from Putnam County, Remains Largely Unknown

Sun Tzu, the sixth century BC military genius behind *The Art of War*, knew the value of a good spy. "What enables the wise sovereign and the good general to strike and conquer, and achieve things beyond the reach of ordinary men, is foreknowledge," he wrote. "Now this foreknowledge cannot be elicited from spirits; it cannot be obtained inductively from experience, nor any deductive calculation. Knowledge of the enemy's dispositions can only be obtained from other men. Hence the use of spies."

As long as hominids have been fighting one another, they have been snooping on one another. Espionage has been called the world's second-oldest profession. Famous spies, both real and fictional, have been lauded by their sponsors and vilified by their enemies from the Trojan horsemen up to James Bond and George Smiley. During the Revolutionary War, Benedict Arnold became the very model of the turncoat, and his name has lived in infamy here for more than two centuries.

But Arnold had a counterpart, a man from the Hudson Valley who is considered the first American spy. And you most likely have never heard of him.

A Man of "Special Abilities"

His name was Enoch Crosby. He was born in Massachusetts on January 4, 1750, and moved to what is now Putnam County when he was an infant. He became an apprentice shoemaker in Kent at the age of sixteen and was plying his trade in Danbury, Connecticut, when the Revolutionary War broke out. He enlisted with a Connecticut regiment and took part the invasion of Canada in 1775. He then returned to Danbury to make shoes, but the call of war drew him back to the army in 1776. He was on his way to an encampment in White Plains when he found his true military calling.

Westchester County was, at that time, a kind of no-man's-land, with the British army in New York City and the colonial militias to the north. Supporters of both sides roamed Westchester. Crosby was mistaken as a Loyalist and asked to meet with others to join the Tory cause. He took what he learned to John Jay, who was a member of the local Committee of Safety, and together they had the Loyalists arrested.

Jay asked him to become a full-time spy, reportedly telling him that "our greatest danger lies in our secret enemies. A man of your special abilities is entitled to greater credit than a regular soldier." Crosby in fact became a double agent, pretending to be a British spy in order to infiltrate the Loyalists. No one, not even his family, knew he was working for the United States, and Crosby asked the Committee of Safety to promise that, if he were killed, his name would be cleared. He also received a special pass in case he was captured by American forces.

Crosby was quite successful. He roamed the Hudson Valley from Westchester County to Lake Champlain, infiltrating Loyalist groups and returning with valuable information. He was also captured by Americans at least four times. One of those times, "he was traveling to Kings Bridge, with men who said they were going to enlist with the British army," says Willa Skinner, historian for both the town of Fishkill and the First Reformed Church of Fishkill. "He led them to the church, where they were all arrested—including Crosby."

All the while, he posed as an itinerant cobbler and peddler. He spent the better part of six years moving between American and British sympathizers, living in deprivation—he sometimes had to hide and sleep in caves—and suffering beatings and even condemnations of death. He had to slink about at night, with few people to confide in or find safety with.

One of his only places of respite was the home of Colonel Henry Ludington, the commander of the 7th Dutchess County Militia. Ludington's daughters helped their father communicate with Crosby and other spies, serving as both guards and liaisons; Crosby employed secret signals known to Sybil and her sister Rebecca.

"Spy" versus Spy

After the war, Enoch and his brother Benjamin bought 276 acres of farmland near Brewster from the Commission of Forfeiture. He married Sarah Kniffen in 1785, and after she died in 1811, he married Margaret Green, who died in 1825. Crosby died on June 26, 1835, and was buried next to his first wife in the Old Gilead Cemetery, in Carmel. Near the end of his life, he wrote in a letter, "Having been spared to enjoy these blessings—independence and prosperity—for half a century and see them still continued, I can lay down my weary and worn out limbs in peace and happiness."

He also enjoyed a small amount of fame. After the war, John Jay, who became the first Supreme Court chief justice, had an equally famous neighbor: James Fenimore Cooper. In 1821, Cooper published *The Spy*, a book that chronicles the exploits of a fictional character named Harvey Birch, who is remarkably like Crosby. It is supposed that Cooper learned about Crosby from Jay, and the book earned Crosby a bit of notoriety. He is further honored now with a portrait in the National Gallery in Washington, DC. Locally, he is remembered at the Van Wyck Homestead in Fishkill, where he was once tried and which is considered the setting for *The Spy*. There is also a marker outside the First Reformed Church in Fishkill, where he was confined after the trial, and another on the west side of Route 6 in Southeast, between Drewville Road and Route 312, that reads, "Enoch Crosby, patriot spy of the American Revolution, lived on a farm, given him for his service, on the west side of this reservoir." "There are a lot of Crosbys still around the region," Skinner says, along with an Enoch Crosby Chapter of the Daughters of the American Revolution in Putnam County.

What made him such a good spy? "It must have been his personality," Skinner says. "He pretended he was a humble shoemaker, and it allowed him to get in with all the locals, whether they were patriots or not." It's unknown how many Loyalists Crosby helped capture. "My answer would be, a lot," says Skinner. And though he never earned the fame that the Founding Fathers and other better-known patriots enjoyed, his service as a covert operative was greatly appreciated. "George Washington would say he was a hero," Skinner says.

Part 4:
The Birth of a New Nation

Echoes of Big Thunder

America's Other Revolution, the Anti-Rent Wars,
Forever Changed the Valley and the Nation

On July 4, 1776, a small but steadfast group of North American rebels banded together, vowed to fight for their freedom and independence, and led an unlikely but ultimately successful escape from the shackles of Old World European domination.

But you know that.

On July 4, 1839, a small but steadfast group of North American rebels banded together, vowed to fight for their freedom and independence, and led an unlikely but ultimately successful escape from the shackles of Old World European domination.

Bet you didn't know that. Unless, that is, you live around the Hill towns of western Albany County or in other select parts of the Hudson Valley, where you may have some knowledge of the so-called Anti-Rent Wars of the 1830s and 1840s.

You might also know it if you are someone like Bruce Kennedy, a documentary filmmaker living in Asheville, North Carolina. Kennedy is a direct descendant of one of the leaders of this little-known uprising, a man named Dr. Smith A. Boughton but known in this context as "Big Thunder." You'll see why in a bit. Boughton was Kennedy's great-great-great-grandfather. Kennedy grew up in Troy, and his grandmother lived nearby, in the town of Averill Park, near the Boughton ancestral home. "As kids we were marched up to visit my granny, and she told us the story of the rebellion," Kennedy says. "As a kid, it just seemed tiresome. Later on we began to appreciate it." He has been tracking down original source material and conducting interviews for about three years now in order to portray this forgotten but important event. "Doing this story has become an obligation to honor the people who conducted this rebellion," he says, including his ancestor, Big Thunder.

So, Big Thunder? Really?

A Feudal Feud

The backstory: When the Dutch settled the valley, the Crown gave enormous tracts of land to a small group of notables, called the Patroons, whose names ring down from history, like Van Rensselaer and Vanderbilt, and were sometimes subsumed through intermarriage with English notables, like the Livingstons. The land was rented to tenant farmers, who paid their debts with crops and other capital. In this semifeudal but legal arrangement, a few privileged families controlled more than 2 million acres of land from Albany to Delaware counties and the lives of about 300,000 people.

Feudalism was declared illegal in New York State in 1782, but the practice continued. After the War for Independence, many farmers found themselves still beholden to these old aristocrats. Farmers paid all taxes, while landowners paid nothing. Farmers had no right to buy the land, even though in many cases the landlords did not have legal title to the land they were renting out. They could be evicted for failure to pay the rent even if they had enough personal property to cover the debt. In the 1830s, they began to wonder why they or their parents and grandparents had fought for self-government fifty years earlier, only to fall under the yoke of another European master.

According to an 1880 history of Delaware County, "One who remembers the old times tells us he never seriously rebelled against the system under which he lived until its seeming injustice suddenly broke upon him after he had called to pay his rent to the representative of the Hardenbergh estate, and found him living near New York in what appeared to him to be extravagant splendor, on the proceeds of his tenants' toil among the mountains of Delaware." Income inequality! Occupy Patroon Street! Revolution was again in the air!

Stephen Van Rensselaer III, who is still today listed among the ten richest men in American history, had just recently died, and his sons, including Stephen Van Rensselaer IV, tried to collect back rents. But while the father, known as "the Good Patroon," was a more pleasant man who "knew how to play the game," Kennedy says, "the sons were spoiled brats." When the farmers asked to meet with SVR IV about forgiving the debts, he refused and sent his minions to tell them to write up their grievances.

On that intentionally chosen July 4 in 1839, some of these tenant farmers met in Berne, one of the Hill towns, to plan their fight for economic freedom and justice. They issued their own Declaration of Independence, which read in part, "We have counted the cost of such a contest, and we find nothing as dreadful as voluntary slavery. . . . We will take up the ball of the Revolution where our fathers stopped it and roll it to the final consummation of freedom and independence of the masses."

SVR IV responded pretty much as King George III did; he ignored their demands and sent local sheriffs in to collect. The tenants refused. The Anti-Rent Wars were on. They would last for more than a decade, and though Kennedy says, "It wasn't war, it was popular rebellion," people suffered and died for their cause.

Feudal Futility

This early phase of the rebellion is also known as the Heldeberg Wars, for the mountains that overlook the Albany Hill towns, but it spread throughout the Hudson Valley. "Boughton was selected by the farmers to represent them in the legislature and in front of the judiciary, all the normal ways to approach a problem within the law," Kennedy says. But then as now, the corridors of power were hopelessly gridlocked. So Boughton and his coconspirators "decided to try illegal civil disobedience until it was resolved."

Inspired by the Boston Tea Party, the farmers disguised themselves as "Calico Indians," with costumes made from their wives' calico dresses and sheepskin masks, and took names like Big Lion, Black Hawk, Red Wing, Pompey, Thunderbolt, and, yes, Big Thunder. They would sound tin dinner horns, and the "Indians" would gather to disrupt property sales, resist evictions, tar and feather opponents, and cause other acts of mayhem. In January 1845, 150 delegates from eleven counties met at St. Paul's Lutheran Church in Berne to call for political action.

In August 1845, though, things got out of hand. A Delaware County sheriff named Osman Steele was shot and killed at a farm sale. That got people's attention. Governor Silas Wright declared Delaware County in a state of insurrection. The leaders were charged with riot, conspiracy, and robbery. Two were condemned to hang, but their sentences were commuted. One defendant, Big Thunder Boughton, was sentenced to life in prison.

It took several more years for things to shake out, but eventually the feudal system broke down. In 1845, tired of the hassles, many large landholders decided to sell out, including SVR IV, who agreed to sell his rights in the Heldebergs. In 1848, his brother, William, sold out his rights in over five hundred farms in the "East Manor," in Rensselaer County. In the 1850s, the remaining Van Rensselaer leases were sold.

The state legislature, which until that point had done nothing, was forced to act. An anti-rent political party formed and helped elect candidates favorable to its positions, and with newfound political clout the Anti-Renters changed the laws. Some of these progressives even moved out to the Midwest, where in 1854 they were instrumental in organizing the Republican

Party. And when John Young, a supporter of the Anti-Renters, was elected governor of New York in 1847, he pardoned Big Thunder Boughton.

1 Percent versus 99 Percent

All in all, it's a great story. So why has it been mostly forgotten? Kennedy thinks that the participants felt what they had done was dishonorable. A total of four sheriffs were killed, and four hundred people in Delaware County were put in prison for months. "I think people felt shame that they broke the law and killed a sheriff," he says. "I talked to a historian who knew a woman who, as a kid, had found an outrageous Indian costume at her grandmother's house. The grandmother told her, 'You put that away and you never talk about it again.'"

Yet today, with the same issues of class and income inequality simmering but not yet at full boil, he feels the story is more relevant than ever. "The remarkable irony to me is that many extremely conservative people are great fans of this rebellion, but when I try to connect it to a rebellion against the elites of the time, they refuse to see how it relates to today. They want to just leave history back there."

The lesson for the rest of us, he says, is that "what those people did then, that looks like democracy to me. As our rights are being restricted, as they were in that era, direct action is something we all have to routinely engage in. It is not comfortable, and we would rather not, but the only way to keep this thing called democracy going is by direct action. The only way the legislature busted out of gridlock back then was because of this direct action. I believe taking to the streets is the only way people can get democracy."

The title of his film, by the way, is *Righteous Rebellion*.

"The Alarming Cry of Fire"

Albany Burned in 1793,
and Three Slaves Hanged for It

"Sunday, the 17th of November 1793, was a day long remembered by the inhabitants of this city, and the few who still linger among us retain a vivid recollection of the scenes enacted during that night. The greater portion of the then quiet church-going people of the day had retired to rest, and were slumbering upon their pillows, when they were awakened by the alarming cry of fire."

So begins the recounting of Albany's worst fire by historian Joel Munsell in his 1860s *Collections on the History of Albany*. The cry of fire was perhaps the most frightening sound for any city dweller throughout most of urban history. Cities from San Francisco to Chicago to London burned to the ground, victims of highly flammable building materials and a lack of firefighting equipment and know-how. This blaze was the first big fire recorded in Albany, which in itself makes it noteworthy. However, it is even more historic for another reason. It was set by three slaves.

It is an inconvenient truth that slavery was both common and legal in the North until the early 1800s. According to the 1790 census, the city of Albany had a population of about 3,500, of which 572 were slaves and 26 were "free persons of color." Though slaves tended to have more freedoms in the North than in the South, their lives were still harsh. "This wasn't a plantation economy, but urban slaves couldn't move around," says Albany city historian Tony Opalka. "Most were house servants." Slave revolts were much in the news in the 1790s. A large insurrection in what is now Haiti, in 1792, had many Americans worried. The Albany fire seems not to have been an act of insurrection so much as a mercenary act of vengeance. And the facts are in dispute. Nevertheless, when the fire burned out and justice, such as it was, was served, three slaves were hanged.

Pomp's Circumstance

According to a 1977 article in the *Journal of Black Studies*, the sparks for the plot were ignited on November 14, when Pompey, also known as Pomp, a slave belonging to the estate of Matthew Visscher, met two teenage slave girls, Bet, owned by Philip Van Rensselaer, and Dinah, or Dean, property of Volkert A. Douw.

Pomp told the girls that two white men had "a grudge" against a prominent Albany merchant named Leonard Gansevoort. According to Munsell,

Tradition asserts that a young man named Sanders, residing in Schenectady, had been paying marked attention to the only daughter of Leonard Gansevoort, and that, from a just, real or imaginary cause, he had either been jilted by that young lady, or been quietly informed by her father, that his visits to his house were unsolicited and very annoying. This, as it might naturally be supposed, came with crushing weight upon the feelings of a young man, proud in spirit and exalted in his future expectation. His whole mind seemed to have been centered in that direction, and the unexpected bursting of his high hopes and expectations, caused him to become a viper and to return the sting.

Sanders had a jeweler friend who offered Pomp a watch if he set fire to Gansevoort's house and store on State Street between Broadway and Pearl streets. On the night of November 17, Bet and Dean took live coals from the Douw house, placed them in a lantern, and accompanied Pomp to the Gansevoort stable, where Pomp put the coals in a pile of hay. The fire spread quickly, and by the time it had burned out the next morning, most of the block bordered by Broadway, Maiden Lane, and James and State streets was destroyed. In all, twenty-six homes were lost, and only a heavy rain and sleet storm kept the entire city from burning.

"The fire was so plainly the work of an incendiary," Munsell writes, "that not only were several slaves arrested upon suspicion, but subsequently a meeting of the common council was held and an ordinance passed forbidding any Negro or mulatto, of any sex, age or description whatever, from walking in the streets or lanes after 9 o'clock in the evening, or from being in any tavern or tippling house after that hour, under penalty of twenty-four hours confinement in the jail."

"It's interesting that slaves were restricted after this, suggesting they weren't before," Opalka says.

Several slaves, including Bet and Dean, were rounded up and brought to the jail, and Bet confessed first, implicating Pomp as well. She signed a deposition of confession on November 28. The three were tried on January 6, 1794. The girls pled guilty, but Pomp claimed innocence. He was convicted, and three days later they were sentenced to death. For unclear reasons, Governor George Clinton ordered stays of execution. Pomp confessed but cleared Bet and Dean, which may have prompted further investigations. But the stay was only temporary. The girls were hanged on March 14, 1794, and Pomp on April 11, 1794, at a gallows elm tree on the northwest corner of State and Pearl streets.

Times Were Changing

"It's hard to figure out exactly what was going on," Opalka says. "This fire was not set by slaves against their owners. It was a third party. Another author says the grudge may be more speculative than real. There is mystery about their motivation, and the fact that the governor intervened with a reprieve is unusual."

But the event does show how attitudes toward slavery were slowly changing. A 1788 law had allowed slaves due process, and "the fact they had a jury trial is very interesting," he says. Albany became an active abolitionist city in the 1810s and 1820s, and "most people in Albany have no idea the city was a hotbed of Underground Railroad activity." New York State finally abolished slavery in 1827.

Sadly, all this activity came too late for Bet, Dean, Pomp, and the homeowners of a block in downtown Albany.

A Whale of a Tale

*In the Late Eighteenth Century, Whaling
Transformed a Tiny Farming Village of 150
People into the Thriving City of Hudson*

Herman Melville called him Ishmael. As every English major knows, Ishmael joined a whaling crew led by a certain deranged, peg-legged captain and set sail out of Nantucket in search of a very large, very white leviathan. What most English majors—and Hudson Valley residents—don't know is that Melville just as readily could have penned the *Pequod*'s launching its doomed voyage out of Poughkeepsie, or Newburgh, or, most plausibly, Hudson, because from just after the Revolutionary War until the 1840s, that city was one of the most important whaling centers in the country.

Well, blow me down! Who knew?

Ina Griffin-Guilzon, museum teacher at the Columbia County Historical Society (CCHS) in Kinderhook, sort of knew. "I had learned about it as an undergraduate studying history, but there was not that much information at all about it," she says. In 2010, she was hired at CCHS with grant money to develop new lesson plans that teachers could use in state school districts. "We got together and brainstormed, looking for topics, and someone mentioned whaling," she says. The more she researched it, the more she realized just how fascinating Hudson Valley's whaling heritage was. In fact, without it, the city of Hudson might not exist at all.

At the time of the American Revolution, it wasn't even Hudson. It was known as Claverack Landing, a tiny speck of a farming community with about ten families and no more than 150 people living there. Whaling, one of the world's largest and most important industries, was the furthest thing from the community's mind. So was the ocean, which was more than one hundred miles away.

New England had been whaling's colonial center since the first sperm whale was killed off Nantucket in 1712. But when the US Continental Congress voted to suspend trade with England in 1774, the British effectively shut down whaling ports along the coast. The industry suffered greatly, and some forward-thinking whalers and merchants began looking for other bases of operation.

In 1783, two Nantucket merchants, Seth and Thomas Jenkins, gathered up $100,000 and sailed first to New York City and then up the river, looking for property. They found it at Claverack Landing. "At that time there were two bays in the area deep enough for whaling ships, land that was suitable for a port, and nearby farms to supply merchant ships, which was also part of their business," Griffin-Guilzon says. The Jenkins brothers bought the land from Dutch Patroons, and in the fall of 1783 Seth Jenkins and his family arrived, building a house while living on their boat. Other families, known as "the proprietors," soon followed. They formed a company called the Nantucket Navigators and laid out the city's grid, all meticulously thought out to transform Claverack Landing into a major shipping and whaling city. "The thirty men who were the proprietors made it a truly planned city," she says. "They knew they'd need ship-builders, sail makers, rope makers, and all the businesses to support shipping, and you can see it all planned for in their early maps."

They also changed the name to Hudson when the city was chartered in 1785. By 1790, the population had exploded to 2,500, making Hudson one of the largest cities in the state and the twenty-fourth-largest city in the country. The population doubled again, to more than 5,000, by 1820. By then—approximately 1815; records conflict, says Griffin-Guilzon—the proprietors had sailed their last ship.

But their success bred competition. Three other whaling companies soon formed in the valley. Around 1830, a new group called the Hudson Whaling Company started in Hudson. The Poughkeepsie Whaling Company began operations in 1831, and the Dutchess Whaling Company set sail from Newburgh in 1833. At their peak they had a combined fleet of thirty-five ships. Not bad, but not even close to what New England ports, which flourished again after the Revolutionary War, could boast. "There were tall tales of Hudson being the greatest and largest port, but it was small and short-lived," Griffin-Guilzon says.

Indeed, the entire industry was short-lived. By the mid-nineteenth century, whale blubber was being replaced by other fuels, such as kerosene, and whaling began its slide. Both the Poughkeepsie and Dutchess companies

Whaling Timeline

1690—Ichabod Paddock of Long Island brought to Nantucket to teach whaling.

1712—Nantucket sailor Christopher Hussey kills the island's first sperm whale, beginning the deep-ocean whaling industry.

1740—Fifty whaling ships sail from Nantucket.

1765—New England whaling towns Bedford, New Bedford, and Fairhaven founded.

1766—British parliament places duty on whale oil shipped to Britain.

1774—US colonies ban trade with England.

1783—Several whaling businesses, shaken by the destruction of the war, relocate their operations from Newport, Providence, and Nantucket to Hudson, New York, which is more than one hundred miles from the open ocean. A group of proprietors called the Nantucket Navigators purchase Claverack Landing, a village of ten families and about 150 people.

November 14, 1784—To honor the river and its discoverer, the proprietors change the name of their settlement from Claverack Landing to Hudson.

1785—The city of Hudson is chartered.

1785—The city's first newspaper, the *Hudson Weekly Gazette,* is published on April 7.

1790—Hudson named a port of entry. The population reaches 2,584.

1793—War between France and England; ships seized.

1810—Hudson population reaches 4,048.

1812—War between the United States and Britain.

Circa 1815—Last ship owned by the Nantucket Navigators sails.

1820—Population reaches 5,310.

1829–1830—A new group of whalers, called the Hudson Whaling Company, forms.

Circa 1844—The last whaling ship out of Hudson sails.

1850—Hudson's population reaches 6,286—about the same as today.

folded in the 1840s. The Hudson Whaling Company sent its last ship to sea circa 1844. Start to finish, whaling in the Hudson Valley lasted just sixty years.

But those sixty years are remarkable. "Who would think these merchants would come 150 miles up the Hudson River to start a whaling company?" Griffin-Guilzon asks. "It's a great topic, especially for children, because it's an adventure story. The spirit of these people who came here to make a new life and build this city is as amazing a story as what they did on the ships." Even Ishmael might agree with that.

Sunken Treasure

Schooners, Sloops, Barges, and Steamships Rest
in Peace at the Bottom of the Hudson River

Above the waterline, the Hudson River is a gorgeous thing to behold. Below the surface, it's a wreck. Literally.

As long as humans have been riding floating objects on water, those objects have invariably sunk. The Hudson is no exception. From colonial sloops and sailboats to war boats and steamships, somewhere north of three hundred known vessels rest on the river bottom. Countless others no doubt have met the same briny fate.

To shine a light on the darker depths of the river and its ghostly remains, the Hudson River Maritime Museum created an exhibit titled "Troubled Waters: Wrecked and Sunken Ships of the Hudson River." The exhibit was first mounted in 2013 by Allynne Lang, curator of the museum, and reprised in 2014. It features relics, sonar images, and information on shipwrecks spanning much of the river's maritime history.

According to the museum, what is thought to be a nineteenth-century sloop was found at the bottom of Haverstraw Bay, and Revolutionary War gunboats may lie near the Bear Mountain Bridge. Many of the wrecks are probably canal boats and barges, such as the ten or so that joined Davy Jones's locker in 1902.

Lang conceived of the exhibit because, she says, "steam boats are one of my particular interests, and there were many bad accidents because of racing." Two of them, however, were worse than bad. They were epically catastrophic.

Just Sit Right Back and You'll Hear a Tale …

Some boats sank in storms; others collided or ran aground in the decades and centuries before modern navigation equipment. Many were scuttled after being damaged beyond repair. More than a few burned while in winter layup. But the most famous Hudson River shipwrecks involved the steamboats *Swallow* and *Henry Clay*.

The *Swallow*, built in New York City and put in service in 1836 as a nighttime passage between New York City and Albany, had a wooden hull nearly as long as a football field and weighed 426 tons. And it was fast.

So was a similar vessel called the *Rochester*. They were known as "Hudson River Flyers" and often raced one another, a common practice of the day. On April 7, 1845, a race was on. The *Swallow*, with Captain A. H. Squires at the helm, left Albany at 6 p.m. on a scheduled run to New York City. The *Rochester*, under a Captain Crittenden's command, and another side-wheeler called the *Express* soon followed. All were loaded with passengers, including about 350 on the *Swallow*, many unaware that racing would be involved.

April in upstate New York being what it is, they sailed in a heavy gale peppered with snow squalls. As the *Swallow* neared Athens, the pilot lost his bearings, and the boat smashed onto a rocky outcropping near shore. The crash was reportedly heard more than a mile away. The hull broke apart, the boilers flooded, the ship burst into flame, and the *Swallow* quickly sank.

A few of the passengers escaped to the bow and dropped to the ground. Many jumped into the river but were unable, in the dark, to find the shore. The city of Athens quickly responded, as church bells tolled and hundreds of people came forward, built fires to provide light, and rescued as many as they could.

The other boats soon came upon the scene and joined in the rescue, saving about 150 people. But at least fifteen others—exact numbers are unknown because passenger records weren't kept—perished.

Though steamboat racing remained legal, one important change was enacted in the wake of the tragedy. Riverboat travel was held off until May.

... a Tale of a Fateful Trip

Warmer weather didn't prevent another tragedy just five years later.

On July 28, 1852, the steamships *Henry Clay* and *Armenia* left Albany on a similar passenger trip–slash–race. Thomas Collyer, who built both ships, was in command of the *Clay*, while the *Armenia* was owned and piloted by Captain Isaac Smith. The *Armenia* reportedly skipped past one landing and left passengers stranded. The *Clay* powered full steam ahead in pursuit, to the growing fear of some of its riders. According to articles that ran in the Greene County *Examiner-Recorder* in 1959, "Sparks shot from her stacks and blew skyward, soot settled the decks, and the increased tempo of her throbbing engines set the whole vessel to shuddering and shaking."

"They were burning woodwork and furniture because they had run out of fuel," says Lang.

Near Kingston, the *Clay's* pilot, Jim Elmendorf, "guided by some maniacal impulse," according to the *Examiner-Recorder*, cut directly into the *Armenia's* path, splintering the hull and foredeck. The *Armenia* slowed down. The *Clay* did not. Near Riverdale, the boiler exploded in flame. Elmendorf turned the *Clay* toward the east bank, which it hit at full speed, running twenty-five feet up and into a railroad embankment.

Those lucky enough to be at the bow, including Elmendorf and his wife, were thrown ashore. But most of the passengers were in the back, cut off from escape by the roaring fire amidships. They jumped into the water, but many couldn't swim, and others were weighed down by the fancy dress of the era.

"In twenty minutes there was nothing left of the *Clay* but a slow burning section of her bow," the *Examiner-Recorder* reports. "All along the shore lay the bodies of the recovered corpses; stumbled the dazed, stunned survivors searching for the bodies of family and friends. The *Armenia* hovered on the scene, picking up survivors. Under a full moon, passengers dragged the river all night long. Eighty were dead."

Among them were some famous and prestigious people of the time, including a former New York City mayor, a well-known Philadelphia attorney, a sister of Nathanial Hawthorne, a granddaughter of President John Adams, and, perhaps best known, Andrew Jackson Downing, a landscape architect from Newburgh who was at the forefront of the emerging movement to build parks in cities and was designing the grounds of the Smithsonian Institution at the time. The wreck made all the papers—the *New York Times* called it a "melancholy disaster"—and although the owners and officers of the *Henry Clay* were acquitted on charges of manslaughter, the New York State Legislature soon thereafter passed the law prohibiting steamship racing on the Hudson.

The Weather Started Getting Rough, the Tiny Ship Was Tossed

That didn't end shipwrecks, of course. The museum chronicles sunken tugboats from the early 1900s, and its most recent wreck is from the 1930s, Lang says. Along with ship parts, anchors, and other flotsam and jetsam, the show features Currier and Ives lithographs of the *Swallow* and *Clay* fires. There is also a diorama of an underwater scene, with boat and anchor submerged, which was designed, as was the rest of the exhibit, by a designer from the Museum of Natural History in New York.

Kids really like the diorama, Lang says, but adults are intrigued as well. "People are interested in disasters. It's a popular topic and there is always an audience for it."

Ladies First

Celebrating Five Female Hudson Valley Treasures

"Well-behaved women seldom make history."

Historian Laurel Thatcher Ulrich's famous maxim now adorns T-shirts, coffee mugs, fridge magnets, and other inspirational tchotchkes, but it's far from a frivolous idea. In 1987, the National Women's History Project petitioned Congress to expand Women's History Week, first proclaimed in 1981, to the entire month of March. Since then, the National Women's History Month Resolution has been approved every year with bipartisan support in both the House and Senate, proving that Democrats and Republicans can indeed agree on something.

You could name plenty of well-known women from the Hudson Valley who behaved badly and made history (I'm looking at you, Eleanor). Of course, there are even more history makers, some familiar and some not-so-much. Here are five to thank for their bad behavior and the legacies they left behind.

Catheryna Rombout Brett

"Women's history," unfortunately, mostly means white, European women's history. But given that, Catheryna Rombout Brett (1687–1764) stands out. She was one of the first white, European women in the valley.

Brett's father, who was in America before the British were, received 85,000 acres in what's called the Rombout Patent. (The original document is on display at her home, now a museum, today.) He left one-third of the land to Catheryna (pronounced Katrina). After she married British navy lieutenant Roger Brett in 1703, the couple, with their children and slaves, moved from New York onto the land in what is now Beacon in the summer of 1708, making her the first white woman to settle the Hudson River Highlands.

In 1709, they hired a Long Island architect to build a Dutch-style house. That home, now known as the Madam Brett Homestead, remained in the family over the next seven generations and for almost 250 years.

Brett was widowed at a young age and became a successful business-woman. She legally defended her boundaries and managed her estate personally, which was no easy feat in the early eighteenth century. "After her husband died, many people encroached her property and even hired natives to scare her off her land," says Lorraine MacAulay, curator of the homestead. "But she was friendly with the natives. She met in the woods with local judges to look over the surveys and confirm her boundaries. And she rode her property lines every day."

She also ran successful gristmill, mining, and waterpower endeavors and made money selling off her land. And she raised three sons, one of whom fought in the Revolutionary War after her death. During the war, her home served as a shelter and storage facility for colonial troops, and George Washington, the Marquis de Lafayette, and other notable figures were guests.

In 1800, Brett's great-granddaughter, Alice Schenck Teller, bought and remodeled the house, and it became known as Teller's Villa; it was then turned into a boardinghouse—or the Teller Mansion. It stayed in the Teller family until 1954, when it was nearly demolished for a supermarket. In the nick of time, the Melzingah chapter of the Daughters of the American Revolution bought it and turned it into a museum.

MacAulay says that Brett should be remembered for more than simply being the first. "She was educated, successful in marriage and as a single mother, and successful in business. She is a good role model."

Martha Washington

Though he had already defeated the British army at Yorktown in 1781, George Washington knew that the Revolutionary War was far from over. The enemy still had 13,000 troops in New York City and another 17,000 in Charleston and Savannah. A peace treaty would not be signed until 1783. That made the years in between perilous. In fact, it was during this time that Washington said the Revolution came as close to being lost as at any time since it began.

It was during this time that he made his headquarters in Newburgh, where he made some of the most important decisions regarding the end of the war and the beginning of the new republic. And he did this with his beloved wife, Martha, at his side.

Martha Washington spent a total of twelve months in the Hudson Valley in these years, says Kathleen Mitchell, interpretive programs assistant at the Washington Headquarters State Historic Site in Newburgh. "She came here on April 1, 1782, left in July to manage their home in Mount Vernon, and returned in November," Mitchell says.

While here, she was a major influence on the events of the time. "Their personal life is not recorded much, but she must have been his sounding board," Mitchell says. She was also a valuable and trusted assistant, performing clerical duties such as copying military orders and letters, maintaining his personal letters and expenses, and managing the household, which included entertaining the important military officers, political figures, and guests who visited constantly.

And she did it all with an amiability that belied her difficult living conditions. "This was a very stark environment, and she was very wealthy and could have wanted to go home," Mitchell says. "But she was willing to make any sacrifice to be there for him."

She also had many friends in the area and traveled to visit with them when she could. And though there is no record of her returning to the area after she left, her time here is critically important to the valley and the country. Perhaps her greatest legacy, along with her husband's, was setting the precedents that formed the character of the new nation. Though General Washington could have anointed himself king, he understood the direction the country should take. So did his wife.

"They were very conscious of not being royalty," Mitchell says. "They were American, not aristocratic."

Janet Livingston Montgomery

One of Martha Washington's local friends was Janet Livingston Montgomery. Both she and her husband, Richard Montgomery, came from some of the earliest and wealthiest families in the New World who settled in the valley. They were the ultimate power couple of the day. But when Richard was killed in one of the first battles in the War for Independence, at the Battle of Quebec in 1775, she took on an even more important role: as the country's First Widow.

Richard has come to be called America's first national hero, and his wife "became an eighteenth-century Jackie Kennedy," says Ray Armater, site director of Montgomery Place, in Annandale-on-Hudson. "With his death, the nation starts to mourn the war, and the family represents the ultimate patriots."

Just thirty-five years old at the time, Janet would outlive her husband by fifty-three years. And much like Jackie, Janet helped preserve her husband's memory while still making a life of her own. The memorial is Montgomery Place. "She builds the place as a shrine to her husband," Armater says. "And time is good to her cause, because the house is finished in 1804, and soon after that Fulton's steamboat comes to the river. The Hudson Valley became a place of pilgrimage for tourists. Boat tours would slow down at Revolutionary War sites like West Point and Kingston, including Montgomery Place."

But Janet was far more than just an icon. She was also a descendant of early Dutch landowners, and the Dutch, unlike the British, empowered women to be strong businesspeople. Her estate was a working farm, and she produced fruit trees, lumber, and other products of the land. Indeed, Montgomery Place is still a working farm, one of the last great, historic riverfront estates that remains in business.

She also stayed interested in the business of the new country. She visited the Washingtons often and attended the ball after the first US president's first inauguration—which was presided over by her brother and certified Founding Father Robert Livingston. In 1825, the Marquis de Lafayette made a respectful trip to her home on his return visit to the United States.

But perhaps the most telling image dates to 1818, when her husband's remains were moved from Quebec to New York City. On July 4, the boat carrying him passed by her home, and Janet, standing on her porch to watch, fainted at the sight, forty-three years after his death.

"Hers is a politics-slash-love story," Armater says. "Here's this young couple, amazingly in love, he's killed, she never remarries, remains totally devoted to his memory, and also plays an important role in the political and economic growth of the country."

Kate Mullany

Kate Mullany was born in 1841 to Irish parents living in England. The family sailed to New York in 1850 and settled in Troy in 1853. Like most immigrants, she endured a harsh life and went to work at an early age. In Troy, in the 1860s, that meant working in a shirt collar factory.

Troy produced about 90 percent of the nation's detachable collars, a fashion fad that earned it the nickname it still bears today: the Collar City. At its height, the industry employed 3,700 women who worked exhausting, fourteen-hour days in stifling heat for pay as low as $2 a week. When factory owners installed new, scalding-hot machines that increased production but made working conditions more dangerous, twenty-three-year-old Mullany stepped in and organized a union.

In February 1864, Mullany and about three hundred other workers formed the Collar Laundry Union. At noon on Wednesday, February 23, 1864, the women went on strike at the fourteen commercial laundry establishments, demanding a 20 to 25 percent wage increase. The business owners denied the union's requests, and the strike lasted six days. On February 28, a few owners gave in; the next day, the others did too.

At the time, most unions lasted only as long as a certain issue was being addressed; once it was resolved—one way or the other—the unions disbanded. But the Collar Laundry Union remained in force for six years. "She led the first bona fide woman's union," says Paul Cole, executive director of the American Labor Studies Center at the Kate Mullany National Historic Site in Troy. "It had staying power. This union became institutionalized."

That a young, female, Irish immigrant would lead such a union was remarkable at the local level, but Mullany wasn't done. "The collar union saw themselves as part of the broader labor movement," Cole says. "They worked closely with the iron molder's union and other unions, and helped them out with contributions. I think that's very significant—they looked at themselves as an important cog in the labor movement."

At a July 4 picnic that year, Mullany presented an embroidered banner with a picture of the interior of a furnace on one side and a picture of "Justice" with an eagle on the other to the president of the Troy Iron Molders. The president of the Iron Molders' International Union, William H. Sylvis, was at the picnic, and Mullany sought him out and introduced herself. That paid off a few years later.

After another strike, with which the Collar Laundry Union negotiated another pay increase, from $8 to $14 per week, and a successful 1868 ironers strike led by Mullany, she attended the National Labor Congress meeting, now led by Sylvis, in New York. During the conference, she was nominated for and elected to the post of second vice president—becoming the first woman elected to a national labor post. Though she declined to serve because the first vice president was also from New York State, Sylvis appointed her assistant secretary. It was the first time a woman had been appointed to a national labor union office.

In 1869 Mullany moved into a three-story, brick double row house on Eighth Street. She lived there until 1875. She also led another strike in 1869, but this time the laundry owners opposed the union and effectively killed it. The Collar Laundry Union dissolved in February 1870. By then Mullany was married to ironworker John Fogerty, and after 1875 she just about disappears from the records. She may have moved with Fogerty as he found work in the burgeoning iron industries of Buffalo and Pittsburgh.

Kate Mullany died, back in Troy, on August 17, 1906, and was buried in St. Peter's Cemetery. Her house was declared a National Historic Landmark in 1998 and became a National Historic Site in 2008. In 2000, Mullany was inducted into the National Women's Hall of Fame. All of this would probably astonish her.

"One could speculate that she had some sense she was more than just a local labor leader, but most people then just saw themselves as doing a job," Cole says. "If she were to come back, I think she'd be pretty surprised at the attention we are giving her."

Margaret Corbin

If you've ever driven into Fort Tryon Park in upper Manhattan, you took Margaret Corbin Drive and looped around Margaret Corbin Circle to get in and out. Corbin earned her naming rights there, in blood, during the Revolutionary War. Severely wounded in battle, she became the first woman to receive a military pension from Congress and the only female veteran of the War for Independence buried at West Point.

That much is known. Much of the rest of her life is harder to confirm, says Frank Licameli, an independent historian who taught military history at the US Military Academy and continues to work at West Point. "It's hard to sort the fact from the fiction," he says, "but legends are important to our image of who we are."

Although Licameli, who has researched her extensively, has been unable to prove it convincingly, Corbin's legend probably begins with her birth, as Margaret Cochran, on November 12, 1751, in Pennsylvania. It is believed that her father was killed and her mother captured by Native Americans when she was five years old and visiting a distant uncle, who raised her after the attack. In 1772 she married John Corbin, who enlisted in the First Company of the Pennsylvania Artillery. She joined her husband in the war effort, as did many wives of soldiers, who did the cooking and washing and nursed the wounded. Many of these women were nicknamed "Molly Pitcher" for bringing pitchers of water to cool the hot cannons during battle. As a result, her story may be confused or conflated with those of other Molly Pitchers, including a famous one at the Battle of Monmouth, Licameli says.

After the British forced the Continental Army into New Jersey following the battles of Long Island and White Plains, about 3,000 soldiers, including Corbin and his wife, remained on the hill that is now Fort Tryon Park. On November 16, 1776, 4,000 Hessian mercenaries attacked the redoubt. John Corbin, a cannoneer, was killed, and Margaret, who had been cleaning and loading the cannon, took over. She managed to fire at the enemy for some time, until she was shot in the arm, chest, and jaw and taken prisoner. She was released after the British won the battle and, severely disabled by her arm wound, which never healed, went to Philadelphia.

She couldn't work, and life was a struggle until after the war. In 1779, Pennsylvania granted her $30 and passed her case on to the Continental Congress's Board of War. Later that year, the board granted her half the monthly pay of a soldier in the Continental Army and a new set of clothes or its equivalent in cash every year. The deal included becoming part of a newly created Invalid Corps, where wounded vets served and supported the military to whatever degree their abilities allowed. The corps was consolidated at West Point, and Corbin moved and lived there—she was known around town as "Captain Molly"—until her death in around 1800.

Mostly forgotten, her story resurfaced around the fiftieth anniversary of the Declaration of Independence. "Many veterans started to write their memoirs, and that's where she may be confused with other Molly Pitchers," Licameli says. "People in the area, though, remembered her. There is one record of a child eyewitness who recalled a stout, red-haired woman and called her Captain Molly."

In the 1920s, the Daughters of the American Revolution looked harder into her case and even found her grave on what had become J. P. Morgan's estate, Licameli says. In 1926, the DAR moved her remains to West Point, where forensics confirmed, from the wounds, that they indeed belonged Corbin. She was buried in the West Point Military Cemetery, next to a monument erected by the DAR.

Like other women of history, Captain Molly may not have been the most polite person around. According to the National Woman's History Museum, the Philadelphia Society of Women had planned to erect a monument honoring Corbin soon after the battle. "However, when they met with her they discovered that she was a rough woman who was poor and drank too much and decided to cancel the monument," the museum notes.

"It appears that when she was younger she was a favorite among a lot of people," Licameli says, noting a friendship with General Henry Knox, who was instrumental in getting her a pension, including a ration of alcohol, which was usually denied women. "Later on it appears she was pretty surly, maybe had an alcohol issue, though there is nothing definitive on that." People who were paid by the government to care for her had difficulty, he says, both because of her personality and because payments slowed down. "Somebody who was severely disabled and had to rely on others for years, it's not very surprising she was a little on the surly side."

But that's to be expected of history makers. "She is pretty unique," he says. "There is nobody like her."

You Call That a War?

O Say, Can You … Explain What the War of 1812 Was All About?

There are wars, and then there are wars. In 2011, we honored the sesquicentennial of the start of the Civil War, the war that, as historian Shelby Foote remarked, turned the United States from a plural "are" to a singular "is." In 2014 we marked the centennial of World War I, the "war to end all wars."

In 2012, however, we were stuck with the two-hundredth anniversary of the War of 1812. "Like Avogadro's number or the rules of subjunctive verbs," notes James P. Lundberg on slate.com, "the War of 1812 is one of those things that you learned about in school and promptly forgot without major consequence."

Sure, you may remember some things about the war. The poem that inspired our national anthem was written during the battle for Fort McHenry. (Or maybe you thought that was the Civil War.) Andrew Jackson became the hero of New Orleans. (Ditto.) The White House burned. (OK, you get the point.)

Here in the Hudson Valley, there is even less reason to hail the war. No battles were fought here. Few hardships were felt. Some local militias did participate, and commendably so, but … what's Avogadro's number again?

Indeed, there are, as far as we can tell, but two significant and lasting local products of the War of 1812. Unlike with subjunctive verbs, we hope you remember these consequences long after you move on to the next chapter.

Cannon Fodder

What was the War of 1812 all about? Well, it was about several things, including land borders with Canada and naval rights with European powers, and it involved several players, including the British, the French, Native Americans, and us. For the Brits, it was an annoying sidebar to their much larger war with Napoleonic France. The main battles were fought on the high seas, along the Saint Lawrence River and Great Lakes, around the mid-Atlantic states, and in the "Southwest," which in the early nineteenth century was Louisiana and the Gulf Coast.

The war came to an inconclusive end with the Treaty of Ghent in 1814 (though fighting continued into 1815), with no territory won or lost and little resolved on any of the participants' sides. It's really no wonder the conflict is so memorably unmemorable.

But the war did reveal a startling weakness in our still-young nation's ability to defend itself. Militias were controlled by the various states. There was no national army or navy to speak of. When the British navy started seizing American merchant ships and grabbing their cargo and sailors for their tussle with France, President James Madison declared war. But he had precious little to fight with—"only 7,000 scattered members of the regular army, and a navy that numbered only sixteen ships," according to research from the Hudson River Valley Institute. If France and Britain hadn't settled their differences, one or the other might have easily turned our young democracy back into a colony.

Having dodged this bullet, the federal government looked to invigorate the military. To do that it needed to rectify a glaring vulnerability in the nation's defenses—not enough cannons. There were only two cannon foundries operating in the United States during the war. Madison ordered the creation of four other foundries. One was in the Hudson Valley, across the river from the US Military Academy. (See Lost and Foundry, page 107.)

Along with its proximity to the academy, the Hudson Highlands site also had strategic natural resources, including deposits of iron, forests to feed the furnaces, and water to provide both power and transportation. The foundry was incorporated in 1818 and immediately began making weapons for the navy. Cannons cost about $130, cannon shot from five cents to eight cents a pound, and guns $8 a ton.

In the following years it also produced locomotives, ship engines and boilers, equipment for mills, and more. During the Civil War, the foundry made guns, projectiles, and gun carriages. But by the end of the century, iron was out and steel was in. The foundry went bankrupt in 1889 and closed for good in 1911.

Born on the Fourth of July

Soldiers need to eat, and the warriors of 1812 ate, among other provisions, beef and pork packaged in barrels by a Troy meat packer named Sam Wilson. All incoming rations were stamped with the producers' name, where they came from, and where they were headed, and these meat barrels bore the stamp "E.A.—U.S." The "E.A." stood for Elbert Anderson Jr., the contractor who hired Wilson. The "U.S." stood for the United States, but soldiers from Troy thought it meant their local butcher, and joked it was from Uncle Sam.

It didn't take long for Uncle Sam and the United States to become synonymous. The character Uncle Sam first appeared in print in an 1816 allegory and took hold over the next decades, both in word and image, as the Uncle Sam who adorns recruitment posters and patriotic tchotchkes to this day.

The current image, in fact, dates to a century after the War of 1812, when an artist named James Montgomery Flagg published a magazine cover in 1916 with the ultimate representation of Uncle Sam, asking, "What are you doing for preparedness?" He was asking, of course, about preparedness for World War I.

Now, *that* was a war . . .

Part 5:
The Civil War

War and Remembrance

A Century and a Half after It Ended, the Civil War Still Reverberates throughout the Lower Hudson Valley

"The Civil War was fought in 10,000 places," writes Geoffrey C. Ward, Ken Burns, and Ric Burns in their epic history of that conflict, "from Valverde, New Mexico, and Tullahoma, Tennessee, to St. Albans, Vermont, and Fernandina on the Florida coast." Not one of those 10,000 places was in New York State. In America's bloodiest war, no blood was spilled in battle on New York soil.

Yet New York played a critical role in America's defining conflict. New York was at the time the nation's wealthiest and most populous state. It was considered by many to be the intellectual center of the war's predominant arguments over abolition and secession. New York State sent more money, more supplies, and more soldiers and suffered more casualties than any other state. In fact, the very first of an estimated 620,000 soldiers to die in the Civil War was from New York State, killed accidentally when a pile of ammunition exploded during a one-hundred-gun salute marking the lowering of the US flag at Fort Sumter before the Confederates took over.

Despite this heroic effort, the lower Hudson Valley had, at best, conflicted feelings about the war. Both Westchester and Putnam counties voted against Abraham Lincoln in the 1860 election and were labeled "secessionist" in more than a few newspapers. While the war's biggest draft riots occurred to the south, in New York City, and to the north, in Troy, lesser insurrections occurred here as wealthy residents of those two counties spent upward of $4 million to hire others to take their places in the draft.

The fighting ended more than 150 years ago, but many would argue that the war has never really ended. So it's worth remembering how Westchester County and the rest of the valley was in many ways the most emblematic region in the country of both the better and the worse angels of our nature.

Antebellum Westchester

In 1860, Westchester County was twice as big as it is now (it included all of the Bronx), but with about 100,000 residents it had one-twentieth of today's population. To the north, farmland; to the south, industries such as iron foundries, sawmills, textile makers, and gun factories. Those geographic and economic differences, much as they do today, colored political views. The rural North supported Lincoln, but the more populous, industrial South sided with New York City, and the three major Westchester newspapers, the *Eastern State Journal* of White Plains, the *Yonkers Herald*, and the *Highland Democrat* of Peekskill, in opposing him.

"Westchester more than any other county in the state was divided in sentiments to south and north," says Vernon Benjamin, author of *The History of the Hudson River Valley from Wilderness to the Civil War*. "The county was a sort of Mason-Dixon line for the state, running roughly through Tarrytown."

The *Eastern State Journal* was particularly virulent in opposing abolition, stating, "The Black Republicans ... have declared that Negroes are the equals of white men, and entitled to the same political and social privileges. Let white men, on Tuesday, repel this foul slander by their votes." And after the 1860 election, the newspaper ran a large-print notice under its masthead that read, "Mr. Lincoln is not the United States Government. The Government is ours, and we owe allegiance to it: Mr. Lincoln is not ours, and we do not owe allegiance to him. Mr. Lincoln's term of office is brief and fleeting; the Government, we hope, will last forever."

The new president made his first of just two "official" visits to Westchester County on February 19, 1861, when he stopped in Peekskill on his way to his inauguration as a favor to William Nelson, a former US congressman and friend. (Lincoln also passed through the county on the way to West Point for a secret, "unofficial" visit during the war.) It's unknown if the crowd was for or against Lincoln; he had lost the county's vote, to the Union-Electoral "anti-Lincoln" party, by a wide margin.

The attack on Fort Sumter, though, changed everything. The call for volunteers from both the federal and state governments was heeded throughout the state, including the lower valley. "Plenty of men joined the war even if they were not fond of Lincoln," says Patrick Raftery, librarian for the Westchester Historical Society. "They didn't feel that they were fighting for abolition. They were more likely to describe themselves as fighting to preserve the union."

A company of men, designated Company B, 17th Infantry, was mustered in Port Chester and became known as the Westchester Chausseurs. (*Chausseur* is a French word, meaning "hunter," used to describe light infantry.) In Yonkers,

---

Fun Fact

Charles B. Rouss, a southerner and Confederate army veteran, was a successful businessman who found himself in deep debt after the war. He decided to move north to, as he said, "fight the Yankees with brains instead of bullets." He again grew rich, operating auction houses and mail-order catalogs. He bought a building on Broadway in Manhattan and liked it so much he made "Broadway" his middle name. The building, in SoHo, is still called the Charles Broadway Rouss Building.

Rouss also led a Confederate veterans group to purchase a four-hundred-square-foot cemetery plot in Hastings-on-Hudson "where today more than fifty sons of the south and their family members lay in eternal rest," writes Michael S. Bennett, codirector of the Daniel Sickles Civil War Roundtable. Rouss paid $5,000 himself for a sixty-foot obelisk. When he died, in 1902, he was worth an estimated $10 million. "He truly did beat the Yankees, hundreds of thousands of them, with his brains, a little business sense and lots of determination, instead of bullets," Bennett writes.

---

the 6th New York Heavy Artillery formed. The 4th New York Cavalry, the 5th Independent Battery, and the 1st Mounted Rifles also included large contingents of Westchester volunteers, as did other companies that mustered in Connecticut, New Jersey, New York City, and farther upstate.

Along with losing men gone off to war, many local industries suffered economic losses initially. Some sold their goods to southern markets, while others needed southern supplies, and all of them lost a lot of business. As early as November 1861, the Westchester County Board of Supervisors began receiving petitions for war relief, and on March 1, 1862, the board passed a $50,000 bond to help families of volunteers. They were given between $1 and $4 a week, and some got an additional $1 per child—up to a cap of $7. Eastchester then had to pass a resolution after it was discovered that only three of the families receiving relief were actually residents of the town. War fraud: it was ever thus.

"Fueled by Booze and Fury"

In March 1863, the state passed its first draft law, calling all men between the ages of twenty and forty-five. However, they could avoid service by paying a $300 fee or finding someone else to take their place. This of course favored the wealthy—it, too, was ever thus—and the less well-off, already fearful of losing jobs to freed southern slaves and returning soldiers, rioted.

"The potential for chaos and violence was much greater in Westchester than anywhere else in the state, particularly below Croton," Benjamin says. A Westchester resident at the time named Daniel MacFarlan wrote in his journal, "Here is a dreadful state of affairs. The Government is responsible for the whole of it. The $300 clause is where the trouble lies. Rich men can get clear of the draft while the poor are obliged to go."

The most famous riots were in New York City and Troy, but enrolling offices in Westchester were looted by mobs that burned draft lists and destroyed railroad tracks as far as Yonkers. Another mob marched from Tuckahoe to Mount Vernon intending to burn the houses of all Republicans. They stopped at Gould's Hotel for a drink, though, and were talked out of their rampage. Newspaper editor Horace Greeley's wife, who lived in Chappaqua, rigged her own house with explosives to protect it from a mob of three hundred or so, "fueled by booze and their own rising fury," as Benjamin writes, who were bent on revenge for Greeley's support of the draft and criticism of the New York riots in that week's *Tribune*. Fear of more rioting led the towns of Yonkers and Tarrytown to form local militias "to defend the Persons and Property of the Citizens of Westchester from riotous persons and mobs."

The situation changed when local and state governments switched to a bounty system, in which they paid men to volunteer and avoid the draft. Towns such as Eastchester levied a tax "sufficient to raise the sum of three hundred dollars for such & every person drawn and accepted in the service of the United States." That sum went up to $450 per man by 1864. The town also added a resolution requiring those—who clearly had paid attention in math class—who took the local bounty, paid $300 to avoid the draft, and then pocketed the difference, to refund their profiteering. (All together now: it was ever thus.)

On the Home Front

While the war raged elsewhere, Westchester residents helped where they could. This included the sizable African American population, which numbered 2,000 in the 1850 census. Freed by New York law in 1817, they lived throughout the county, in New Rochelle, Ossining, Rye, Yonkers, and, most notably, The Hills, a community in Harrison that began in the 1770s, when Quakers freed their slaves and settled them in the area near Silver Lake. Some of these free blacks enlisted in so-called colored regiments formed in Rhode Island, Massachusetts, and Connecticut and fought in important battles in Louisiana, Virginia, and Tennessee.

Fun Fact

Admiral John L. Worden, the first commander of the famed ironclad *Monitor*, was born in Westchester County, grew up in Dutchess County, and is buried in Pawling. Along with the many ships, forts, and fields named in his honor, you can also buy a home on Admiral Wordens Lane, in Briarcliff Manor. It will cost you more than the $275,000 battleship did, though.

Women also pitched in. Some served as nurses in army hospitals, one of which operated on Davids Island from 1862 to 1867 and also became a prison hospital for captured Confederates after Gettysburg. They also headed up fund-raising and relief efforts and formed "lint societies"—collecting lint off old cotton clothing and bedding when cotton became scarce.

As in all wars, some businesses profited off this one. "The Bronx River was an important industrial stream," says Stephen Paul DeVillo, author of *The Bronx River in History and Folklore*. "It is one of the few streams near New York City with enough [vertical] fall to produce water power and power mills." Already a center for textiles, rubber and leather goods, and explosives, the region experienced "a general uptick in all kinds of industries related to the war," DeVillo says. "Not everybody got an army contract, but enough did."

"Peace, Magic Word"

Lincoln won reelection in 1864 but again lost convincingly in Westchester County, which preferred George McClellan, the dithering former head of the Union army. McClellan's eventual replacement, Ulysses S. Grant, however, orchestrated General Robert E. Lee's surrendered at Appomattox Courthouse soon thereafter. Upon hearing that happy news, Rye resident Cornelia Jay, the great-granddaughter of John Jay, the first chief justice of the US Supreme Court, wrote in her diary, "Last night I stayed awake till midnight. The silence of the street was broken by the cry of 'Extra,' 'Surrender of Lee's Army'... Peace, magic word, is on everybody's lips."

A week later came tragic words: Lincoln had been assassinated. Jay wrote another diary entry after attending church the following Sunday, Easter: "As [the bishop] began the bright sun clouded up and he said it was a fit emblem of the cloud that had come over our Easter joy."

Though divisive in life, Lincoln was unifying in death. "He was deified as the Great Emancipator, and Westchester County shared that with everyone else in America," Benjamin says. Lincoln's funeral train passed through West-chester County on April 25, 1865—his second official visit—on its way to his burial in Springfield, Illinois. Residents crowded every station along the line up the Hudson River to pay respects. The Ossining station unfurled a floral arch over the tracks that read, "We Mourn a Nations [*sic*] Loss," and at the Peekskill station, the *New York Times* reported, "flags and mottoes were here displayed, and a band of music performed a funeral march, greatly adding to the solemnity of the scene."

Postbellum Westchester

In the five years after the war, Westchester boomed. Total population grew by 30 percent as the Industrial Revolution took hold and the county's rural roots steadily withered and eventually died. "The end of the war helped spur sub-urbanization of the Bronx River Valley," DeVillo says. "A lot of money went to the mercantile class during the war, so a lot of them had new or increased wealth and began buying miniature country estates."

War veterans became a powerful force. They established a national asso-ciation, the Grand Army of the Republic (GAR), which had at least ten posts in the county. The GAR was subsumed by later wars and later associations, such as the American Legion. Veterans also began erecting monuments, and more than a dozen still stand throughout the county—including one dedi-cated to the Confederates in Mount Hope Cemetery, in a burial ground for those who left the ravaged South after the war (see "Fun Fact"). The monu-ment on Broadway in White Plains was built in 1872 despite the objections of the man whose home it fronted. J. Warren Tompkins even got a court order to stop construction, but the veterans sponsoring it had it built anyway,

---

Fun Fact

Two men with ties to Westchester County were directly involved with Lin-coln's assassination. Dr. Charles Sabin Taft, who later retired to Mount Ver-non, was in the box below the president's at Ford's Theater that evening and helped tend to Lincoln while he lay mortally wounded through the night. Taft is buried in St. Paul's Cemetery.

Colonel William Withers, of Rye Beach, was the orchestra leader at the fateful performance of *Our American Cousin*. He was offstage when John Wilkes Booth escaped, and he was stabbed by Booth while trying to stop him. Withers was the first person to accurately describe Lincoln's murderer to the police.

---

in just two hours, by firelight, after midnight. They made sure to turn the statue's back to Tompkins's home.

If there is a lasting legacy to the county's involvement in the Civil War, it may be dedication to military service. "That started in the Revolutionary War. In the Civil War, they weren't abolitionists but felt that the preservation of the Union was important," Raftery says. "They came back and put up monuments because they were quite proud of their service. You can imagine the veterans of World War I and II as children, seeing these men hobbling around. I think it's reflective of the county's service to the country."

Lost and Foundry

An Important Historic Site in Cold
Spring Gets a Major Makeover

On June 24, 1862, with the Civil War going badly for the North, the *New York Tribune* reported, somewhat breathlessly, "It is stated on the authority of passengers from West Point today that President [Abraham] Lincoln and General [John] Pope arrived at Cozzens Hotel, West Point, at an early hour this morning, and the fact that a special train passed over the Hudson River Railroad after midnight leaves little reason to doubt the truth of the report. As General [Winfield] Scott is now residing at West Point it is to be presumed that the President and General Pope have gone to consult him in regards to affairs of the army."

One US congressman later wrote that the president's trip upriver "startled the country and quite as much startled the Cabinet, as not a single member of it had any intimation of his intended journey." Speculation was that Lincoln was considering changes to Union army leadership and wanted Scott's advice, but to this day no one knows exactly what Lincoln was there for; in his own inimitable words, he said in a speech on the way back to Washington,

> *When birds and animals are looked at through a fog they are seen to disadvantage, and so it might be with you if I were to attempt to tell you why I went to see Gen Scott. I can only say that my visit to West Point did not have the importance which has been attached it.... Now, I can only remark that it had nothing whatever to do with making or unmaking any General in the country. The Secretary of War, you know, holds a pretty tight rein on the Press, so that they shall not tell more than they ought to, and I'm afraid that if I blab too much he might draw a tight rein on me.*

What is known, however, is that the president not only conferred with generals but also toured West Point and attended a dinner party where he "charmed all the ladies with his conversational powers and affability." And he took a side trip to Cold Spring, where he inspected the most important munitions factory in the nation and one of the first representations of the burgeoning Industrial Revolution. The West Point Foundry, an ironworks built in the wake of the near-disastrous War of 1812, played an enormous role in supplying the Union army with state-of-the-art weaponry and steam engines for trains. It went on to forge pipes for New York City's water system and machinery for the cotton and sugar industries.

The foundry's owners also were perhaps the first to understand "vertical integration," controlling every aspect of the process from mining to manufacturing to distribution. But with the advent of steel, iron quickly fell out of favor, and the West Point Foundry foundered and died in the early twentieth century. Fallen to ruins and reclaimed by the woods, it sat unappreciated—until 2013, when its new owners, Scenic Hudson, opened the restored and reclaimed property to anyone wishing to step back in time.

Guns A-blazing

After the British nearly ended the American Experiment in 1812, largely because the country had no military to speak of, President James Madison sought to increase the country's might, which included establishing munitions manufacturers to produce more armaments. The area around Cold Spring was perfect for such a factory. It had numerous iron-ore mines nearby, there was plenty of timber for fuel, local waterways could power the machinery, and the Hudson River provided an important shipping lane. And, of course, West Point, just across the river, offered military protection.

Incorporated as the West Point Foundry Association by a merchant named Gouverneur Kemble, the ironworks opened shop in 1817, but its most influential figure came on board in 1835. That's when a West Point graduate, Captain Robert Parker Parrott, was appointed inspector of ordnance from the foundry. A year later he resigned his army commission to become superintendent, and under his leadership the factory became a leader in munitions making. He and his brother, Peter Parrott, also managed the Kemble-owned furnaces and eventually bought one of them. And, why not, he married Kemble's niece, Mary, in 1839.

In 1843, the foundry built the USS *Spencer*, the first iron ship built in the United States, but Parrott's experiments in new ways to build artillery, bullets, and bombs led to his greatest invention, which carried his own name. The Parrott rifle, which debuted in 1860, was actually a cannon and came in several sizes, the largest of which was called the 300-pounder—it weighed 26,000 pounds itself and could launch a 300-pound cannonball.

The foundry peaked during the Civil War, naturally, and its 1,400 workers transformed Cold Spring into one of America's first "company towns." The foundry built houses, churches, and a school in town, and shops sprang up on Main Street; many of these buildings still stand. During the war the foundry produced 2,000 cannons and 3 million shells, including another Parrott invention, an incendiary shell used in an 8-inch Parrott rifle known as the Swamp Angel to blast Charleston. Though powerful, the guns were also dangerous—given to exploding—and often inaccurate. To test them, they were fired at Storm King Mountain. During Lincoln's visit, Parrott fired one across the river, but the president was reportedly unimpressed: "I'm confident you can hit that mountain over there, so suppose we get something to eat. I'm hungry," he said.

Back in Business

Parrott resigned as superintendent of the foundry in 1867 but kept experimenting with artillery shells and fuses at West Point until his death at Cold Spring in 1877, at the age of seventy-three. By then, innovations in iron and steel production were making the foundry obsolete, and it declared bankruptcy in 1889. It was sold in 1897 to a company that made sugar mills but closed in 1911 and was left to fall to ruin. Leftover pollutants turned the grounds into a Superfund site. Between 1996 and 2009, Scenic Hudson stepped up, purchased the eighty-seven-acre site over several acquisitions, and began reclamation.

In October 2013, the $3.6 million West Point Foundry Preserve opened, with many of the ruins now stabilized, interpretive signage and audiovisual tours, and an accessible half-mile trail that connects directly to the Metro-North train station at Cold Spring.

"I think it's a perfect combination of interpretive elements, and it helps bring the foundry to life," says Rita D. Shaheen, director of parks for Scenic Hudson. The audio narration includes experts like noted Lincoln scholar Harold Holzer. "He speaks of Lincoln's visit there, and you can stand in about the same location where Lincoln stood," Shaheen says.

Equally important is the recovery of Foundry Cove and the surrounding acreage. Replanted with native wetlands vegetation, it has become a beautiful natural preserve of woods, creek, and wondrous river views. "The industrial past has once again been returned to its natural state," says Ned Sullivan, president of Scenic Hudson. "It's a beautiful place to visit in all seasons, and the site has such importance in the history of the Hudson Valley and indeed the history of the entire nation."

The Godfather of Soil

Meet James F. Brown: Former Slave, Master Gardener,
Hudson Valley Diarist, and American Icon

Dr. Myra Young Armstead, a history professor at Bard College, took one look at the diary sitting on a table and knew she had found a treasure. This was around 2005. Armstead had been hired as a consultant to help create educational programs for Mount Gulian, the eighteenth-century Dutch colonial home of the Verplanck family in Fishkill that is now a national landmark and museum. Elaine Hayes, the executive director, was giving a tour. "I asked what this book was," Armstead says. "She said it was the diary kept by the gardener in the 1800s named James F. Brown. And then she said, 'By the way, he was African American.' I immediately knew I had to look at it."

For any historian, she says, a diary is intriguing. This one covered forty years, from 1826 to 1866. "A diary that long made it doubly intriguing," she says. "And most diaries were kept by the elites, so to learn that this was by a gardener, and an African American, when most at the time were illiterate, made it triply or quadruply intriguing."

The book at Mount Gulian is actually a photocopy, so she went to the New York Historical Society, which holds the original. And what she found was . . . pretty boring, actually. "The diary is very flat and uninspiring to read," she says. "Most readers would put it down after five minutes." Brown writes almost nothing of his inner thoughts and feelings or about his remarkable life story as a former slave who became a successful, middle-class, free man in the Hudson Valley. Instead his entries mostly record mundane daily events and "an awful lot about planting," she says. "I had a friend read it, and he said it's a fantastic weather report."

Nevertheless, Armstead had a hunch there was something more to be learned and a bigger story to be told. She was looking for a new research project, and here it was. That serendipitous stumbling onto a forgotten diary resulted in her 2012 book *Freedom's Gardener: James F. Brown, Horticulture, and the Hudson Valley in Antebellum America.* A review in the *New York Times Book Review* called the book "beautifully researched" and "bursting with detail." Though the diary itself may be a snooze, James Brown's life was anything but.

Say It Loud

The biography of a slave is hard to pin down, and James F. Brown's early story is no different. He was born, as best can be determined, on October 1, 1793, in Maryland, probably in Fredricktown, now called Frederick. He was sometimes known by other names—Anthony Fisher or Anthony Chase. By 1818, he was living in Baltimore, still owned by the Williams family but living as a "quasi-free" slave, as Armstead writes, being hired out to others, living on his own, paying taxes, and saving money.

In 1826, his master, Henry Lee Williams, fell gravely ill and wrote a note stating his desire to free Anthony Chase upon his death. Based on this promise, James/Anthony married another slave named Julia.

But when Henry Williams died, his sister, Susan Williams, Brown's legal owner, failed to honor her brother's dying wish. James pled his case and even offered to buy his freedom from her. When she still refused, he wrote a letter (as Anthony Chase) to a man to whom he had been hired out and explained that he had decided to run away. He promised that he would reimburse his owner, Susan Williams, to prove "that I dont mean to be dishonest but wish to pay her every cent that I think my Servaces is worth." And then he fled to New York City, leaving Julia behind.

He found work with the Verplanck family in 1827. He was waiting on the family at a dinner party around this time when one of the dinner guests recognized him as an escaped slave and demanded that he be returned to his owner in Maryland. The Verplancks help arrange for his manumission from Susan Williams, and Brown was free. He also began journaling around this time. He probably didn't know it, but his was one of only a very few journals kept by black people anywhere in the North. And it gets off to a rollicking start; an early entry tells of his secretive return to Maryland, where he purchased Julia's freedom for $100, which he had saved while working up north.

Papa's Got a Brand-new Bag

Mount Gulian, the colonial-style fieldstone house built around 1730 at Fishkill Landing on the Rombout Patent land, was first used as a summer retreat for the Verplanck family, which lived in Albany and Verplanck Point in Westchester County, and as a working plantation. During the War for

Independence, the family turned the estate over to the Continental Army because of its strategic location on the Hudson and across from Washington's headquarters at Newburgh. In late 1782 through the summer of 1783, Mount Gulian was the headquarters of army general Friedrich Von Steuben, who, along with other American officers, created the Society of the Cincinnati, America's first veterans' fraternal organization, on May 13, 1783.

In the early 1800s, part of the Verplanck family took up full-time residence, and by 1829 James Brown was working there full-time as the estate's gardener, coachman, and general laborer—and chief diarist. His journal entries record daily chores, local news, business receipts, favorite recipes, church sermons, and, predominantly, his work tending the landscape.

Brown also became very active in the burgeoning nineteenth-century horticulture movement, attending meetings, corresponding with important white horticulturalists like Andrew Jackson Downing and Henry Winthrop Sargent, and gaining influence in what was then considered as much an art as an occupation. As such he was more than just a rich family's gardener; he was a middle-class, upwardly mobile, socially as well as racially integrated citizen. As a free and well-paid man, he was able to buy his own house and land, and that gave him the right to vote. On November 8, 1837, he wrote in his diary, "James F Brown voted for the first time."

Living in America

As he aged through the Civil War years, his work and journaling fell off, and he died in 1868 at his home in Beacon. His wife kept his diaries until her death (they are buried together in the Beacon St. Luke's Church cemetery), when they passed to a Verplanck family member with whom she had kept in contact. Eventually they were donated to the New York Historical Society, where they remained pretty much undisturbed for a century or so, until Armstead and Hayes began their recent collaboration

What makes this dry, dusty diary important? Hayes, for one, had wanted to look into it since she joined the museum twenty years ago. "We have no idea what he looked like. He left no heirs. Yet his story and the story of Mount Gulian are pretty much a microcosm of all of American history," she says.

For Armstead, Brown's journal offers an entry into "the development of national citizenship." "This guy lived from 1793 to 1868, the first generation of Americans after the Revolution, the generation that forged the American identity," she says. "The idea of freedom was up for grabs; we were trying to figure out the meaning of it." Brown, she says, "wasn't a flamboyant character," but he exemplifies three important markers in the struggle to define freedom.

"First, there was personal freedom versus slavery, which of course he lived," Armistead says. "Second, with the economic changes of industrialization of the nineteenth century, there were 'wage slaves' versus independent labor, and as a master gardener he escaped wage slavery. Third, there was the burgeoning freedom of political expression. De Tocqueville wrote that Americans were are all joiners, joining societies to improve health, politics, temperance, and this idea that ordinary people can join groups and shape society was unknown in Europe. Brown exhibits this as well—he writes about temperance societies, antislavery talks, horticultural societies, volunteer firefighters, fraternal societies, orphan asylums. He is one of the ordinary citizens affecting larger policies. Through that, he is helping define what freedom is."

Seeking Truth

*Few Remember That Sojourner Truth, Renowned
Former Slave Turned Abolitionist and Woman's Rights
Activist, Started Her Sojourn in Ulster County*

Even if she hadn't changed her name, Isabella Baumfree would likely still be remembered now, nearly 140 years after her death, for the brave and life-changing work she did. But Baumfree did change her name—wonderfully so—and it has permanently cemented her in the pantheon of American historical figures. Indeed, today's best marketing and branding experts could not improve on the moniker she chose: Sojourner Truth.

Even those who aren't quite sure what she did can tell, by that name, what she stood for. And yet, many of those who are able describe her self-chosen mission to "travel up and down the land" speaking truth to power may not remember that she began her travels in Ulster County, where she lived the first thirty years of her life.

When the library at the State University of New York–New Paltz was named after her in the early 1970s, history professor Carlton Mabee (now retired) and librarian Corinne Nyquist began digging into her local connections. "Carlton and I walked out of a library planning session and said, 'She came from here, and we ought to know more about her,'" says Nyquist. "There was not much information about her early years in other books about her."

They both met with local historians and tracked down family names associated with Truth's history. Mabee, who won a Pulitzer Prize for his biography of Samuel Morse, used his research to write *Sojourner Truth: Slave, Prophet, Legend*, published in 1995. Most of what we know about her Hudson Valley days comes from his book and Nyquist's research and is collected at a page on the State University of New York–New Paltz website (newpaltz .edu/sojourner_truth).

"I Walked Off, Believing That to Be All Right"

Isabella Baumfree was born circa 1797, one of thirteen children of slaves named Elizabeth and James Baumfree, who were owned by Colonel Johannes Hardenbergh and worked his estate in Swartekill, near what is now Ripton. This was still a heavily Dutch settlement, and Baumfree spoke only Dutch until around the age of nine. She had a typically horrific slave's life. She was sold from her family at about age nine, along with a herd of sheep, for $100 to a man named John Neely. The Neelys spoke English, and Isabella was savagely beaten for being unable to communicate. She said that Mrs. Neely once whipped her with "a bundle of rods, prepared in the embers, and bound together with cords." She learned English here but spoke with a Dutch accent for the rest of her life.

She was sold twice more, finally ending up with the Dumont family of New Paltz. Here too she was abused, and around this time she started turning to religion and began, she claimed, hearing the voice of God. She also fell in love with a slave named Robert in her late teens. One night, while Robert visited her, his owner followed him, beat him brutally, and dragged him away. She never saw Robert again but soon gave birth to her first child. A few years later, her owner forced her to marry another slave, and they had four children, one who failed to survive, between 1822 and 1826.

The Dumonts had promised to free her when New York officially abolished slavery in 1827 but broke that promise. Not long after, she escaped with one daughter. "I did not run off, for I thought that wicked," she said later, "but I walked off, believing that to be all right."

Adrift, Isabella and her child wandered to the home of Isaac and Maria Van Wagenen. When Dumont found her and threatened to take her baby if she didn't return, Isaac Van Wagenen bought her services, until emancipation took effect, for $20.

The Van Wagenens treated her well, insisting she not call them "master" and "mistress." Here she became "overwhelmed with the greatness of the Divine presence" and became a devout Methodist. She also began her first fight against injustice by trying to retrieve her five-year-old son, Peter. She learned he had been illegally sold to a slave owner in Alabama. A Quaker denomination helped her track Peter down, and she then sued to get him back in a case held at the Kingston courthouse.

"As she tells it, she didn't know what a grand jury was, so she walked up the courthouse steps and asked someone," says Nyquist. "She found them and told them about her son. Think about the courage this woman had to do that."

Remarkably, she won her suit and got Peter back. She was the first black woman to go to court against a white man and win. And the event is memorialized by a plaque at the courthouse, near the door, the first of many, that she walked through.

"The Spirit Calls Me, and I Must Go"

Around 1829, she and her two children traveled to New York City. She supported herself as a housekeeper and began street preaching with an odd and eventually unsuccessful ministry called the Retrenchment Society. Over the next thirteen years, she became known as a powerful and persuasive speaker. When her group floundered, she decided to become a traveling preacher, telling her friends, "The Spirit calls me, and I must go." And she changed her name to Sojourner Truth.

She wandered east, eventually finding a utopian community in Massachusetts called the Northampton Association of Education and Industry, where she stayed from 1844 to 1846. The association was strongly abolitionist and tolerant and supported women's rights. Truth even met and worked with abolitionists such as Frederick Douglass. When the association disbanded—it failed to make enough money to support itself—Truth went to live with one of its founders, George Benson. Unable to read or write, she dictated her life story, and *The Narrative of Sojourner Truth: A Northern Slave* was published by noted abolitionist William Lloyd Garrison in 1850. Truth sold copies at her speaking and preaching stops, giving her enough money to buy a home in Northampton for $300.

"After moving she seldom visited the mid–Hudson Valley again," says Mabee. "When she later talked against slavery in New York State, it was likely to be in New York City and across the central part of the state from Albany through Utica, Syracuse, and Rochester. In these areas there were strong antislavery societies. There were none in Ulster County."

"Ain't I a Woman?"

In her fifties, her legend really began to grow. In 1854, she gave perhaps her most famous speech at the Ohio Woman's Rights Convention in Akron. It became known as the "Ain't I a Woman?" speech and pulled together her personal story of slavery, abuse, and degradation.

During the Civil War, she spoke about and aided the Union cause, enlisted black troops (her grandson enlisted in the 54th Regiment, Massachusetts), and helped emancipated slaves adjust to their new freedom. She

Statue-esque

In 2009 the town of Esopus Board established the Sojourner Truth Memorial at the corner of Route 9W and Salem Street in Port Ewen. The memorial includes a statue of Truth as a young girl.

even met President Abraham Lincoln. In 1863, Harriet Beecher Stowe wrote a praise-filled article about her in the *Atlantic Monthly*.

After the Civil War ended, she continued working to help newly freed slaves and traveled to preach and speak. In 1874, she developed ulcers on her leg, and by 1880 she could no longer travel widely. She continued to preach around Michigan, speaking for temperance and against capital punishment. She died on November 26, 1883, at eighty-six years old and is buried in Michigan.

Mabee used to give tours of select local sites that were important in Truth's life but no longer does so. Along with the courthouse, there are churches, gravesites, and homes from her past. Some of them are in private hands or in fragile states, so Nyquist is reluctant to say where they are. "But if people want to visit them, I can contact the owners and try to arrange a visit," she says. "Ulster County should have some kind of tour on her life here. That would be fascinating."

Part 6:
The Valley Transformed

"The Pride and Joy of Po'keepsie"

Matthew Vassar's Rise from Immigrant Brewer to Founder of America's First Female College

Matthew Vassar was an enormously successful businessman, a political force, a pioneer in women's rights, a hobnobber with the stars, and, of course, the founder—more than 150 years ago—of the college in Poughkeepsie that bears his name. But what he really wanted, when all was said and done, was a statue. It finally arrived far too late for him to enjoy it, one of the few failures in his remarkable life.

Vassar was born on April 29, 1792, in the village of East Dereham, England, the son of Ann Bennett and James Vassar, farmers and religious dissenters from the Church of England. When Matthew was four, his family left for America. "They were the first of the Family name that left their Fatherland and were induced to seek this new Western continent more for the love of civic and religious freedom than from any pecuniary consideration," he later wrote.

The family settled in Dutchess County, where a family they knew was living, and bought a farm on Wappinger Creek, near Manchester Bridge. James's brother, Thomas, a brewer, also came. "But he forgot to bring hops, so he sailed back to get them," says Elizabeth Daniels, PhD, Vassar College historian and emeritus professor of English. In 1799, Thomas Vassar planted Dutchess County's first-ever acre of barley, and in 1801 he and James began the family's American brewing concern.

Ten years later, when the brewery burned to the ground and Matthew's elder brother, John Guy, was killed by the fumes, James went back to farming. Matthew, already running an oyster house in town, started his own brewery. He also became, at age nineteen, the de facto head of his family.

"He Wanted to Make Money"
Driven to succeed—"he was ambitious and wanted to make money," Daniels says—Vassar went on to buy a stake in a successful cloth-cutting machine,

invest in real estate, help incorporate Poughkeepsie Savings Bank, become president of the Hudson River Railroad, dabble in the whaling industry, and develop an aqueduct (selfishly, to bring water to his brewery, which continued to thrive). At a time when Poughkeepsie was a powerful and established metropolis, "no one was more active than him," says Colton Johnson, PhD, professor emeritus of English and dean emeritus at Vassar.

He was married in 1813 to Catherine Valentine (or Valantine; both spellings appear in the record). They had no children. In the ensuing decades Vassar was elected a trustee of the village of Poughkeepsie and, later, its president. He hosted the likes of the Marquis de Lafayette and Ralph Waldo Emerson.

And he did all this without the benefit of formal schooling, says Johnson. "He went to night school briefly but was kicked out for throwing an inkstand at the schoolmaster." Two specific events, however, led education, specifically women's education, to consume the rest of his life.

In 1837, his niece, Lydia Booth, moved her girl's seminary from Fredericksburg, Virginia, to a building on Garden Street in Poughkeepsie owned by Vassar. In the following years she impressed upon Vassar the urgent need for educational opportunities for women. And in 1845, Vassar and his wife visited Europe. While in London, he later wrote, "I visited ... the famous 'Guy' Hospitall, the founder of which a family relative, '[Thomas] Guy'... had the honor of being named after. Seeing this Institution first suggested the idea of devoting a portion of my Estate to some Charitable purpose."

"This trip struck him forcefully," Daniels says. And not just the charitable purpose; he was most impressed by the statue of Thomas Guy in front of the hospital.

"More Lasting Than the Pyramids"

In 1854, Lydia Booth died, and her school was purchased by a man with the wonderfully nineteenth-century name of Milo P. Jewett. A northerner by birth, Jewett had run a girl's seminary in Alabama but, as southern animosity grew ever fiercer leading up to the Civil War, came back to New York. In an unpublished manuscript titled "Origin of Vassar College," Jewett claimed he suggested the idea of a college for women to Vassar: "If you will establish a real College for girls and endow it, you will build a monument for yourself more lasting than the Pyramids; it will be the pride and joy of Po'keepsie, an honor to the state and a blessing to the world."

And the perfect place for a statute. Vassar bought land two miles east of Po'keepsie in 1860 and a year later incorporated Vassar Female College. At

Vassar College: A Timeline

1792—Matthew Vassar born in England.

1796—His family immigrates to the United States and settles in Dutchess County.

1845—Vassar visits Guy's Hospital in London, founded by an ancestor, and is impressed with the importance and permanence of properly endowed public philanthropy.

Vassar's niece, Lydia Booth, proprietor of the Cottage Hill Seminary in Poughkeepsie, suggests her uncle consider enabling "enlarged education for women."

1855—Milo P. Jewett tells Vassar that, in founding a woman's college, "you will build a monument to yourself more lasting than the Pyramids."

1861—Vassar Female College is chartered by the New York State Legislature.

Vassar donates $408,000 in securities and two hundred acres of land.

Vassar turns the first spadeful of soil for Main Building, designed by James Renwick Jr., architect of the Smithsonian Institution Building in Washington, DC, and St. Patrick's Cathedral in New York City.

1865—Vassar Female College opens, with 353 students—including a Civil War widow—between the ages of fifteen and twenty-four. Tuition: $350.

1867—The word "female" is removed from both the institution's name and the front of Main Building.

The college colors, rose and grey, are chosen, symbolizing the rose of sunrise breaking through the grey of women's previous intellectual life.

The first four students graduate from Vassar

1868—Matthew Vassar dies as he delivers his farewell address to the board of trustees.

1915—In the college's fiftieth anniversary year, President Henry Noble MacCracken proposes to the presidents of Mount Holyoke, Smith, and Wellesley a "four college conference," leading eventually to the Seven College Conference (the "Seven Sisters").

1968—Vassar College goes coeducational, as trustees approve admitting male students beginning in 1970.

1974—The first coed class graduates.

1999—Vassar is named "College of the Year" by *Time* magazine and the *Princeton Review*.

2006—Matthew Vassar's statue is unveiled.

the first trustee's meeting, he presented a small tin box containing securities worth $408,000 and a deed for two hundred acres for the college site and farm. "It occurred to me, that woman, having received from her Creator the same intellectual constitution as man, has the same right as man to intellectual culture and development," he told the trustees.

Vassar himself put the first shovel in the ground on June 4, 1861, to begin construction of Main Building. Though it was ready to open in 1864, Vassar wanted to wait until the end of the Civil War. "A women's college was a rather controversial experiment," Johnson says. There were those who thought it would destroy American womanhood and the fabric of the American family and that studying could lead women to infertility or insanity. "Vassar knew he needed as calm and favorable a public climate as possible," he says.

Milo P. Jewett, the first president of the college, wanted to open immediately and resigned. Reverend John H. Raymond, a charter trustee, became the president, at a salary of $4,000, and was in place on September 26, 1865, when Vassar Female College welcomed its first 353 students, from as far away as California, between the ages of fifteen and twenty-four. The annual fee for tuition and residence was $350.

"A woman's college was a sensation around the country. Tongues were wagging about what was happening," Johnson says. "This was a life-changing experience for the students, but they had such uneven preparations that it wasn't known who was a freshman and who was a sophomore until the next year."

That next year, the word "female" was removed from the college's name, and tuition, already beginning its persistent climb, was hiked to $400. And in 1867, the first four graduates of Vassar College graduated with "certificates of completion"; the board was still wrangling with the suitability of awarding "bachelor's" degrees to women.

Matthew Vassar died a year later, on June 23, 1868, while addressing the board of trustees, still pining for his own personal Rosebud. He never got his statue, even though he posed for models and offered to loan local sculptors $25,000—at 7 percent interest—to create one (but had no takers). His likeness didn't take its rightful place on campus until a few years ago.

Never mind that, though. Time will tell if his college is "more lasting than the Pyramids," but it is certainly "the pride and joy of Po'keepsie, an honor to the state and a blessing to the world."

My Old School

From Ministers and Poets to Musicians and Politicos, Bard College Has Been Fostering "Liberal Education in Action" for More Than 150 Years

John Bard was a product of what we'd now call "overachievers." His ancestors were renowned physicians and businessmen, founders of, among other things, New York Hospital and New York Life Insurance. His grandfather operated on George Washington during our first president's first term in office. John, who came into the world in Hyde Park in 1819, was born into money and prestige. But he took a different path, one that led to the founding, more than 150 years ago, of the Annandale college that now bears his name.

Bard, the eleventh of fourteen children, "almost certainly did not have the hard-driving power" of his forebears, writes Reamer Kline, former Bard president, in his book *Education for the Common Good: A History of Bard College, the First 100 Years, 1860–1960*. But he was devoutly religious and felt, as the proper nineteenth-century country gentleman should, that he had a responsibility to improve his community. For Bard, that meant building Episcopal churches.

In 1849, Bard married Margaret Taylor Johnston, member of another prominent and even wealthier family. Her father was a founder of New York University. "He married very well," says Michele Dominy, vice president and dean of the college, and she means more than just the money. "They both had in their genealogy a commitment to education and health."

They bought an estate called Blithewood, which they renamed Annandale, after Margaret's ancestral home in Scotland, and commenced building churches and schools there and in Tivoli. But there was a shortage of Episcopal ministers. Two prominent members of the church—John McVickar, a clergyman who taught for fifty years at Columbia University and was superintendent of the Society for Promoting Religion and Learning (and Bard's uncle), and Horatio Potter, an Episcopal bishop—joined with Bard to fix that shortage by creating a preparatory college for the seminary. The church (represented by Potter) would recognize the college and help support it, as would McVickar and his society. Bard would provide the land and buildings, including one called St. Stephen's Hall. Thus was St. Stephen's College born in 1860. Six students entered that year.

The college struggled in the early years. "It was never well supported by the church," Dominy says. But Bard put his money where his beliefs were to keep it going. He had paid $60,000 for the Annandale property and spent $80,000 on the college, and he carried annual subsidies of his schools and the college of $3,000 per year. College instructors that first year—there were four—were paid $1,000 a year, which was good money. "He does not seem to have been shrewd or particularly astute in money matters," Kline writes, and his fortune rapidly declined.

Worse, in 1868 his fourth child and only son, Willie, died of a fever at age twelve. Distraught, the family moved to England, where Bard lived for the next thirty years. (Kline suggests that financial worries as well as the death of his son may have motivated the move.) He returned to Annandale only occasionally. His wife died in 1875, and Bard, who remarried, came back to the United States to live, in Washington, DC, in 1895. But his fortune had deteriorated so that in 1897 his thirty-acre estate was in foreclosure. It was sold to the college, for about $38,000. Bard died February 12, 1899. His nephew called him "a gentleman to his fingertips. Hospitable, kind, gentle, sweet in thought to all, and a lovely refined personality."

Flaming Liberals?

In 2005, the *Princeton Review* ranked Bard College as the second-most liberal college in the United States (after Mills College in California), declaring that Bard "puts the 'liberal' in 'liberal arts.'"

But Michele Dominy, vice president and dean of the college, much prefers the term "progressive." "We are represented as being to the left politically, but that's really a conflation of progressive education being liberal," she says. "For us, progressive education is very much about a breadth and depth of intellectual training and an expectation of engagement in the world. But many parts of our curriculum would belie our being called left. We have worked with West Point for a number of years, and our faculty is not universally liberal."

The college does foster a culture of risk taking, she says. "That elasticity and willingness to experiment makes us seem liberal in that sense."

Bard College: A Timeline

1819—John Bard born at his family estate, Hyde Park.

1853—John and Margaret Johnston Bard buy Blithewood, which they rename Annandale.

1860—St. Stephen's College is chartered by the New York State Legislature. Six students begin their classical training in preparation for the seminaries of the Episcopal Church.

1866—The college begins granting degrees in the liberal arts and sciences, in addition to the preseminarian program.

1868—Twelve-year-old Willie Bard dies, and John Bard moves his family to England.

1899—John Bard dies.

1928—St. Stephen's becomes an undergraduate college of Columbia University.

1929—Franklin Delano Roosevelt becomes a trustee and serves until 1933.

1933–1944—A number of distinguished European émigrés join the Bard faculty, including political editor Felix Hirsch, violinist Emil Hauser, economist Adolf Sturmthal, and psychologist Werner Wolff.

1934—The college's name is changed to Bard College.

1944—Bard withdraws from affiliation with Columbia in order to become coeducational. The first women students arrive in September.

1946—Mary McCarthy joins the Bard faculty, the first of a long list of writers to teach at Bard during the late 1940s and 1950s, including A. J. Ayer, F. W. Dupee, Ralph Ellison, Franco Modigliani, William Humphrey, Theodore Weiss, Anthony Hecht (Bard class of 1944), Saul Bellow, and Dwight Macdonald.

1973—Former Bard students Donald Fagan and Walter Becker, as Steely Dan, release "My Old School," vowing "I'm never going back to my old school" because of a drug bust on campus in 1969.

1985—Donald Fagan goes back to his old school to receive an honorary doctorate. '"Well, you know. I'm not one to hold a grudge," he tells *Entertainment Weekly*.

1990—The Bard Music Festival begins its first season.

1991—Undergraduate enrollment reaches 1,000.

2002—The Human Rights Program is established, the first full academic concentration in human rights at a US college.

2003—The Richard B. Fisher Center for Performing Arts, designed by Frank Gehry, opens.

2005—The Bard College Conservatory of Music opens.

2006—The Hessel Museum of Art opens.

For its first sixty years, St. Stephen's offered men a classical curriculum and prepared more than six hundred ministers. But in 1919, the college hired Dr. Bernard Iddings (B. I.) Bell, a well-known educator, writer, and churchman, as warden (that's what they called the dean back then). St. Stephen's began to adopt a broader, more secular curriculum that included the social and natural sciences. And in 1928 the college took a more radical new step when it became an undergraduate school of Columbia University. Donald G. Tewksbury of Columbia was appointed dean in 1933 and instituted his "program," or curriculum, for the college.

"Dean Tewksbury formed the curriculum that still stands, in many ways, today," says Dominy. "His charge was to make the change, but his goals were similar to those when it was a church school in the 1860s, and those goals still stand in the twenty-first century. At our one-hundredth anniversary, in 1960, the college's mission statement was 'liberal education in action.' It still is today."

But it no longer is St. Stephen's College. In 1934, Tewksbury put John Bard's name on the front door.

The Birth of a County

In 1812 Putnam County Seceded from Dutchess County

As revolutions go, this one is, frankly, kind of lame. It won't ever be confused with the American colonies' war for independence from a tyrannical monarch. It inspired no glorious mottos like "liberty, equality, fraternity." It failed to foment similar uprisings around the globe, like the "Arab Spring." No, the revolution, two hundred years ago, that resulted in the bisection of Dutchess County and the creation of Putnam County was precipitated, mostly, by mud.

Still, a bicentennial is worth celebrating, as Putnam County did in 2012 to mark that day, June 12, 1812, when it came in to being. To fully appreciate this event, however, requires dipping into history. And into the aforementioned mud.

The first peoples to get muddy in what would become Putnam County were the Wappinger, Native Americans who thrived on the region's fertile lands and abundant waters. The Dutch, of course, eventually got hold of the land, which became part of Adolphe Philipse's patent. It was incorporated into Dutchess County, one of just twelve New York State counties, in the early eighteenth century. Back then, Dutchess included all of the future Putnam and a small bit of the future Columbia counties. It was named for the Duchess of York, whose husband became King James II. And its business was administered by Ulster County until 1713, when Poughkeepsie became the seat of government in the county.

The south end of the county grew slowly, because the Philipse heirs still owned most of the land. Yet its location made it valued territory during the Revolutionary War. Both sides wanted to control the Hudson Highlands, and had it not been for Paul Revere, the most famous midnight rider in our history might have been an area teenager named Sybil Ludington. In April 1777, the sixteen-year-old daughter of Colonel Henry Ludington took to her horse and mustered her father's militia to march to Connecticut, where they forced the British to retreat to Long Island. The redcoats continued to attack the area, though, and its defense by the colonists was commanded, for a time, by General Israel Putnam. The area was so critical that Benedict Arnold was outed as a traitor here, trying to help the British advance at West Point.

After the war the population grew, and by the end of the century there were enough residents to start complaining about the Dutchess County government. And here's where the mud comes in.

Everything governmental had to be transacted in the city. Legal work was done there. Deeds were filed there. Grievances were adjudicated there. Banking was conducted there. Every male between the ages of sixteen and sixty had to be in the militia, and every officer had to go there once a year to be sworn in. Town supervisors had to spend several days there, unpaid, every year. The problem? "In the late 1700s and early 1800s, Poughkeepsie was just too darn far away," says Sallie Sypher, Putnam County's deputy county historian and former county executive.

It took a full day to get there. While there, travelers had to find a place to stay, stable their horses, pay for meals, and conduct their business. Then it took another day to get back home. If they were carrying cash—electronic funds transfers were two centuries down the road—they were subject to literal highway robbery. "It was a big drag," Sypher says.

The drag was worst in spring and fall—mud seasons. And there was no Department of Public Works to maintain the thoroughfares. "People were chosen to work stretches of the road when needed, to push the mud out of the way," Sypher says. They weren't paid and in fact were fined if they didn't do their job.

Those in the southern half of the county began debating separation at the end of the eighteenth century and, in 1806 and 1807, asked the state legislature to allow their own town clerks to conduct business. They were turned down. Then, when the Poughkeepsie courthouse burned down, the county hoped to pay for a new one through, among other revenue streams, a new tax on dogs. "Farmers in the southern part of the county needed their dogs for work, and they found this and other bits of overregulation very annoying and irritating," Sypher says. Taxation without canine representation was the last straw.

In 1812, a petition to create the new Putnam County was approved. The paper trail as to how this happened is, well, muddy. Records are sparse, Sypher says, and there was no newspaper there at the time. "We don't even know how they chose the name Putnam."

We do know that, once the dust had settled, Dutchess tried to stick it to Putnam one last time. "They sent the Putnam supervisors a bill for $222.70 for outstanding fees and services," Sypher says—about $12,000 in today's money. "It was just one more irritating thing, and the Putnam legislature said, 'Forget it. You lost.'"

Air Pure and Dry

In the Nineteenth Century Cornwall Became
the Nation's Premier Health Retreat

I wish I were Nathaniel Parker Willis. Not just because he was the highest-paid magazine writer of his time—that time being the mid-nineteenth century, when magazine writers still made money worth mentioning—though there is that. And not just because he belonged to an overachieving family of editors and publishers and poets and musicians, though that would be nice too. And not just because he hung with the likes of Henry Wadsworth Longfellow, shared rum and oysters with Charles Dickens, and was praised by his friend Edgar Allan Poe for writing "by far the best play from the pen of an American author," though, come on.

No, I really wish I were Willis, who was born in 1806, in Portland, Maine, because he took a boat ride about forty miles up the Hudson River from his New York home and spotted a patch of land near the banks of Canterbury Creek in the town of Cornwall. The property's owners told him it was virtually worthless, "an idle wild of which nothing could ever be made."

Willis bought it anyway in 1846 and hired the most famous architect of the day, Calvert Vaux, to design a fourteen-room house, sited at the edge of a plateau by Moodna Creek next to a two-hundred-foot drop into a gorge, which would afford him glorious river and mountain views. (Did I mention that Willis was the highest-paid magazine writer of his time?)

He called his home Idlewild, of course, and from there he edited his new magazine, the *Home Journal*, you may have a copy on your coffee table, though it is now known as *Town & Country*. Willis often wrote about his new home in the magazine, about the clean country air and vast natural beauty and healthful climate, at a time when privileged New Yorkers, his readership, were growing especially tired of the dirty city air and vast, ugly unhealthiness of urban life. Travel was generally hard in those days, but boating to Cornwall Landing was relatively easy, and Willis's friends and readers came to check it out.

Many liked it so much, they came every year and in time bought their own idle wilds, and for a short while Cornwall was perhaps the nation's first health retreat. Boardinghouses took visitors, and modern conveniences like a telegraph office and library sprang into being. "Many made it an annual trip and eventually bought property and made Cornwall home," says Village of Cornwall historian Colette Fulton. In a very real sense, this began the migration to the suburbs that has resulted in the region we all know and live in today. "To this very day," Fulton says, "there are people who own property in both places and others who live here but commute to New York to work."

That's why I wish I were Nathaniel Parker Willis, the father of the lower Hudson Valley.

"Malaria and Mosquitos Unknown"

I certainly don't wish for Willis's other legacy. His magazine nearly failed during the Civil War, he grew very ill from epilepsy, and he died in 1867 with a diminished reputation that has faded such that his biographer noted in 2001 that he is now merely a footnote to his more lasting friends and acquaintances.

But in turning Cornwall into a health haven and, further on, a suburb, Willis lives on. The town itself had humble beginnings. It was settled in the 1740s by two branches of a family named Clark, who bought five hundred acres to farm, Fulton says. Their children purchased more land and slowly built the town, but it was still very much a rural community in the 1840s. The city to the south, meanwhile, was becoming ever more crowded and dirty. "Doctors were aware of the fact that the mountain air, the elevation, and being away from city smog was healthful," Fulton says. At the turn of the nineteenth century, though, it was hard to reach from distant Manhattan because the roads, if they existed at all, were lousy. Commercial traffic trawled the river, however, and "passengers on those boats saw how beautiful the area was, and that they could get out of the city and relax," Fulton says. "Then steam ships made it easier for passengers to travel." Regularly scheduled departures allowed for a manageable day trip for those looking to escape city life.

Willis's articles spurred many to visit, though it wasn't Club Med. "There were no big hotels," Fulton says. "A few small hotels and boardinghouses advertised mountain air and access to fresh fruits and vegetables. People would clear out rooms and rent them in summer. It was a common practice, and a nice little income."

The Smith House, for instance, boasted of "Large, Airy Rooms, Elegant Shade, Extensive Verandas," a view of "the broad bay of Cornwall," and convenient access to the post office and bowling alleys, for $8 to $16 a week. The Moodna Mansion, in Orr's Mills, advertised "fine spring water running through house."

As its popularity grew, Cornwall saw smaller and larger hotels open to cater to the new health-conscious vacationer. For example, the Cornwall Mountain House, a large hotel that resembled the Mohonk Mountain House, sat on the west side of "famous Storm King Mountain, commanding a river and landscape view not surpassed in this country for beauty and extent, air pure and dry, nights cool, malaria and mosquitos unknown."

These hotels also offered music and dancing, and the town built a bandstand at which members of John Philip Sousa's band, who were frequent visitors, gave concerts. The library hosted plays and lectures. It was a scene. "A couple hundred visitors came every summer, maybe more," Fulton says, and while that's not exactly Cancun-at-spring-break busy, it was very upstate-1850s busy, as one local guide wrote: "With the advance of summer, the usual change has come about, in the character of our population. The farm-houses are peopled with city-boarders—butter scarce; horses in great demand; a tree an exception which has not a nurse and baby under it; and the roads, at evening, quite holly-hocked with young ladies in gay ribbon."

The Birth of a Notion

Like all good scenes, this one had only a short fine time of young ladies in gay ribbon. After the Civil War, the railroads were built, allowing travel to more distant lands, and Cornwall's days as a health retreat "fell by the wayside," Fulton says.

But many of those who had visited decided to stay. They built homes and raised families. Some were artists and musicians who, like artists and musicians today, found the area inspirational. Others became early commuters, taking the morning train or boat into Manhattan and returning in the evening. They started schools and opened local businesses. In 1884, the village of Cornwall-on-Hudson was incorporated. The rest, as we all know, is lower Hudson Valley history.

For good (and, yes, ill), we can thank Nathanial Parker Willis for that.

A (Man-Made) River Runs Through It

The D&H Canal Was the Engine of Growth for the Lower Hudson Valley

Here's a quick Hudson Valley quiz: What do the Ulster County towns of Port Jervis and Wurtsboro have in common? Hint: Consider the names Jervis and Wurts.

Stumped? Then also ask yourself why the towns of Phillipsport, Port Orange, and Port Jackson (now called Accord) are called ports. Why, for that matter, does Port Jervis have a Canal Street and Ellenville and Wawarsing a Towpath Road? And what is Summitville the summit of exactly?

The answers to all these questions relate to the early-nineteenth-century engineering marvel and economic stimulus package known as the Delaware & Hudson (D&H) Canal.

New York's better-known canal, the Erie, had a song written about it, and the more famous Barge Canal system linked the Erie to other canals in the Finger Lakes, Oswego, and Champlain Valley regions. But the D&H Canal is of special value to the lower Hudson Valley.

It's hard to remember, in these days of superhighways and high-speed freight trains, that when this country was still in its infancy in the early 1800s, it was hard to get stuff from here to there. Roads were primitive or nonexistent, railroads hadn't been invented yet, and the new country was really, really big. That presented an interesting problem for the brothers Wurts, William and Maurice, two merchants from Philadelphia who owned land in northeastern Pennsylvania that contained rich deposits of anthracite coal.

The War of 1812 had virtually shut off the supply of bituminous (soft) coal from the United Kingdom, sparking America's first energy crisis. The Wurts brothers believed their harder form of coal offered a new and cheap—but as yet untested—fuel source for the area's biggest energy consumer, New York City, and the rest of the growing country.

Dig This

But how to get it there? Believe it or not, in the 1820s building an artificial river was more economical than building a road. Yes, it was more expensive upfront. Digging and blasting through wilderness required the labor of thousands of men. (It took 2,500 men and two hundred teams of horses just to complete the section between Cuddebackville and Kingston.) But once it was done, a canal moved a lot more product. A two-horse barge could transport one hundred tons of coal a lot faster than a two-horse wagon could move just one ton.

So the Wurts boys built themselves a canal. In 1823, they hired Benjamin Wright and John Jervis, engineers of the new Erie Canal, to design a canal from Honesdale, Pennsylvania, to Eddyville on the Rondout Creek near Kingston. From there, the coal could be sent down the Hudson to New York City or upriver to Canada. Wright and Jervis designed a canal 4 feet deep, 32 feet wide, with 108 locks, 137 bridges, and 26 basins, dams, and reservoirs. The cost: $1.2 million, which was serious money then.

The state kicked in some of this serious money, but to raise the rest, the Wurts brothers needed to prove that anthracite coal would work. On January 7, 1825, they convinced several business and financial leaders to meet at the Tontine Coffee House on New York's Wall Street to watch anthracite burn. And burn it did. Within hours, their freshly minted stock had sold out.

Armed with cash, the company set to work, and in less than three years it had built the 108-mile link between the coal mines and the Hudson River. The locks, which could accommodate up to thirty-ton boats, could raise or lower the boats between eight and twelve feet apiece. (The canal reached its apex at what became, you guessed it, Summitville.) The original canal included two major aqueducts to carry boats over the Neversink River and Rondout Creek. And when the canal was enlarged between 1847 and 1851, the company added four new aqueducts, engineered by John A. Roebling, who took much of what he learned here to build a rather famous bridge connecting Brooklyn to Manhattan several years later.

Follow the Money

While the canal made its Pennsylvania owners and New York City investors wealthy, it also proved a boon to the vastly unsettled counties through which it passed. "It helped enrich people all along the canal, especially in Ulster County," says Stephen Skye, a historian and president and CEO of the Neversink Valley Area Museum, in Cuddebackville. "People worked to build the canal, to run it, and to maintain it. The county's population exploded.

Kingston's major industry was the canal, and it grew from a village to a major New York and American city. Esopus went from a tiny village of hundreds to a town of thousands."

The canal began as a way to move coal, but as it was widened, deepened, and improved over the years, it quickly added other products, including human passengers.

During the canal's peak years at mid-century, thousands of boats floated up and down the canal at any one time. "It was the economic highway for the entire area," says Eileen Camasso, president of the board of trustees, D&H Canal Historical Society and Museum, in High Falls. "A lot of people today know it was there—there are so many places with the word 'canal' in their name, and they know there are little villages seemingly in the middle of nowhere because of the canal. But I don't think they understand how powerful an engine of the economy it was for one hundred years."

End of an Era

By the end of the century, though, railroads had become the preferred means of transportation in the country. In 1898, only two hundred coal-carrying boats were still in operation. That year, the Delaware & Hudson Canal Company, which had been investing in trains since the 1860s, officially became the Delaware & Hudson Railroad Company. Still in operation, the D&H is now America's oldest continuously operating transportation company.

What of the canal? The company sold the land, which was filled in over time. "Once it closed, many of the villages along it had to find new roles," says Camasso. "Some may have disappeared, but many redefined themselves." Today, only a few fragments of the canal remain, protected as National Historic Landmarks. The best place to see these remains is at the D&H Canal Museum and its Five Locks Trail. When you do, remember that this scenic path once supported a lot more than hikers—it supported the entire lower Hudson Valley.

Train Kept A'rollin

E. H. Harriman Rode Tall over the Nation's Railroads—and the Lower Valley

WOODCOCK: You're the Wild Bunch, Mr. Cassidy. I understand that, but you gotta understand that Mr. E. H. Harriman himself of the Union Pacific Railroad gimme this job and I never had such responsibility before and since he entrusted me to get the money through, I got to do my best, don't you see?
BUTCH: Your best doesn't include getting killed.
WOODCOCK: Mr. E. H. Harriman himself, he had the confidence in me —
BUTCH: Open the door. Or that's it. . . . Ya think he'd die for you, ya lousy amateur? . . . Now, Woodcock!
WOODCOCK: I work for Mr. E. H. Harriman of the Union Pacific Railroad—
[Railroad car explodes.]
—Butch Cassidy and the Sundance Kid

Downstaters, especially those who live in the town or play in the park named after him, know the name Harriman. So do those who lived through the 1940s, 1950s, and 1960s, when the name was at the center of state, national, and international politics. For the rest of us though, that name was most likely first heard in doomed defiance of Paul Newman.

Woodcock, of course, crawled from the wreckage, only to go through the same near-death experience later in the movie. Who was this Mr. E. H. Harriman, who inspired such loyalty? Woodcock, for one, would not have been surprised to learn how he came to have a town, a park, and much more named after his family. After all, at that time—the turn of the twentieth century—E. H. Harriman was as well known as J. P. Morgan, John D. Rockefeller,

Andrew Carnegie, and other captains of American industry during its most prosperous, albeit gilded, age. He is less iconic today among the general public; according to his biographer, Maury Klein, that may be because "he was a fairly colorless individual in terms of personality, and he died fairly young of stomach cancer. But in this period, he was the undisputed titan of the railroads."

"Do as I Say, and Do It Damn Quick"

Railroads, banking, oil, and steel were the major paths to great wealth from the end of the Civil War to the Great Depression, and Edward Henry Harriman had his hands in two of them. He was born on February 20, 1848, in Hempstead, New York, the son of an Episcopal deacon. He had business in his blood, though; his great-grandfather, William Harriman, emigrated from England in 1795 and became successful in commercial trading.

E. H. quit school at age fourteen to work as a Wall Street message boy. He soon became a managing clerk, and by age twenty-two he owned a seat as a stockbroker on the New York Stock Exchange. He saw the promise of railroads and invested his own money. He also saw the promise of merging railroads with banking, both professionally and personally; in 1879 he married Mary Williamson Averell, daughter of William J. Averell, a banker in Ogdensburg who was also president of the Ogdensburg and Lake Champlain Railroad Company. They eventually had two sons, E. Roland, whom you probably don't know of, and W. Averell, whom you probably do.

Harriman was a "small, sort of bantam rooster type," says Klein, author of *The Life and Legend of E. H. Harriman* and professor emeritus of history at the University of Rhode Island. "He was full of fight, full of energy, full of confidence, pretty curt. He was also utterly and completely devoted to his family, but he was one tough guy who did not suffer fools and did not like his time wasted." Indeed, one quote attributed to him is "Cooperation means 'Do as I say, and do it damn quick.'"

In 1881, he bought a small, bankrupt, thirty-four-mile railroad company called the Lake Ontario Southern, reorganized management, renamed it the Sodus Bay & Southern, and sold it to the larger Pennsylvania Railroad Company—making a hefty profit. This, he realized, could be the start of something big.

And it was. Though still a banker by trade, he was invited to become a director of the Illinois Central at age thirty-five, and by thirty-nine he was its vice president. "He got quite involved in its operations and management, and he began to think of that as something he would like to do," says

Klein. He helped pull the line through a severe recession, the Panic of 1893, and his insightful management skills brought him wealth and acclaim. Both would grow exponentially, though, when he purchased control of the bankrupt Union Pacific (UP) in 1897. "He was asked to come in to manage the UP," Klein says. "He was not the lead man at all, but it became clear that, of all the financiers involved, he had the most time and interest in overseeing the railroad."

Harriman toured the entire western region that the UP ran through. "He talked to people everywhere, and came home convinced that times were brightening, and that the railroad would do well," Klein says. "If someone took over and upgraded it, he thought it would be a very, very good investment. Most people thought he was crazy, but he did it, and in the process of reorganizing virtually every aspect of the company, he created the model for a new era of railroad history." In 1901, he merged the UP with his new purchase, the Southern Pacific, to create the largest railroad company in the nation, a source of jobs for men like Woodcock and ill-gained cash for men like Butch and Sundance.

Parks and Recreation

Like other titans of the era, Harriman needed a colossal estate. He had begun buying land near Tuxedo in 1885 and by 1900 had acquired 20,000 acres. In 1905, he decided the top of a 1,300-foot ridge overlooking the Ramapo River was just the place, and by the summer of 1909, the house, which he called Arden, was finished. Sadly, nearly so was he. On September 9, 1909, he died unexpectedly at Arden House. He is buried at the St. John's Episcopal Church cemetery in the hamlet of Arden. At the time of his death, he not only controlled the Union Pacific, the Southern Pacific, and the Illinois Central but also owned the Saint Joseph and Grand Island, the Central of Georgia, the Pacific Mail Steamship Company, and the Wells Fargo Express Company.

His net worth at the time was between $70 million and $100 million—in 1909 money. It all went to his wife and their two children, E. Roland, "a kind, gentle soul," according to Klein, who worked in the family business, and W. Averell, who also worked in his father's railroad business until 1940, when he became the political force that we know him as today.

The family legacy has never diminished in the area. "Once E. H. moved to the Hudson Valley, he became a leading benefactor of the era," Klein says. When the state wanted to build the Sing Sing prison on his stretch of the river, he "persuaded" it not to by building a park instead. His family also gave to many local charities, especially those helping underprivileged children, for whom he had a soft spot in his heart. And in 1910, his widow donated 10,000 acres to the state of New York for Harriman State Park.

"The Hudson Valley owes a lot to him and his family," Klein says.

A Nineteenth-Century Utopia

*The Shakers Made Mount Lebanon, Columbia
County, the Center of Their Spiritual World*

Ask most people about the Shakers, and they'll mention two things: furniture, and that lovely hymn "'Tis the Gift to Be Simple." Beyond that? Um, they were celibate, a fatal design flaw that explains why they aren't around anymore, right? Yes. What else?

Stumped? Well, there is quite a lot else, actually. "I offer this challenge to people," says Jerry V. Grant, director of research and library services at the Shaker Museum and Library in Mount Lebanon. "I rarely have anyone come to the museum that I can't connect the Shakers to an interest of theirs. This was a fully functioning society that did everything a society does. So food, diet, agriculture, health care, dress, the arts—there is something here to learn about. There are a variety of ways to access the Shakers, and if you spend any time with them, they become relevant."

The Shakers were more than relevant in Columbia County in the late eighteenth and nineteenth centuries. Indeed, Mount Lebanon was to the Shakers what Salt Lake City is to the Mormons. This village, the first fully formed Shaker community in America, was home to the Central Ministry and governing community for the entire Shaker movement from 1787 to 1947.

Mother Ann Lee led her United Society of Believers in Christ's Second Appearing from England and settled near Albany, in what is now the town of Colonie, in 1775. In England, they had been known as the "Shaking Quakers" for their ecstatic church ceremonies, and the shortened name followed them here. After Lee's death in 1784, leadership fell into the hands of Father James Whittaker. "By then, the society, which held revivals out in 'the frontier' to gain new members, had many converts in the Mount Lebanon area who owned land," says Grant. "They donated or consecrated their land to the church."

Beginning in 1785, Whittaker built the communal society model that he thought all other Believer societies should follow. The community was first known as New Lebanon, after the town, but the name was changed to Mount Lebanon in 1861. The federal government even gave them their own post office, because for 160 years, until 1947, the Shakers at Mount Lebanon led the largest and most successful utopian communal society in America. At its peak, it consisted of six hundred members and hundreds of buildings spread out over 6,000 acres.

This community also developed the Shaker ideals of equality of labor, gender, and race, communal property, freedom, and pacifism, Grant says. Its buildings, furnishings, and even urban-planning schemes represented the Shaker aesthetic of simplicity. Father Joseph Meachum, who took over when Whittaker died, standardized plans for subsequent communities. The meetinghouse, built in 1785, went up first. The village then expanded to provide living and working quarters for the original eight families. Construction was based on simplicity and functionality.

As it grew, the village was divided into smaller "family" groupings, called Center, Church, Second, North, and so on. Each family had its own leadership, members, and commercial activities. And the Shakers were quite commercial. Their businesses, which included seed production, herbal medicine, and chair manufacturing, were lucrative, and they were savvy salespeople. "They embraced the name Shakers, and by the 1870s everything they sold had the Shaker name on it," Grant says. "It was easier to say than their full name, and it made for snappy marketing." They even started a mail-order catalog business by the 1840s—long before Sears ever met Roebuck.

But the Industrial Revolution, coupled with their, um, lack of coupling, brought about the Shakers' demise. By the early 1930s, their presence in the area was minimal. The last Mount Lebanon Shaker died in 1947. Over the following years, the village was broken into three sections and sold to various private owners, including the Darrow School, which still inhabits Mount Lebanon's Church and Center families.

The North Family was purchased by the Shaker Museum and Library in 2004 as its future home. Now known as the Mount Lebanon Shaker Village, the site was named a National Historic Landmark in 1965. It consists of ten buildings, including the remains of the Great Stone Barn, a four-story, 10,000-square-foot testament to the Shaker worldview that was, sadly, destroyed by a fire in 1972.

If you haven't considered the Shakers worth your time, remember Grant's challenge. "Even though their life was anything but simple, the Shakers are the banner holders for living the simple life," he says. "Today, when living a committed life is becoming less common—families break apart, your bank cancels your mortgage, government is failing us—they give a rallying cry for a life of commitment to each other, to the poor, to civil rights. They kept the faith."

Part 7:
Business Straight and Crooked

Valley of the Barons

*Vanderbilt, Rockefeller, Gould—the Hudson Valley
Boasts a Wealth of the Wealthy's Historic Mansions*

The rich are different from you and me. They have bigger houses. And some of the richest people's biggest houses can be found on the banks of New York's Hudson River.

Fun fact: the Hudson Valley has the largest concentration of nationally recognized historic places in the United States. Since before there even was a United States, the river has been drawing the wealthiest artists, politicians, and captains of industry to its uncommonly beautiful shores. Here they built their "country cottages"—"ginormous mansions" to you and me. All the big names are represented: Vanderbilt, Roosevelt, Rockefeller. So are less-remembered titans. Some lived in them full-time; others used them as a temporary escape from New York City. At least a dozen of these estates are now public museums that give us commoners a glimpse of how the other half lived.

And boy, did they live.

The Lower Valley

Three grand estates can be found in Westchester County, minutes from Midtown Manhattan. Just hop on Route 9 heading north, and before you hit the Tappan Zee Bridge, you'll find Sunnyside, the home of writer Washington Irving.

As with all these homes, the first thing you notice is the view. Here the river widens into what the early Dutch explorers named the Tappan Zee (sea), with the Catskills off in the distance, all spreading gloriously before Irving's front door. The house itself is a landmark of the romantic period Irving loved. The stone structure, still covered in the dreamy wisteria Irving planted himself, has an eclectic mix of Dutch, English, Spanish, and Scottish influences. The gardens are purposefully informal, with winding paths surrounded by flowering trees and shrubs.

Inside, many of the family furnishings remain in place. Tour guides are dressed in elegant early-nineteenth-century attire, giving you a sense of life at Sunnyside, which Oliver Wendell Holmes called "next to Mount Vernon, the best known and most cherished of all the dwellings in our land."

Right next door—you can actually walk there from Sunnyside on the lovely Croton Aqueduct Trail—sits the imposing Gothic-revival castle known as Lyndhurst. First occupied in 1842, it was bought in 1880 by the robber baron Jay Gould, who gave it its present name.

The sixty-seven parklike acres surrounding Lyndhurst present more formal nineteenth-century landscaping, with wide, rolling lawns, specimen trees, and rose gardens. But it's the castle itself that commands attention. The towers and turrets seem ready to unleash volleys of flaming arrows or cauldrons of boiling oil on invading Huns. Inside, enormous stained-glass windows illuminate the period European furniture and artwork from such painters as Corot, Courbet, and Bouguereau. Robber baronry, obviously, had its rewards.

Of course, so did tycoonery, and just north of Lyndhurst you'll find the Rockefeller estate, Kykuit. "It's what God would have built," the saying goes, "if only He had the money." Kykuit, pronounced "KIE-cut," is Dutch for "lookout," and the six-story Georgian mansion looks over the Tappan Zee (and on a clear day, the Manhattan skyline) from the high point of the Pocantico Hills.

For many visitors, the best part of Kykuit is the artwork. Nelson Rockefeller, New York governor and US vice president, was a modern art lover, and he dotted the grounds with sculptures by Picasso, Moore, Calder, Nevelson, and many others. A tour of the private, underground galleries includes a collection of Picasso tapestries. And the Coach Barn (barn? Only a Rockefeller would call this mammoth outbuilding a barn) houses classic cars and horse-drawn carriages.

No visit here is complete without a side trip to Union Church of Pocantico Hills. No, not to pray you someday marry into money, though that's worth a shot. This simple stone church features stained-glass windows by Henri Matisse and Marc Chagall, commissioned by—who else?—the Rockefellers.

The Mid-Valley

My favorite mansion cluster is centered mid-valley. Just south of Hyde Park, two families you may have heard of—the Roosevelts and the Vanderbilts—came upriver to get away from it all.

The Franklin D. Roosevelt Historic Site and Library (the family called it Springwood) was bought by FDR's father in 1867. As both governor of New York and president, FDR used Springwood as his emotional and political home. Everyone from state hacks to Winston Churchill and King Edward VI visited here. In 1944, as both the war and his life neared their end, he said, "All that is within me cries out to go back to my home on the Hudson River."

The guided tour is a fascinating blend of history and sociology, an insightful look into FDR's personal (still on hand: his collections of stuffed birds, coins, and model ships) and political worlds. The grounds, on which Franklin and Eleanor are buried, are of course gorgeous too. But not quite as gorgeous as their friendly neighbors to the north.

The Vanderbilt Mansion may have the finest river views of all these homes. Indeed, the grounds have been voted the region's best picnic spot ten years running by the readers of *Hudson Valley Magazine*. The 212-acre estate is perched on a towering bluff overlooking the river. Its sweeping lawns are the perfect spot to spread a blanket, open the cooler, and soak in the river waters flowing gently past the Shaupeneak Ridge and Catskill Mountains.

The shack ain't too shabby either. Designed by the famed architects McKim, Mead, and White, the fifty-four-room, 55,000-square-foot beaux arts mansion was one of the first steel-framed houses in the United States. It drips Gilded Age grandiosity, from the Louis XV bedrooms to the hand-carved wooden dining room ceiling and the marble columns in the drawing room.

After the tour, you'll find it hard to believe that this is in fact the smallest and least expensive of the four Vanderbilt mansions. But then, its owner, Frederick William Vanderbilt, grandson of Cornelius "Commodore" Vanderbilt and son of William Henry Vanderbilt, spent only a few weeks here each year, so it's not like he needed a really nice house or anything.

The last stop on this leg of the tour—though not the last big house on the block by any means—is Montgomery Place. My wife and I love this place. It's not as grand as the Vanderbilt manse or as historic as FDR's crib. But there's something about how the home interacts with the landscape. Every porch points you toward a breathtaking view. The 380-acre property features stunning perennial, annual, and herb gardens, working fruit orchards, and natural woodlands through which century-old trails meander, up to and along the Saw Kill River, which tumbles through a postcard-perfect waterfall down to the waiting Hudson.

Nature, not furniture, is what really impresses here.

The Upper Valley

Nature also wins at the final destination on this tour. Its owner and builder, Frederic Edwin Church, was perhaps the premier artist of the Hudson River School of nineteenth-century landscape painting. And many of his paintings were composed right here from his hilltop estate.

He called it Olana, meaning "treasure house" in ancient Persian, and designed every last detail—down to mixing the paint colors himself—in Persian-Moorish style. He also meticulously oversaw the landscaping on his 250-acre spread to frame and highlight the views of the river and mountains. "I can make more and better landscapes in this way," he wrote, "than by tampering with canvas and paint in the studio."

This spring my wife and I made the trek up the hill for our second visit and our daughter's first. We took the child-friendly but shorter family tour, which points out all the stuff Church collected over thirty years of world travel, including furniture, tapestries, rugs, bronzes, paintings, sculptures, and even sombreros. Coolest of all is looking out the wide, Middle Eastern–style windows and seeing the very vistas he painted. Following a long walk over the roads he himself cut, through the woods, and then along a ridge overlooking the river, we had a small sense of what it must have been like, 150 years ago, to live like the rich and famous in New York's stunning Hudson Valley.

Nice Ice

Before Refrigerators and Freezers, the
Hudson Valley, Particularly Rockland Lake,
Supported a Thriving Ice Industry

What makes a commodity valuable? We all learned in Economics 101 that it's supply and demand. Those, of course, can change dramatically over the course of history. Wars were once fought over salt. It's now one of the cheapest products in the grocery store. Today, we all have freezers filled with more ice than we can use. But in the nineteenth century, people paid good money for big chunks of frozen water. And most of that frozen water came from the rivers and lakes of the Hudson Valley.

New York City was the nation's biggest consumer, buying 285,000 tons of ice a year by mid-century. The river itself, from north of Poughkeepsie all the way to Albany, provided some of the product, but the best ice around came from Rockland Lake. The spring-fed lake was renowned for its clean, pure water, and in 1831 the Knickerbocker Ice Company was formed; it soon became the region's largest supplier of ice and a major Hudson Valley industry, earning Rockland Lake the nickname "Icehouse of New York City."

By the 1850s, the company owned a dozen steamboats and seventy-five ice barges and employed about 3,000 people to harvest and ship ice all over the world. The harvesting typically began in January, when the ice was about a foot thick. A horse-drawn plow made deep cuts into the ice, and teams of men pulled out ice blocks of about two feet by three feet. They were then dragged to storage units called icehouses measuring more than 350 feet long, 100 feet wide, and 50 feet high, located at the northeastern corner of the lake. These icehouses could store more than 50,000 tons of ice, most of which stayed frozen well into the summer thanks to wooden walls insulated with sawdust.

In 1860, a cog railway was built to connect the lake and dock. A spur line of the West Shore Railroad also ran to the icehouses. When warm weather arrived, the stored ice was placed on inclined railroad cars, transported to barges on the Hudson River, and shipped to New York City. There it was transferred to icehouses all over the city and then distributed to customers via ice wagons.

By the 1880s, about 1,500 ice wagons, including Knickerbocker's signature bright yellow ones, rattled up and down the streets of New York, and icemen would deliver as much as eighty tons a week, block by tong-gripped block, up narrow staircases to anxiously waiting housewives. Or to disappointed housewives; see the Three Stooges classic where iceman Curly runs up a huge flight of stairs on a hot day only to deliver an ice cube. The iceman cometh, indeed.

The Ice Age

Rockland Lake was the biggest but by no means the only ice company in the valley. The area around Castleton and Schodack, in Rensselaer County, was another big provider, with a dozen or so icehouses located on the banks of the Hudson or the islands just offshore. All this ice brought with it significant social and cultural changes. It helped keep meat, fish, and dairy products safe, improving both food quality and public health. It helped kick-start the nation's beer industry; ice meant beer could be brewed and stored all year long, and more than 120 breweries were up and running in Manhattan and Brooklyn by 1879. Ice was even used medicinally, as hospitals dispensed it to fever victims to lower body temperature.

There was even a market scandal in ice. In the 1890s there were accusations of price fixing. In 1896, the major ice companies, including Knickerbocker, were consolidated in a national trust and prices doubled, leading to public outcry and ice demonstrations. New York's mayor, Robert Van Wyck, and other city officials were accused of conspiring to create a virtual ice monopoly, and the public learned that the mayor and his brother had been given $1.7 million in the trust's stock. Not surprisingly, the scandal led to the mayor's defeat in the 1901 election.

Closer to home, the ice industry contributed to the growth of Rockland County, says Gretchen Weerheim, former curator of education for the Historical Society of Rockland County. "The actual harvest only lasted about three weeks a year, but it gave farmers some extra income in winter," she says. And it drew seasonal workers, many of whom settled in the area and raised their families there. "Longtime residents here generally have someone who worked in the ice industry or knew someone in it," Weerheim says.

But many newer and younger residents have no idea there ever was such an industry, she says. "I love the whole spirit of enterprise, that a couple of guys came to the lake and figured out how to make this pure water work as ice. These guys figured out how to make an icehouse that kept ice into the summer and ship it around the world."

It wasn't scandal that killed the ice industry. It was electricity and refrigeration. Artificial ice replaced the natural kind, and home freezers meant supply could rise and demand fall. The Knickerbocker Ice Company closed in 1924. In 1926, one of the icehouses caught fire during demolition, and the fire spread and destroyed much of the village of Rockland Lake. The foundation of the ice company remains today, marked by a historical plaque, but not much else exists to remind us of this once flourishing industry.

With one big exception. Why do you yell at your kids to "close the freezer"? It's probably because your parents or grandparents used to yell it at you. If you're old enough, they probably even called it "the ice box." They yelled because they remembered the days of delivered ice. "You couldn't leave the ice box open very long, or the ice would melt," Weerheim says. And that was a big deal in those days.

Pough-cough-sie

The Smith Brothers Made Cough Drops, and Poughkeepsie, Famous

Poughkeepsie has produced its share of eclectic and unusual famous people: Samuel Morse, he of the eponymous code; Ed Wood, considered the worst film director ever; the inventor of Scrabble; and assorted artists, athletes, musicians, and their acolytes, including the guitar player for Velvet Underground and "Mountain Girl," Grateful Dead leader Jerry Garcia's wife and muse. But perhaps no two Poughkeepsie natives are better known than William and Andrew, the Smith Brothers.

For almost 150 years, their prodigiously bearded faces adorned the package of their singular product, Smith Brothers Cough Drops. Their first names may have been a mystery to many—indeed, because the words "trade" and "mark" appeared beneath their pictures, many nineteenth-century customers thought that they were Trade Smith and Mark Smith. But that is only because that trademark, registered in 1877, is one of the oldest and best known in American history.

In fact, many consumers still recognize the brothers, even though their cough drops have been largely unavailable for decades.

"For the Cure of Coughs, Colds, Hoarseness, Sore Throats, Whooping Cough, Asthma, &C, &C"

The Smith family made its way from Scotland to Quebec, where William Wallace Smith (1830–1913) and Andrew Smith (1836–1895) were born, and then, in 1847, to Poughkeepsie. Their father, James, opened a restaurant and ice-cream shop called James Smith and Sons. In 1852, legend has it, fate introduced him to a salesman with the delightfully Dickensian name of Sly Hawkins, who sold him a recipe for a cough drop. Smith the elder cooked it up in the restaurant kitchen, called it "James Smith & Sons Compound of

Wild Cherry Cough Candy," and pitched it "for the Cure of Coughs, Colds, Hoarseness, Sore Throats, Whooping Cough, Asthma, &C, &C." That was a stretch of snake-oil proportions. But the concoction did offer actual benefits. It increased salivation and soothed irritated throats, a symptom common to upstate New Yorkers then and now. And it tasted like candy.

William and Andrew helped make the drops and sell them in the streets of Poughkeepsie. When their father died in 1866, they shifted their attention to the growing cough drop trade and renamed the company Smith Brothers. The drops were immensely popular throughout the region, and, as *American Heritage* magazine put it, "there, on the banks of the Hudson River, two canny Scots made the throat lozenge an American institution, rivaled in popularity only by the town's next most widely known product, Vassar girls."

Success spawned competition. Companies called Schmidt Brothers, Schmid Brothers, Original Smith Brothers, Improved Smith Brothers, and even a pair of Smith Sisters tried to muscle in on the action. So, in 1872 William and Andrew, marketers well ahead of their time, put their hirsute visages on their wrappers. They also got their trademark, a mere seven years after the US Congress had first passed legislation providing for the registration of trademarks.

"Other trademark portraits followed in various lines of consumer goods," *American Heritage* wrote, "but no indicia of ownership produced more millions of dollars' worth of free publicity than the chin whiskers of Trade and Mark, subjects of countless editorials, favorite topics of newspaper columnists, standard fare for funny fellows from the days of vaudeville to the coming of the standup radio comic. At one time the company kept sets of whiskers and wigs to outfit cutups who wished to attend costume parties as Trade Smith or Mark Smith. Knowing they had a good thing going, the brothers never shaved."

Thus was a major brand born.

"The Delicious Odor of Licorice Is Wafted through the Air"

The brothers built a factory on Church Street, capable of producing six tons of drops a day, and the company built a newer facility, increasing production fivefold, on North Hamilton Street, in 1915. Older Poughkeepsians can still remember the smell. "Today," the Vassar *Chronicle* reported in 1944, "as one approaches the modern factory on Hamilton Street . . . the delicious odor of licorice is wafted through the air." By then the company also had another plant in Indiana. At its zenith, Smith Brothers was making sixty tons of cough drops—1 million packages—a day.

Andrew—aka Mark—the more likeable of the brothers, was a bachelor who liked a whiskey now and then and was such a soft touch that he was known as "Easy Mark." William—Trade—on the other hand was a Victorian through and through. According to the *Chronicle*, "He was a staunch prohibitionist and never allowed liquor to be served in his restaurant, a policy which still is in effect today. The shop was never open on Sundays, and no doubt William Smith would raise his eyebrows at the recent innovation permitting smoking."

He was also a community leader, a friend of Matthew Vassar and an early steward of the college, an unsuccessful politician, and a very generous philanthropist who, it has been reported, "assessed his brother Andrew for half of all charitable donations whether he knew of them or not."

Andrew died in 1895, and William continued as president of Smith Brothers up to his death in 1913. (Both are buried in Poughkeepsie Rural Cemetery, and their plots are featured in the cemetery's walking tour.) William Smith's son, Arthur G. Smith, then took over and expanded the company, adding more products like menthol drops, cough syrup, and wild cherry drops. Arthur's sons, William Wallace Smith II and Robert Lansing Smith, followed, and during the company's centennial celebration in 1947, they put on swallow-tailed coats, grew bushy beards, and put themselves and their company back in the spotlight.

They kept the company in private hands until 1964, but after four generations, the family sold out to Warner Lambert, which sold the concern to F&F Foods of Chicago in 1977. Production in Poughkeepsie was discontinued. And Smith Brothers nearly coughed its last.

"They Were the Innovators"

The brand languished over the next few decades, victim of poor corporate management and increased competition. In 2010, F&F Foods went bankrupt. By 2012, with the product essentially off the shelves of all major retail outlets, annual revenues were down to $1 million.

In 2010, though, New York–based private equity firm York Capital Management bought the assets of F&F, including the Smith Brothers brand, for about $10 million. It teamed with minority partner Steven Silk, who has a long and Clio Award–winning history of reviving tired brands like Lea & Perrins, Hebrew National, and Armour hot dogs. As the CEO of the new Smith Brothers company, Silk worked hard at modernizing the production facilities and retooling the Smith Brothers products and image.

"I never knew the Smith Brothers brand was dormant," he says of learning about the opportunity in 2011. "I thought it was in Walgreens that day. There were still many references to the brand in pop culture. I saw it in *Boardwalk Empire* and in an Adam Sandler movie. It still had high brand awareness, even though it had been off the shelf for twenty years."

That kind of awareness was the foundation on which he hoped to rebuild the company. "This brand is older than Levi's," he says. "It's older than Heinz ketchup. But we are not rebuilding based on nostalgia. We want to be relevant to today's consumer needs."

Sadly, they weren't. By 2015, with sales well below projections, the reborn company went under. According to the *Chicago Tribune*, "The ambitious plan to revive the dormant 168-year-old brand with aggressive marketing and a new line of cough drop and wellness products never gained traction, and the company has once again fallen into insolvency." Silk had stepped down from the company several months earlier "to pursue other brand building opportunities," he told the paper.

The Smith Brothers and their bodacious beards live on only in memory.

Cementing Its Reputation

*Modern America Could Not Have Been
Built without Rosendale Cement*

Ask any middle schooler to name the important figures of the Industrial Revolution, and if she was paying attention in history class, she'll rattle off names like Eli Whitney, Robert Fulton, Samuel F. B. Morse, and Elias Howe. But even her teacher probably wouldn't include the name Canvass White. That's a serious omission, especially in these parts. Canvass White was almost singularly responsible for the success of such revolutionary nineteenth-century engineering feats as the Erie Canal, the US Capitol, the Brooklyn Bridge, the Delaware Aqueduct, the Statue of Liberty, Grand Central Station, and, according to one historian, the modern incarnations of New York City and Boston.

What do those things have in common? None of them could have been built without natural cement, and White was to cement what Whitney was to cotton and Fulton was to watercraft. Along the way, he helped make Rosendale both the eponym and the center of the natural cement world.

In a technical journal article titled "An Overview of the History and Economic Geology of the Natural Cement Industry at Rosendale, Ulster County, New York," authors Dietrich Werner and Kurtis C. Burmeister tell how the early years of the nineteenth century "sparked a number of large-scale building projects, including the construction of regional canal networks. These canal projects required quantities of high-quality mortars unavailable in North America prior to the introduction of natural cement." Unlike other binding agents of the time, cement can harden under water. It is made from clay-rich dolostone or limestone, and the Hudson Valley was geologically blessed with large quantities of these stones.

Canvass White, more than anyone, used this resource to transform the nation and the lower Hudson Valley. As author Bill Bryson writes, "The great unsung Canvass White didn't just make New York rich, more profoundly, he helped to make America."

Cement Mixer

Canvass White (1790–1834) was born in the central New York county of Oneida. He was an engineer working on the Erie Canal when he went to England to study canal construction in 1817 and learned of natural cement. He earned his own cement patent back home and began the first natural cement factory in Chittenango in 1819.

The product proved so successful he quickly expanded operations wherever he found limestone. And the area around Rosendale had the best rocks around. They were unearthed in 1825, while the Delaware & Hudson Canal was being dug near there. Those limestone deposits were vast: twenty-two feet deep, three miles wide, and extending thirty-two square miles between High Falls and Kingston. The cement turned out to be so good that the term "Rosendale cement" became a trademark lawyer's worst nightmare: it became synonymous with natural cement, like Kleenex for tissues.

By then, the cement business was fiercely competitive. "This competition sparked Rosendale's nascent natural cement industry," Werner and Burmeister write. White and his partner and brother, Hugh, knew they couldn't compete from far-away Chittenango. In 1836, the Whites relocated to Whiteport, near Rosendale, "a time of considerable growth in the natural cement industry."

By the early 1840s, thirteen companies operating sixteen cement works produced 600,000 barrels of cement annually. Thanks to the Delaware & Hudson Canal, Rondout Creek, and the Hudson River, these companies were able to ship concrete to markets and import fuel more cost-effectively than inland cement producers. Rosendale cement eventually found its way to every major port on the Atlantic Ocean and even to the West Indies, and it was used in just about every significant construction project of the era. For example, from 1884 to 1886 Rosendale cement from the Widow Jane Mine was carried to Liberty Island, where it was used to build the base for the Statue of Liberty, the largest nineteenth-century concrete structure in the United States. The foundation comprises massive concrete walls eight to nineteen feet thick and twenty feet deep, behind the granite walls of the pedestal.

In the final year of the nineteenth century Rosendale's cement industry peaked, producing nearly 10 million barrels a year. But as the new century began and engineering became ever more ambitious, builders needed even stronger cement, and a new product called Portland cement rapidly became more popular. In just a decade, from 1900 to 1910, the two products essentially exchanged market share. Natural cement production across the United States shrank from 10 million barrels annually to 1 million, while Portland cement production grew from 1 million barrels to more than 12 million by 1910. Natural cement held on for a while as a specialty product, but in 1970, the Century Cement Manufacturing Company in Rosendale, the last natural cement works in North America, closed.

All in all, it had been a good run. Thirty-four different cement companies filed a property deed prior to 1900 at the Ulster County Clerk's Office, says Gayle Grunwald of the Century House Historical Society. "This did not count unincorporated family businesses," she says, of which there were probably many. During most of the 151-year span of the natural cement industry, Rosendale produced nearly 50 percent of all the natural cement manufactured in North America.

Postproduction

The empty mines have been used for a number of endeavors—some successful, some foolhardy. Mushroom cultivation and storage for sweet corn were naturals, but "the trout-raising experiment was doomed almost from the start," Grunwald says.

The rest of the community has adapted as well, of course. "There are no more guesthouses and resorts of the 'temperance type,' no more mules plodding along the remaining sections of the towpath of the Delaware & Hudson Canal through Rosendale," she says. "You won't see the workers leaving the mine exhausted at the end of the day, but you could see bats in the area that now call it their home."

What is left is the Widow Jane Mine, the only historic cement mine open to the public. An example of the "room and pillar" method of mining, the Widow Jane Mine is relatively horizontal (most followed the seam of limestone at angles that approached ninety degrees) and therefore easy to access. And its mysterious, otherworldly essence plays evocative host to musicians, poets, New Agey celebrants, and the just plain curious. "Some say the cave feels spiritual," Grunwald says. "They have come here to toast their happiness as they wed and sometimes to share the most supreme sadness of death. They come to celebrate the summer solstice, hear Taiko drummers, serve as an extra in a movie shoot, or just to see the mine and perhaps pay tribute to the cement miners who left us such beauty along the way. Unintentional beauty, but certain beauty all the same."

Cheesy

Monroe is the Birthplace of Two Great Cheeses—
One of Which Isn't Really Cheese

American ingenuity is a remarkable thing. Among our greatest gifts to the world are products that, how shall we put this, resemble real things but are themselves wholly unreal. Twinkies come immediately to mind. So does reality television, an oxymoron taken to the second power. I am old enough to remember Beatlemania, a 1970s Broadway show whose marketing slogan was "Not the Beatles, but an incredible simulation!" Yet one of the most enduring fake-real "incredible simulation!" products ever to infect the land was invented right here, in the Orange County town of Monroe, in 1918. I am talking, of course, about Velveeta.

This "pasteurized prepared cheese product," as it must be described by FDA fiat, is, to paraphrase *Monty Python*, certainly uncontaminated by cheese. But it wasn't always thus. Indeed, it was invented by a cheese-making prodigy, and Monroe was once home to some of the leading cheese makers in the land—real cheese, made by Old World craftsmen. That line begins, in 1873, with a man named Julius Wettstein, a German cheese maker who immigrated to the United States from Germany. According to Monroe town historian James Nelson, he opened the first cheese factory in Monroe, which produced "a fine line of German, French and Swiss type cheeses," Nelson writes in a history of the town's cheese industry. "Wettstein was amply rewarded for the long hours expended in building his company. He acquired a solid business reputation and his cheeses commanded a high market price."

Owing to his wife's poor health and return to Germany, Wettstein sold his Monroe Cheese Company in 1878 to Messrs. Gross and Company, for $16,000. The new proprietors, principal owner Lena Gross and the cheese makers Leonard R. Gross, John Hoff, and August Gross, acquired a two-story frame house, a two-story factory, a barn, two carriages, one truck, one black horse and equipment, and the rights to a formula for a cheese known as fromage de Brie. In 1884, they in turn sold the business, including trademarks for fromage de Brie and two other styles, Neuchatel and d'Isigny, to Adolphe Tode and Ferdinand Wolfe for $25,000. And four years later, the new owners hired a cheese genius named Emil Frey.

Eureka! Liederkranz

Emil Frey, the son of a farmer and cheese maker, was born in Switzerland in 1867. He and his father came to America, and in 1887 Emil worked briefly for the Neuesswanders Cheese Factory at Slaterytown, in the Orange County town of Blooming Grove, before being hired at the Monroe Cheese Company.

As Nelson tells it, Adolphe Tode was also the owner of the Manhattan Delicatessen in New York, and in 1889 he challenged his cheese makers to produce a popular style called Bismarck, because his imported product often spoiled on its way from Europe. "Frey experimented for two years before he stumbled on a new product," Nelson writes. No, this was not Velveeta; that was his second great invention. This wasn't Bismarck cheese, either. It was a soft-ripening, spreadable cheese that was so good, Tode told Frey to forget Bismarck and send more of his new creation. The cheese was given the name Liederkranz after a famous New York City Singing Society that included Theodore Roosevelt, Leopold Damrosch, and Jacob Ruppert. It was soon one of the most popular cheeses in the land. "It became very famous and was served in the best restaurants and hotels from New York to San Francisco," Nelson says. He writes that the *Monroe Gazette* of May 15, 1915, reported that over 1,000 boxes of Liederkranz, weighing about 2.5 tons, were shipped from the factory in a two-day period and that the factory averaged over a ton per day.

The cheese was successful, but Adolphe Tode wasn't. Financial problems put his company and property into foreclosure, and both were bought by a New York City wholesale grocer named Jacob Weisl, whose family ran the company for the next thirty-eight years. It was under Weisl's leadership that Frey came up with his second cheesy breakthrough.

Eureka! Velveeta

The company opened a second factory in Covington, Pennsylvania, where it made mostly Swiss cheese. But there were problems; many of the cheese wheels broke or were misshapen. "They didn't like to waste anything," Nelson says. "They also had a lot of whey, another waste product, which they didn't know what to do with." So the broken bits were shipped back to Monroe, where Frey spent the next two years tinkering on his home stove. In 1918, he had his second eureka moment. He discovered that mixing the whey with the broken cheese created a smooth end product with a velvety consistency. He named it Velveeta.

The Weisls spun this brand off into the Velveeta Cheese Company, incorporated on February 14, 1923, and together the two companies were successful—for a while. In the mid-1920s, under the strong hand of one Max O. Schaefer, sales extended to "practically every hotel and restaurant in America and some European countries," Nelson writes. Schaefer was also an early enthusiast of another new invention of the time—the automobile— and helped establish the Monroe racetrack and the Monroe Driving Park Association. After he died in 1925 in, not surprisingly, a car crash, both the racetrack and the cheese company were doomed.

In January 1926 the Monroe Cheese Company closed both its Monroe and Covington plants and moved to Ohio, where milk was more plentiful and less expensive. The Velveeta Cheese Company remained in Monroe until the next year, when it was sold to Kraft Foods.

And that was the end of industrial cheese making in Monroe.

One Last Slice

Nelson says that after Velveeta left, the Monroe plant was bought by Ray and Joseph George to make and bottle natural fruit beverages. Prohibition, however, gave them other ideas. In July 1932 the New York State Police raided the building and found a still, which produced "another type of natural beverage which was much more popular than the former," Nelson writes.

The Monroe Cheese Company was bought out by Borden in 1929. Liederkranz continued to be quite popular, and Emil Frey worked for Borden as the general manager until he retired in 1938. He died on January 11, 1951.

In 1989, the Monroe Historical Society honored the Monroe Cheese Company at the site of the former factory on Mill Pond Parkway. Among the distinguished guests in attendance was Emil Frey's son, Robert, who donated and unveiled a marker to commemorate his unsung father's contributions to the world of cheese. And to Velveeta, which, as Nelson says, "we really can't call cheese, can we?"

Let There Be Light

And There Is Light in the Lower Hudson
Valley, Thanks to Roscoe W. Smith

If you flipped on an overhead light or a reading lamp to peruse this book, think for a moment not of the book but of the light. Most likely you didn't give that part of the reading equation any consideration. Electric light has been a part of our lives for so long, no one still living likely remembers a time without it. We take it for granted, but it wasn't granted until men like Roscoe W. Smith granted it to us.

Smith brought electricity to Orange and Rockland counties with his own two hands. A descendant of the first person to settle what became Monroe, Smith turned his early proclivities in both mechanical tinkering and business to pioneer electric service, eventually forming the company that morphed into Orange and Rockland Utilities. The delivery of electricity today is a complex, computerized system of power generation. But when Smith jumped into this new field at the turn of the last century, it was still a primitive, hands-on endeavor involving digging holes, erecting power poles, stringing wires, and shoveling coal into boilers. Smith did all that and more in his half century of lighting the valley. And then he turned his attention to bringing even more civic-minded light to the community he lived in for nearly a century.

"A Foolhardy Venture"

"Grover Cleveland was President of the United States when I was born," he writes in his biography, "Brief History of My Life—a Country Boy," written when he was eighty-seven and published in *The Life and Times of Roscoe William Smith, 1877–1976*, edited by his granddaughter Margot Mayer Richter. "To a boy living on a farm in the country, as I did, a twenty-mile radius comprised my world for years." During his long life, as he helped power the valley with electricity, he witnessed the birth of the airplane, the automobile, gas engines, radio, television, movies, and "on the debit side, the atomic bomb."

"Life, however, was very simple when I was born on August 1, 1877," he writes. Born in a farmhouse on a back road between Monroe and Turners, now known as Harriman, he was named Roscoe, he writes, "because my mother decided that with a name as universal as Smith, I should have an uncommon first name." His middle name came from his maternal grandfather. His ancestor, David Smith, was the first to settle Monroe, purchasing a plot of land from Philip Livingston and building a gristmill in what is now Crane Park in 1741. Future Smiths were farmers and undertakers, the progenitors of Smith, Seaman & Quackenbush, Inc. Funeral Homes, the oldest funeral firm in New York.

The Smith farm, now the site of the Pine Tree Elementary School, was without any modern conveniences. The oldest of seven children, Roscoe Smith suffered "most of the children's diseases," like whooping cough and diphtheria. "We knew little or nothing of what was going on as far away as Newburgh and Goshen," he writes. He walked three miles to school in Monroe. It was Little House on the Hudson.

At a young age, he turned his head to business. By his early teens he had built a poultry barn and incubator to sell eggs, tapped maple trees to make syrup, sold newspapers, and worked in a restaurant. His siblings went to college and became doctors, lawyers, engineers, and artists, but at fifteen, he writes, "I became unhappy in school and finally decided to leave." A natural mechanic, he taught himself how to wire barns and houses for doorbells and alarms. At eighteen, he got a job at the famed Tuxedo Club's on-site power plant, earning $30 a month plus board at the club. He worked twelve hours a day, with no holidays and no Sundays off, wheeling coal and shoveling it into the boilers that provided the power.

At the time, small power companies were springing up to deliver electricity to local communities. When the Tuxedo plant shut down a few years later, he went to work at the new Rockland Electric Company in Hillburn. There, he maintained the boiler, engines, power wheels, and switchboards and also helped build the power lines, digging postholes and stringing the wires to new parts of the area. When the company built a newer, larger gas-powered plant, he was promoted to engineer; for $85 a month, he was, "largely devoted to carrying the long spouted can to fill the many oil cups constantly."

He was also devoted to bringing electricity to his hometown. His experience, he writes, "made me feel confident that I could plan, lay out and supervise the electric pole lines for the new little company I formed at Monroe." First, he got married in 1903 to Ina Miller, "the only girl I ever courted." They moved into a house he built in Suffern. (Smith was also handy at construction and had a side business buying land and building houses in Tuxedo and Sloatsburg. At twenty-eight, he was elected a director of the Suffern Building and Loan Association, the youngest such bank director in the state.)

He planned his company and convinced investors to buy stock in it, and incorporated the Orange Utilities Company in 1905. Looking back, he writes, "I wonder how I ever had nerve enough to try such a foolhardy venture." He and his associates began digging holes and erecting poles made of chestnut trees he bought and hewed. He bought land on Spring Street for $500 to build a 240-square-foot, 200-horsepower plant. "We had plenty of problems and troubles without end," he writes. He took no salary for a year and a half, and financial stresses were so serious, "I began to keep off the streets as much as possible."

The Dean of Utility Presidents

The plant finally started operating on February 8, 1906. Current was available from 5 p.m. to 6 a.m. (It didn't operate twenty-four hours a day until 1909.) With few homes and stores yet wired, his total receipts for March 1906 were $41.96. But by August that was up to over $550 a month, and his little company grew bigger. In 1907, he bought Goshen Light and Power. He had to borrow money to do that, and many of the stockholders, thinking "this mortgage was the beginning of the end," sold out. To this day, their heirs are asking how they could have been so stupid. That year, the company paid its first dividend. "I might state here," Smith writes proudly, "that dividends of this amount and larger have been paid continuously and without interruption from the very beginning to the present time.'"

He was making $75 a month—less than his line foreman. He lived off sales of the seven houses he owned by that time. On snowy days, he had to don snowshoes to walk to the plant to fix things. The office was his home; the bookkeeper, his wife; their desk, the dining room table. By 1909, the company, now known as the Orange and Rockland Electric Company, was flourishing, grossing $25,000, and it bought its first company car, a used Cadillac, for $120. Smith began acquiring other power companies in Warwick, Buttermilk Falls, Tuxedo, and elsewhere and over the next forty years became the dominant utility in the area. In 1955, in honor of the company's fiftieth anniversary, General Electric called Smith "the dean of all utility presidents in the United States."

Then seventy-eight, though, he was ready to "lay down the burden" of running the company. In 1958, he merged it with Rockland Light and Power to create what is known today as Orange and Rockland Utilities, Inc. He turned his attention to philanthropy. Over the rest of his long life he donated property for the Monroe Woodbury Youth Center, Smith's Clove Park, and the site of Village Hall. His abiding passion, though, was Museum Village at Old Smith's Clove. A lifelong collector of bygone artifacts such as tools used by wagon makers, blacksmiths, and harness makers, he had built sixteen buildings to house them all and opened the museum in 1950. He devoted much of the final years of his life to the museum and was honored with the Award of Merit from the American Association for State and Local History and the George Washington Honor Medal for Village Restoration from the Freedoms Foundation. He died on October 10, 1976, at age ninety-nine, having lived long enough to see two great-grandchildren born—seen, no doubt, with the help of electric light.

Up the River

One of America's Most Famous Prisons, Sing Sing,
Has Been Around Almost Two Hundred Years; yet
Most Locals Know Little about Its Colorful History

The aboriginals who lived there called themselves the Sint Sink, which meant "stone upon stone." The seventeenth-century Dutch interlopers appropriated their land and altered the name to Sinck Sinck or Cinque Singte. In the mid-1800s it became known as Ossin-sing, from another Native American word, ossin, also meaning stone. Then, Ossin-ing, and now Ossining.

But criminals have always called it "up the river."

Sing Sing, the prison, and Ossining, the town, are inextricably linked. Indeed, the town changed its name only because the prison had become so notorious. And that's just one of a multitude of facts, stories, and myths surrounding the nearly two-hundred-year-old star of stage, screen, song—and grisly executions.

Its age was one of the things that inspired Guy Cheli, a writer who lives in Mahopac, to research and write *Sing Sing Prison*, a book in the Images of America series published by Arcadia Publishing in 2003. "It was built in 1825, and there aren't many things still standing now from 1825," says Cheli, a member of the Ossining Historical Society. Like many who work or live in the region, Cheli was aware of the prison but not its history. "It's right there in Westchester County," he says, "but I never really knew the story behind it."

You Dirty Rat . . .

Sing Sing most immediately conjures images of the gangster era of the 1920s and 1930s, of Jimmy Cagney movies and cops-and-robbers radio serials. During that time it housed the infamous Willie Sutton, Lucky Luciano, members of Murder Incorporated, and other well-known ne'er-do-wells. But by then, bad guys had been sent "up the river" from New York City courthouses for one hundred years.

When New York State's first two prisons, one in Greenwich Village dating to 1797 and the other in Auburn built in 1816, became overcrowded, the legislature commissioned Auburn Prison warden Elam Lynds to build a new and more modern facility. He decided to locate it in Mount Pleasant, near a small village called Sing Sing, because the stones that gave it its name were still being quarried nearby.

In 1825, Lynds transferred one hundred Auburn inmates by barge along the Erie Canal to freighters down the Hudson River and forced them, at gunpoint, to build the new prison. It opened in 1826 and was fully completed in 1828. But with crime a growth industry, it continued to expand for the rest of the 1800s. By the turn of the century, it housed more than 1,200 prisoners.

Old Sparky

A nineteenth-century prison was barbaric, and Sing Sing was no exception. Prisoners were expected to keep absolute silence. Beatings—and worse— were commonplace. "Bread and water" and "ball and chain" weren't metaphors; they were a fact of life.

"There really was torture," says Cheli, until prison reform took hold in the country, led in large part by Sing Sing's warden during the 1920s and 1930s, a man named Lewis Lawes. "Lawes believed that prison was punishment enough and that he would send prisoners back into the world as better people than when they came in," Cheli says. Lawes educated prisoners, taught them trades, and entertained them with visits from the likes of Babe Ruth, Harry Houdini, Edward G. Robinson, and other stars of the day. "He helped change the way prisons were run," Cheli says.

Lawes also abhorred the death penalty, which propelled Sing Sing into the spotlight many times during its history, perhaps most famously with the 1953 execution of Julius and Ethel Rosenberg. They were two of a total of 614 men and women who were put to death in the electric chair, known as Old Sparky, up until 1963, the last execution conducted in New York.

Rooms with No View

Today, Sing Sing houses about 2,000 inmates as a maximum-security prison. But it's essentially hiding in plain sight. Its impact on the village has been minimal. "It has supplied jobs, but many of the workers don't live locally anymore," Cheli says. There have been only a handful of escapes. In 1980, prisoners held some guards hostage. "Most famously, in 1941, a village police officer and a corrections officer were shot and killed during a prison break," Cheli says. The escapees were caught and executed.

The prison may come out of hiding, however, if plans for a museum and visitor center ever come to fruition. "In my opinion, that would be great," Cheli enthuses. "The train from Times Square goes right past it. Imagine how many millions of people would go there—it could be like Alcatraz. It would be a boon for the village and the state."

Cheli is biased, of course. "Sing Sing is my favorite subject that I ever covered," he says. In fact, he has a personal collection of artifacts, including old books, photos, artwork, and letters from wardens and prisoners, some items more than a century old. "I have a beaded necklace made by a prisoner in the late 1800s," he says. "It looks like a Native American necklace."

But his collection isn't available for public viewing. As of now, only the Caputo Community Center in Ossining, which has a small exhibit, and the Ossining Historical Society, which is more library than museum, openly acknowledge the place where bad guys are sent when they are sent up the river.

No Shrinking Violet

Violets Were Once the Nation's Most Popular Flower—
and Rhinebeck Was the Violet Capital of the World

One of the best things about living in the Hudson Valley is its rich and colorful history. The past is ever present here. But that history is so deep, sometimes it can get buried and forgotten. Literally.

They say that if you dig in just about any yard in Rhinebeck, you'll find bits of broken glass. Like Native American arrowheads or Dutch pottery shards, the glass points back to a time that most current residents don't know about. This, though, is a much more recent time—the late 1800s to the mid-1900s—when Rhinebeck and its surrounds were the center of a huge, national, now-forgotten industry. The glass is what remains from the greenhouses that powered an industry based on a shy little flower: the violet.

From the Gilded Age through the Depression, the violet was the world's most popular flower, a symbol of the height of fashion. And Dutchess County was considered the "violet belt"—with Rhinebeck its buckle. The city was known as the Violet Capital of the World; its major growers, known as the Violet Kings, and smaller producers supplied about 25 percent of the nation's violets.

Who knew?

Tobe Carey didn't. The acclaimed local filmmaker was looking for a project when he was reminded of something he had been told years earlier. "About ten years ago, Artie Traum's wife asked me if I knew about Rhinebeck and violets," says Carey, of Glenford. "I didn't pay much attention. Then last January she reminded me of it. I wanted a smaller project, and this seemed worth looking into."

His research took him to, among other places, the Museum of Rhinebeck, whose curator and former president, Steven Mann, did know about this history. The museum had an exhibit on the subject in the late 1990s, he said. "We have hundreds of items on violets—it makes up probably 5 percent of our entire collection." But he acknowledges that most people in the region have no clue about this history and hopes that Carey's film, *Sweet Violets*, will renew interest.

Through vintage photographs and postcards, archival film, period popular music and literature, and interviews with historians and the descendants of the area's largest growers (some of whom remember working in the greenhouses as children), Carey weaves a story that moves from ancient Greece and Rome through Europe and Dutchess County, touching on characters as wide-ranging as the Greek Muses, Sappho, Napoleon Bonaparte, Frederic Chopin, Thomas Edison, and Eleanor Roosevelt.

The local connection begins in the post–Civil War 1800s, when a gardener named William Saltford imported violets from England for estates in the area. His brother, George, took some of the plants to Rhinebeck to start his own business, where they seemed, for still unknown reasons, to love the town's soil and flourish.

During the Gilded Age, violets were the flower of choice among the rich, particularly coveted on holiday corsages for Valentine's Day and Easter. The violet business boomed. At its height, in the years before World War I, perhaps four hundred violet greenhouses sprouted in Rhinebeck, many along Violet Avenue—so many that the town was also known as the Crystal City—and in nearby towns like Red Hook, Fishkill, and Hyde Park. During the Easter season, more than a million blooms would be shipped by train—one was named the Violet Special—to New York, Boston, Philadelphia, Chicago, and beyond. For the preppies and their dates attending the Harvard-Yale football game or the National Horse Show, only a violet corsage would do.

The area's biggest growers, the Violet Kings, included Julius Vonder Linden, A. E. Coon, and the Trombini brothers, who had eighteen greenhouses of their own. The work was tough, requiring intense labor to grow, hand-pick, bunch, box, and ship the blooms and constant monitoring of the temperature and humidity in the greenhouses then heated by primitive coal-burning stoves. But it was still lucrative—for a while.

Like most fashion statements, this one faded. In the 1920s, Victorian esthetics gave way to modern, more casual and comfortable clothing styles. Big, bulky corsages had no place on a flapper's dress, and the violet became "your grandmother's flower." There was a brief rebound in the 1930s, thanks mainly to First Lady Eleanor Roosevelt. A big fan of the flower and a champion of local industry, she carried large corsages of Dutchess County violets at FDR's inaugurations.

But soon, reasons both scandalous and economic brought about the flower's downfall. The scandal involved a 1927 Broadway play titled *The Captive*, whose plot involved a love triangle concerning a man, his wife, and her female lover. Their symbol of commitment was the violet. The play closed after five months, with the lasting effect of making violets anathema to correct society. (Lesbians bought them in droves, however.)

Mann, however, thinks the scandal "was only the fourth- or fifth-most important reason" for the industry's demise. First came fashion changes, followed more dramatically by industrialization during the 1940s and 1950s, which offered farmers and their workers a far easier way to make more money. "Why work so hard for ten hours a day when you can make triple the money sitting behind a desk or working on the assembly line," Mann says. "One researcher says the industry really died because of the growth of IBM in the area." Those who did stay in the flower business moved toward blooms like anemones and roses, which were not only more popular but easier and less costly to grow.

By 1979 the last commercial violet growers went out of business. Today, only one local grower, Battenfeld's, continues the tradition, planting one row of cultivated violets every year—most of which now go to culinary establishments for gourmet salads and decorations. Says Fred Battenfeld, in Carey's film, "I don't want to lose that part of the area's history."

A history that, thanks to *Sweet Violets*, more of us now know.

They Got Legs

A Raid on a Kingston Bootlegging Operation Helped Bring Down Gangster Legs Diamond

"Do you know what Legs Diamond was trying to do?" an associate of his asked during an interview. "Well, he was trying to control all the illicit activities in the East. He was trying to be as big as Capone."
—*Jack "Legs" Diamond: Anatomy of a Gangster* by Gary Levine

Legs Diamond, it was said, never met a friend he didn't double-cross. Even by the dubious standards of Depression-era gangsters, he was no good. His enemies pumped so much lead into him that Dutch Schultz once asked his own henchmen, "Ain't there nobody that can shoot this guy so he don't bounce back?"

Yet, by 1930, he was also the Hudson Valley's biggest celebrity, a symbol of the little guy standing up to the heavy government hand of Prohibition. After being forced out of New York City, he set up operations in Catskill, and most of the locals knew he was running booze out of a brewery in Kingston. But government agents charged with enforcing the Eighteenth Amendment could never figure out how.

Raids in the early summer of 1931 finally uncovered the subterranean secret to his operations and led to the beginning of the end for Legs Diamond. The man who may have gotten his nickname for the way he could run for his life ran out of running room. Five months later, someone finally shot this guy so he didn't bounce back.

"A Future in the Catskills"
Jack Diamond was born on July 10, 1897, in Philadelphia to Irish immigrants. His mother died in 1913, and the family moved to Brooklyn. Soon a member of a street gang, Diamond embarked on his criminal path while

still a teenager, when he robbed a jewelry store. After being jailed for desertion during World War I, Diamond went to work for the big-time gangster Arnold Rothstein, the man who fixed the 1919 World Series. He also freelanced as a hit man for Jacob "Little Augie" Orgen, committing his first murder and soon after getting shot himself when Orgen was killed.

Legs began his own bootlegging business, mostly by hijacking trucks loaded with booze to fuel his speakeasies. He was outgoing and flamboyant, a womanizer (though he was married), and a terrific dancer. In fact, that's the more likely source of his nickname, according to Gary Levine (no relation to me), a former professor at Columbia-Greene Community College in Hudson who published *Jack "Legs" Diamond: Anatomy of a Gangster* in 1995. He quickly became a target of other gangsters. By the end of the 1920s, New York had become too hot for him. He'd been shot two more times, and he needed a new base of operations.

In *Legs*, a fictional account of the gangster's life, author William Kennedy envisions Diamond explaining to his attorney, Marcus, that he's "got a future in the Catskills."

> *"Don't you think you ought to get straight first?"*
>
> *"You don't understand, Marcus. You can carve a whole goddamn empire up there if you do it right. Capone did it in Cicero. Sure there's lots of roads to cover, but that's all right. I don't mind the work. But if I slow now, somebody else covers those roads. And it's not like I got all the time in the world. The guineas'll be after me now."*
>
> *"You think they won't ride up to the Catskills?"*
>
> *"Sure, but up there I'll be ready. That's my ballpark."*

The "Million-Dollar" Raid

Prohibition began on January 20, 1920, and killed off thousands of successful breweries around the country. One of those was the Peter Barmann Brewery. The beermaker, located on the corner of what is now Barmann Avenue and South Clinton Avenue in Kingston, had been in operation since 1852. Before it died, though, the Barmann Brewery was in the illicit hands of Legs Diamond.

The Feds knew that beer was flowing to New York and Albany from Kingston but couldn't find the source. On May 1, 1931, while Diamond was in an Albany hospital after being shot in a speakeasy in the Greene County town of Acra—his fourth shooting—local agents hit two warehouses on Bruyn Avenue. They nabbed ten men and about 3,000 barrels and 41,000 bottles of ale, worth more than $200,000. Three elite federal agents, known as "the Flying Squadron," were then assigned to the area, and on June 2, while hiding in the grass near the brewery, they saw a truck leave the yard. One agent jumped on the truck and forced the driver, Diamond associate John Sheehan, to surrender. The other two agents, armed with Thompson machine guns, stormed the brewery. They found so much cash, weaponry, brewing and trucking equipment, and beer that the raid became known as the "million-dollar seizure." It was one of the biggest such raids of the time.

They also discovered how the operation had escaped their attention for so long. Underneath the brewery, local plumbers on Diamond's payroll ran a flexible 2.5-inch rubber hose through the city sewer lines to the Bruyn Avenue warehouses half a mile away. That way, few trucks ever left the brewery, which helped allay suspicion.

City of Kingston historian Ed Ford says his late brother-in-law, a plumber, actually worked in that area and found some remnants of the pipes and hoses. "I wish he had saved some for me," Ford says. He has visited the tunnels himself but never discovered any artifacts.

There are also rumors that victims of Diamond's violence were dumped in the caves and tunnels under the brewery, including the famed Judge Crater, who disappeared mysteriously in 1930. "I never saw any bodies either," Ford notes.

"They'll Never Get Legs!"

Legs Diamond left the Albany hospital on May 31, 1931, to answer kidnapping charges in Catskill. In front of the courthouse, Gary Levine writes, a nine-year-old boy shouted, "They'll never get Legs!"

The trial was moved to Troy and finally held in December. Legs was acquitted—having probably bribed the jurors—and celebrated by getting drunk and visiting his mistress in Albany. In the wee small hours of December 18, he stumbled to his boardinghouse rooms on Dove Street and passed out. The Feds didn't get Legs.

But others did. Two gunmen followed him into the bedroom, where he lay sprawled out in his underwear, fired three bullets into his head at close range, and sped off in a black sedan.

No one knows for sure who finally stopped Legs from bouncing back. He had enemies on both sides of the law. It could have been other gangsters. It may have been the Albany police department under the direction of political boss Dan O'Connell; O'Connell claimed as much in Kennedy's book *O Albany!* As with much of gangster life and death, much remains mysterious.

"There are so many stories," says Ed Ford. "How do you know the truth?"

The Adams Family

Adams Fairacre Farm and the Hudson Valley Have Grown Together, in Business and Otherwise, Over the Past Century

Back in the late nineteenth century, at the height of this country's wave of European immigration, a young family from Padula, Italy, made its way to Poughkeepsie. They were called Adamucci, or perhaps Adamico; the provenance is unclear. What is clear, though, is that the family eventually changed its name to Adams. The boy, Ralph, was born in 1891, and he worked the fields with his father, a vegetable farmer like many of his Italian immigrant brethren.

In 1919, Ralph and his wife, Mary, herself an immigrant of Irish descent born in 1890, borrowed $500 to purchase fifty acres of their own to farm. Located on Pleasant Valley Road—now called Route 44, the Dutchess Turnpike—they named it Fairacre Farm.

How would Ralph feel, seeing their humble farm one hundred years later, now the thriving enterprise known as Adams Fairacre Farms? "He would be shocked to see the evolution of the business to what it is today," says his grandson Patrick Adams, who now runs the company, as CEO, with his brother Steve, the COO. The times and the region have changed dramatically over the past century, of course, and in many ways the Adams' family business has mirrored those changes. Think of it as a living museum of the area's agricultural and business history.

By the late 1920s, the farm was producing enough to sell its vegetables to grocers at a central market in Poughkeepsie's Clinton Square. In the early 1930s, Ralph and Mary started a roadside stand, selling to neighbors and travelers out of the barn that stood along a dirt road. Now armed with a staff of four—their children Diana, Dorothy, Ralph, and Donald—they increased their production to the point that, in the 1940s, they could build a farm stand on the property bearing the name Adams' Market. They also acquired more land in Salt Point that included apple trees, prompting the first use of the plural "Fairacre Farms."

The 1950s brought big changes to the valley and the farm. It acquired its first greenhouse, which allowed the farm to plant seeds in winter for spring transplanting in the fields. It also led to a new line of business: the plants themselves. "One day, we put extra tomato plants in pots—and sold out in hours," said Mark Adams in a talk he gave about the farm's history. "My dad said, 'We got $3 a pot for a tomato plant, and we don't get $3 worth of tomatoes off a plant. Go out in the field and dig them back up."

Many of those shoppers were newcomers, brought to the area by IBM. "We had the produce and starter plants, the people at IBM had money and free time, it was perfect for us," Mark said. "We grew up alongside IBM, and it was really beneficial for us."

Until now the retail business was secondary to the farming, so the store closed after the fall harvest. In 1956 they stayed open year-round, selling produce from other local farmers and peddlers. Then, in 1957, the senior Ralph Adams passed away unexpectedly. The next year, his sons Ralph and Donald took over the business. They also expanded it, building a small store and offering local milk and eggs in addition to produce.

In the coming years, the next Adams generation moved into the family business. Mark Adams and his wife, Sue, started Mark Adams Greenhouses in 1978 to offer bedding plants and poinsettias to be sold in the store. A second store was built on Route 9W in Kingston in 1981. By now, the retail business was so successful, the family no longer had time to farm themselves and sold few if any of their own fruits and vegetables. "The stuff we could grow was like 1 percent of what we could sell," Mark Adams said. "Also, the soil wore out, and deer became a huge problem." Deer, once rare, became so plentiful they ate an entire field of green bean blossoms one year. "My father couldn't believe it," Mark said.

In 1998, the Adams' third store was built, in Newburgh, offering a salad bar, prepared foods, a sweet shop, a gift shop, and a gourmet grocery department. Since then, the Poughkeepsie and Kingston stores have been renovated, a fourth store opened on Route 9 in Wappinger, featuring the company's first hot-food bars, and the newest addition, a bakery, opened at the Poughkeepsie location in 2018. And reaching one hundred years is no reason to stop moving forward. "We try to keep our stores current, and we are always on the lookout for a new location," Pat Adams says.

All of which would certainly befuddle Ralph Adamucci. But if that's not the story of America, what is?

Part 8:
World at Wars

Over There, Back Here

How World War I Was Fought on the Hudson Valley Front

It was called the Great War, but it wasn't. World War I was terrible—one of the bloodiest conflicts in human history, responsible for more than 17 million dead and 20 million wounded soldiers and civilians.

It was called the War to End All Wars, but it didn't—it destroyed the old world order and set the stage for the even more devastating World War II, along with the Russian Revolution and the Cold War and the numerous hot wars that inspired.

When the United States entered the war on April 6, 1917, it was a relatively minor player on the world stage. The war turned it into a world power. New York State and the Hudson Valley played a big part. The state provided the most men, money, and material, says Aaron Noble, senior historian and curator, political and military history, at the New York State Museum in Albany. "One in ten soldiers was from New York State. Fourteen thousand New Yorkers died. Twenty-five New Yorkers got the Medal of Honor," he says, all far more than any other state. New York was the wealthiest and most populous state, it had the most developed industrial base, and it was the financial capital of world. "The war touched every part of the state," Noble says. Here are some of the ways it touched the Hudson Valley.

New York Joins the Fight

On July 12, 1917, President Woodrow Wilson ordered the entire National Guard of the United States into service. The New York State National Guard Division was officially designated the 27th Infantry Division. New York produced several regiments that went off to war, including the 69th Infantry Regiment, known as the "Fighting 69th," and the 369th Infantry Regiment, the first African American regiment to serve in combat in the war.

They trained at Camp Whitman, in Green Haven (now the site of Green Haven Correctional Facility), and at Camp Smith, in Peekskill. The

Hudson-Mohawk river corridor and the newly built Barge Canal were important avenues to the nation's biggest port, New York Harbor, from where 75 percent of the war's manpower and materiel was shipped, Noble says. Iona Island was the site of one the largest naval munitions depots in nation. "The river is deep enough for naval ships to travel upriver to load, but it was difficult for submarines to navigate," he says. "It was used in both World Wars."

The 27th Division comprised 991 officers and 27,114 enlisted men when it shipped out to Europe on April 20, 1918. The men fought with several British and American army units at various fronts. In September it helped in the Somme offensive to break through the German defenses of the Hindenburg Line, forcing the Germans into a general retreat that resulted in the end of the war two months later. The division was sent home in February 1919 and mustered out several months later, having sustained a total of 8,209 casualties during the course of the war.

The Forgotten Hero

The 369th Division—the Harlem Hellfighters—formed in a Harlem armory, a cigar store with a dance hall above it, in 1913 as the 15th New York Infantry. Among the first troops to arrive in Europe, the renamed 369th US Infantry announced that America was in the fight, lifting French morale.

The regiment participated in many of the war's important battles, including the Second Battle of the Marne and the American drive in the Meuse-Argonne. A few weeks after the armistice was signed, it reached the banks of the Rhine, the first Allied unit to get there. The most celebrated soldier in the 369th was Henry Johnson, a private from Albany. In May 1918 Johnson went to the aid of another private named Needham Roberts. They fought off a twenty-four-man German patrol. Though both were severely wounded, they fired until their rifles were empty and then fought with their rifles as clubs. Johnson battled with a bolo knife and, according to the field report, "gave a magnificent example of courage and energy." He became the first American to receive the prestigious Croix de Guerre, France's highest military award. Theodore Roosevelt called him "one of the five bravest American soldiers in the war." His combat nickname was "Black Death."

Then he returned home. At first, the Harlem Hellfighters were heroes, feted with a parade down Fifth Avenue. But his war injuries made it hard to work, and botched paperwork denied him a disability allowance. He lost his wife and three children, took to drinking, and died penniless in 1929 at age thirty-two, largely forgotten.

Only decades later was it discovered that he had been buried at Arlington National Cemetery with full honors. Many of his supporters, including Senator Chuck Schumer, worked tirelessly to restore his good name, earning him a posthumous Purple Heart in 1996, an Albany street named in his honor, and, in 2015, the Congressional Medal of Honor.

However, that work also revealed a surprise. Another supporter was Herman Johnson, a distinguished World War II veteran who served with the Tuskeege Airmen, who had believed he was Henry's son. In researching Henry's genealogy, the army discovered that neither Herman, who died in 2004, nor his daughter, Tara, were his descendants. "The Army believes this to be a case of historical inaccuracy, not fraudulent representation," the army said in a statement when the mistake was announced. "While we appreciate the Johnson family fighting for the award and keeping the memory and valorous acts of Henry Johnson alive, we regretfully cannot recognize them as PNOK," or primary next of kin.

A curious footnote to a courageous and complicated life.

It's a Gas

The war was notorious for inhumane warfare. Poisonous gasses were horrific weapons of mass destruction. The only defense was the Connell Gas Mask, invented by Dr. Karl Connell, who for a time lived in the town of Denning (Ulster County) and in Scarsdale. Born in Omaha, he graduated from Columbia College in 1898 and from the Columbia University College of Physicians and Surgeons in 1900. He was a surgeon at Columbia and at Roosevelt Hospital, along with serving as a major in the National Guard medical corps from 1907 to 1917, when he went to France as chief surgeon of a medical unit at the outbreak of the war in 1914.

"Dr. Connell and other medical personnel set up field hospitals in France to care for all soldiers, no matter the nationality," says Donna Steffens, director of Time and the Valley Museum in Grahamsville. In 1917, he was asked to invent a mask to help protect against poison gas. "He suggested a mask with a metal face piece and sponge rubber against the face, and a canister carried on the back of the head," she says. This proved to be a much more efficient mask than previous gas masks; "soldiers can wear it and still see, speak and shoot," she says. He continued perfecting the mask and by 1918 produced the first American mask that protected against all known gasses. He then worked with others to create the Richardson-Flory-Kops, or RFK, model, which became the go-to mask for the rest of the war. Three million were produced and used in the Second Battle of the Somme in 1918, and the mask was credited with saving tens of thousands of American lives. "Only 2 percent of 72,807 US gas casualties died, compared to 13.4 percent of some other countries," Steffens says. He eventually received the Distinguished Service Medal for his work on the mask.

After the war he moved back to Omaha, where he became a professor of surgery at Creighton University and founded Presbyterian Hospital in 1920. After he retired, he continued his medical tinkering and obtained ten patents on improved anesthetic equipment, which he produced in the Long Island village of Branch, where he founded the Connell Apparatus Company. He lived in Ulster County from 1924, on an estate called Wintoon Lodge, until moving to Scarsdale shortly before his death in 1941.

Birth of a Hospital

If you were sick at the turn of the twentieth century, you were cared for at home, by your family. If you were indigent, you went to the county almshouse. In 1914, Westchester County bought a 520-acre horse farm and built a new almshouse in a building known as Macy Pavilion. When the United States entered the war, the federal government leased various facilities such as this around the country to serve as military hospitals to tend to the returning soldiers. In April 1917, the government paid $190,000 a year for Macy Pavilion, and designated it US Base Hospital 38.

Today, it is known as Westchester Medical Center.

During the war and as late as 1919, the base hospital treated wounded soldiers evacuated from the battlefields of Europe, including those with "shell shock," the term for posttraumatic stress syndrome, and victims of the Spanish influenza pandemic of 1918–1919. The majority of the sick were cared for in large, twenty-bed wards with a total capacity of 850, according to the US Army Medical Department, Office of Medical History. At its peak in May 1919, the hospital had 1,133 sick or wounded soldiers in its care.

But that care was very primitive, says Dr. William Frishman, director of medicine at WMC and its unofficial historian. "There was very little you could do for patients except provide convalescence," he says. The staffing was so short, "the patients who were in better shape helped out as nurses, serving food, helping the ones who were less fortunate." With the discovery of antibiotics still years away, infection was a big problem. Shell shock victims were sedated, but little else was offered. "They didn't really understand it then, and frankly we don't know much more about treating it today," Dr. Frishman says.

After the army no longer needed the hospital, it was returned to the county government, after an extensive renovation of the new building, which the Department of the Army described as "modern in every way" with rooms that were "clean, white and new." It was renamed Grasslands Hospital, situated on the Westchester County Public Reservation, which would also house other government facilities, such as the county jail, the county medical examiner, and the police and firefighters' academies. There was also a working farm and a potter's field.

Grasslands Hospital became Westchester County Medical Center in 1977, then dropped its county affiliation in 1998. It traces its beginnings to that commission as US Base Hospital 38, making 2017 the one hundredth anniversary of not only the war but the medical center. "It gives us pride in being on staff here, knowing that the hospital has served community and country for that long," Dr. Frishman says. "It goes beyond being just a local hospital, and we are very proud of that."

End of an Era
On June 28, 1914, the *Poughkeepsie Journal* reported that noted rich person Ogden Mills had recently purchased a 120-room home in Paris, France. Such was the life of the Gilded Age aristocrats like Mills and his peers, who ruled over the Hudson Valley from their stately mansions. Later that day, the world would learn of another event that would effectively end that age as surely as the meteor that ended the reign of the dinosaurs: the assassination of Archduke Franz Ferdinand of Austria, heir to the Austro-Hungarian throne, and his wife, Sophie, Duchess of Hohenberg, by an anarchist named Gavrilo Princip, the spark that ignited a world war.

That juicy bit of coincidence was uncovered by Donald Fraser, educator at the Staatsburgh State Historic Site, formerly known as the Mills Mansion. In honor of the war's centennial, Fraser curated a thematic tour titled "World War I and the End of the Gilded Age." This tour ran in conjunction with another exhibit dedicated to Ogden Livingston Mills, the son of Ogden and Ruth Livingston Mills, describing his service in the war. A state senator when war broke out, he quit his job to serve in France. "He was certainly born with a silver spoon in his mouth and could easily have led the life of leisure, but he dedicated his life to public service," Fraser says. He became a captain in the infantry and flew reconnaissance missions over enemy lines. The family lent General John Pershing, commander of the American Expeditionary Force on the western front, their newly purchased Paris home to use as his headquarters, after which he presented them with an engraved silver tray as thanks (which was displayed at the exhibit).

But as any dedicated fan of *Downton Abbey* knows, the war signaled the beginning of the end of the era. "Before World War I, millionaires were the movie stars of the day," Fraser says. "How they spent their money garnered the front pages. When war came, the news turned to more serious matters. It didn't end conspicuous consumption, but it did end the fascination with conspicuous consumption. That was looked at with more skepticism."

The war brought other seismic shifts in the landscape that had supported these wealthy families. The income tax became a permanent feature of American life during the war. New opportunities for women to work showed there was more to life than social gamesmanship. "These fabulously rich women might have been talented and brilliant but had no focus for that except social one-upsmanship," Fraser says. "But with the war women start to get into politics and business. You see Alva Vanderbilt become a leader in the suffrage movement. There is much more opportunity for their talents."

Another local aristocrat, young Franklin Delano Roosevelt, used the war to jump-start his political career. After serving as undersecretary of the navy during the War to End All Wars, he of course led the nation through the war that inevitably followed—and helped put the Hudson Valley on the front pages instead of the society pages.

The Picnic That Won the War

The Real Story behind Hyde Park on Hudson

The most famous hot dogs in history were served on June 11, 1939. They were served at a picnic hosted by a well-known Hyde Park family, the Roosevelts. Guests included a well-known British family, the Windsors. The Windsors had never before sampled hot dogs and found them, at first, confounding. "How do you eat this?" Mrs. Windsor whispered to her host. She decided to use a knife and fork, ignoring Mr. Roosevelt's culinary advice to use her hands. Her husband, however, consumed his the American way. The Windsors, by all accounts, enjoyed the tubular treats. And that is how these became the most famous hot dogs in history.

These hot dogs, you see, helped save the Western world from the Nazis.

The hosts, of course, were better known as the president and first lady of the United States, Franklin Delano and Eleanor Roosevelt. The guests were more commonly referred to as King George VI and Queen Elizabeth. The picnic and the events surrounding it were historic in a number of ways. This was the first time a reigning British monarch had ever set foot on US soil, even including colonial times. It came at a time when Europe was at the brink of war. These facts were not mere coincidence.

At that time, US government policy was isolationist. Relations with our cousins across the pond were at best cold and distant. "There was still much anti-British sentiment and anger at dragging us into World War I," says Dr. David B. Woolner, associate professor of history at Marist College and a senior fellow and resident historian at the Roosevelt Institute. But Britain needed our help. FDR wanted to provide that help but needed to persuade the public both that it was a good idea and that the Brits were worthy. "With this new war, the debate over US intervention was intense. It was a very critical time in relations between Britain and the US," Woolner says.

Political genius that he was, FDR invited the royal couple to a picnic at his place.

Simple Country Life at Hyde Park

In 1938, FDR learned that the king and queen were planning to visit Canada—the first monarchal visit there as well—to try to rebuild royal esteem in the wake of the abdication of Edward VIII. He wrote to the king almost immediately. His letter, dated September 17, 1938, and delivered by Ambassador Joseph Kennedy (head of a soon-to-be well known family of his own), stated, "I think it would be an excellent thing for Anglo-American relations if you could visit the United States.... It occurs to me that you both might like three or four days of very simple country life at Hyde Park—with no formal entertainments and an opportunity to get a bit of rest and relaxation." The king's reply, written on Balmoral Castle stationery and dated October 8, 1938, accepted, adding, "I can assure you that the pleasure, which it would in any case give to us personally, would be greatly enhanced by the thought that it was contributing in any way to the cordiality of the relations between our two countries."

Diplomacy is written between the lines. And FDR, a master of the art, planned not only to meet with the king and queen but to present them as "regular people" to the American public. What better way than with a little summer repast, al fresco, at Top Cottage?

"It's fascinating because, when you look at the correspondence, FDR doesn't want him to come to Washington," Woolner says. "He's more interested in them coming to Hyde Park. There is no suggestion of formality, no state dinner. He wanted the public to see the 'essential democracy' of the royals."

The State Department, however, squashed that idea, and FDR acquiesced to a formal visit befitting a head of state. "But he put his own touch on things in a brilliant fashion," Woolner says. The royals sailed to Mount Vernon to visit George Washington's home. They laid a wreath at the Tomb of the Unknown Soldier, significantly a World War I casualty, at Arlington National Cemetery. They stopped by a Civilian Conservation Corps camp, a work-relief camp for victims of the Depression, in Virginia. They attended a music program at the White House replete with folk music, Negro spirituals, and cowboy songs. And then they visited the World's Fair in New York City. "It was all about portraying those essential qualities of US democracy," Woolner says, and letting the public catch a glimpse of the king and queen in the midst of it.

Hot Dogs and Beer

The capper, though, was the picnic. FDR planned every last detail, including the hot dogs—much to the horror of his proper mother, Sara—and inviting gardeners, cooks, and other staffers to dine with the king and queen. "You can still meet people today whose relatives were there at the picnic," Woolner says.

Another attendee was Daisy Suckley. FDR's distant cousin has since become known as his "closest companion," as illustrated in Geoffrey C. Ward's book of that title. At the time, their relationship was seemingly simply professional; she was his secretary. But after her death, letters were discovered that revealed they were extremely intimate emotionally; FDR unburdened himself to her as he could to almost no one else.

"They had a hook-and-eye relationship; they understood each other perfectly," says Cynthia Owen Philip, a freelance writer and historian in Rhinecliff and author of *Wilderstein and the Suckleys*. Did they also have a physical relationship? "Who knows what they did," says Philip, who was a friend of Suckley. "It would not be spoken about in those days. But he took a photograph of her on a tiger rug, which he kept in the Oval Office, and she took one of the few pictures ever taken of him in his wheelchair."

"The public has a hard time understanding this, but both FDR and Eleanor had their own circle of friends," Woolner adds. "They tended to relax with others and had more of a policy relationship, much like the Clintons today. Daisy was part of his circle. People also don't understand how they could be emotionally intimate but not physically intimate. She loved FDR, but so did a number of other women. He was incredibly charismatic. What's most important about Daisy is that, through her diary and correspondence, we have almost the only picture of the private FDR. She was someone he could express his most intimate feelings to."

Suckley was two tables away from the head table at the picnic. She didn't think it was such a big deal. "I saw them bring a silver dish with two little hot dogs on it to the King and Queen. But I was not near enough to see whether they ate them. It's all so silly," she said at the fiftieth anniversary of the event, when she was ninety-eight.

The *New York Times* didn't think it was so silly. The next day's front page read,

KING TRIES HOT DOG AND ASKS FOR MORE; And He Drinks Beer With Them—Uses Own Camera to Snap Guests Photographing Him

HYDE PARK, N. Y., June 11.—King George VI ate his first hot dog, was chauffeured by the President of the United States, and turned his own hand motion-picture camera against his photographers at a typical Roosevelt picnic party today.

Carl Spackler, Defender of Freedom?

In the movie *Hyde Park on Hudson*, millions learned about the historic royal visit of 1939 and the relationship between Franklin Roosevelt and Daisy Suckley. She is played by the great Laura Linney. He is played by Bill Murray.

Yes, *that* Bill Murray. Carl Spackler, the gopher-killing, Dalai Lama–caddying, Masters-dreaming, demented groundskeeper in *Caddyshack*. Cinderella story. Out of nowhere. I have to laugh. Could this really work?

Dr. David B. Woolner, a senior fellow at the Roosevelt Institute, thinks so. "There are certain qualities of Murray that fit FDR's personality," he says, "his wry sense of humor, his ability to enjoy things even in the midst of a great deal of stress."

Indeed, one scene in the trailer depicts Murray as FDR chauffeuring the terrified king and queen at breakneck speed up the steep and twisting roads of his estate in his famous blue Ford Roadster, driving with his hand controls and waving his cigarette holder, looking not unlike another character Murray played, Hunter S. Thompson.

Woolner hadn't seen the film when this was first published, but "folks who have seen it told me they take some artistic license, particularly with his relationships with the women in his life, including Daisy Suckley," he says. "They imply—or more than imply—that the relationship was physical, but there is no actual evidence to prove that one way or the other."

Nevertheless, he looked forward to seeing the film. "I'm pleased to see the drama of Anglo-American relations. It could have gone terribly wrong if the public had reacted differently, but it was handled brilliantly by Roosevelt and the royal family."

So they got that going for them. Which is nice.

Historians have come to realize this event was a very big deal indeed. Three months after the picnic, England declared war with Germany. Roosevelt was able to convince Congress and the American people to take steps to aid the British while still maintaining American neutrality. "There has been greater recognition over the past twenty years about the importance of this visit," Woolner says. "It was an enormous PR success for both governments. I think a genuine warmth emerged between FDR and the king, and it marks a significant turning point in Anglo-American relations."

Thanks, in no small part, to hot dogs.

The Indestructible Man

Beacon Honors the Life—and Implausible Death—of a War Hero

Dixie Kiefer was a bona fide war hero. He was a navy commander who, during World War II, saw fearsome action in some of the worst battles of the Pacific. He was perhaps the most often wounded officer in the navy; one of his crewmen reportedly once said, "He's got so much metal in him the ship's compass follows him when he walks across the deck."

On January 21, 1945, the USS *Ticonderoga*, under his command, was hit by two Japanese kamikaze bomber planes. Despite devastating losses and his own injuries—he was struck by shrapnel in sixty-five places—he brought his ship to safety. After the attack, he was awarded the Silver Star, just one of the many medals he earned over the course of his career, including the Navy Cross, the Purple Heart with Gold Star, the Victory Medal, the American Defense Service Medal, the American Campaign Medal, the Asiatic-Pacific Campaign Medal with two bronze stars, and the World War II Victory Medal.

His fame was such that he was featured as "Captain Dixie" in a navy-produced documentary, *The Fighting Lady*, which won an Academy Award in 1945. When he received yet another award, the Distinguished Service Medal, Secretary of the Navy James V. Forrestal called Kiefer "the indestructible man."

But on November 11, 1945, the indestructible man was destroyed. The war was now over, and still recovering from his wounds, he died when his navy transport plane crashed into Mount Beacon, overlooking Forrestal's hometown. Irony is too small a word to describe the loss.

In 2015, seventy years after the death of Kiefer and five other veterans, a small group of volunteers calling themselves the Friends of the Mount Beacon Six held a ceremony to honor their memory. David Rocco, one of the friends, is a retired carpenter who has volunteered on lots of local projects, including the Walkway over the Hudson and the Mount Beacon Fire Tower restoration. During that last project, he heard, offhand, about "a legend by the name of Dixie Kiefer," he says. "I dug into it and kept getting more and more engrossed in it. It was like peeling an onion. I was fascinated."

As you will be.

"Extraordinary Heroism"

Dixie Kiefer was born in Blackfoot, Idaho, on April 5, 1896. He entered the Naval Academy in 1916 and served in Europe at the end of World War I. After the Great War he became a pilot in the new aviation branch of the navy, and in 1924 he made the first nighttime takeoff from a warship.

As World War II broke out, Kiefer, now a commander, served as executive officer—second in command—of the aircraft carrier USS *Yorktown* in the Battle of the Coral Sea and the critical Battle of Midway, where, on June 4, 1942, he helped defeat the Japanese navy for the first time in 350 years. The *Yorktown* was lost during the battle, and according to the US Navy's official website,

> When the stricken vessel was being gutted by raging fires, [Kiefer], being unable to obtain rescue breathing apparatus from his own smoke filled cabin, entered the photographic laboratory, which was a flaming inferno from burning films, and conducted the first fire-fighting there. Later, while directing the abandonment of the Yorktown, Commander Kiefer, in lowering an injured man into a life raft, burned his hands so severely that when he himself went over the side and descended by line, he was unable to support his own weight. In the resultant fall he struck the ship's armor belt and suffered a compound fracture of the foot and ankle. Despite acute pain, he gallantly swam alongside of and pushed a life raft toward a rescuing destroyer until he became so completely exhausted that he had to be pulled out of the water.

He was awarded the Distinguished Service Medal for "exceptionally meritorious service. . . . [He] contributed greatly toward bringing the ship and her air group to a high state of morale, efficiency and readiness for battle exhibited by the *Yorktown* in her splendid contribution to the victory attained by our forces in the actions comprising the Battle of the Coral Sea." He was also awarded the Navy Cross for "extraordinary heroism as Executive Officer of the USS *Yorktown* in preparations for, during and after action against enemy Japanese forces in the Battle of Midway."

Kiefer was hospitalized until January 1943. In April 1944, he took command of the *Ticonderoga*. On January 21, 1945, two enemy planes struck the ship near Formosa, killing 144 men and injuring 200 others, including him. The first kamikaze started large fires, but, despite his own wounds, Kiefer remained on the bridge for twelve hours and got the ship out of danger. In a reportedly unprecedented maneuver, he deliberately flooded part of the ship to put it on a ten-degree list, which caused the flaming debris to slide overboard. Then he moved the ship away from the burning wreckage. For his services in command of the *Ticonderoga*, he was awarded the Silver Star.

Hallowed Ground

He returned to the United States, and after another hospital stay, he was appointed commander of naval air bases, First Naval District, with additional duty as commander, Naval Air Station, Quonset Point, Rhode Island. On November 11, his arm still in a cast from wounds sustained the previous January, he was flying with five other servicemen from New Jersey to Quonset Point in a navy transport. It was a dreary, rainy morning as the plane flew over Stewart Airfield in Newburgh, and the plane flew so low Beacon residents reportedly heard it over the city. Then they heard an explosion.

The crash site wasn't found until fifteen hours later, in the woods near the northwest ridge of Mount Beacon. All six aboard were dead. Dixie Kiefer was identified, in part, by the cast on his arm. Pieces of the plane still rest at the crash site to this day.

Along with holding the ceremony, the Friends of the Mount Beacon Six hope to get a plaque honoring the dead placed at the town of Fishkill's war memorial park on Route 52. They also want to put a monument at the site, because, as Rocco says, "it is hallowed ground."

Chasing Ghosts

Celebrating an Unusual World War II Unit, the Ghost Army

Children of veterans grow up hearing old war stories, and Liz Sayles is no different. But the stories her father, Bill, told were very different from the tales spun by most soldiers. She didn't quite appreciate just how unusual they were, however, until a documentary filmmaker showed up four years ago to interview her dad about his days in what has come to be known as the Ghost Army. Thanks to an exhibit curated by Liz Sayles at the Historical Society of Rockland County, all of us can learn the remarkable story—which was classified and top secret for fifty years—that she heard as a child.

Just after D-day in 1944, the US Army sent a battalion called the 603rd Camouflage Engineers into Europe. No ordinary grunts these—this battalion was made up of artists and actors and armed with rubber tanks, phony artillery, ersatz uniforms, and a cache of sound effects. Their mission was to deceive the enemy. Their strategy was to impersonate different army units, conjure fake deployments and troop movements, fool spies, and generally create the biggest military deception since the Trojan horse.

Being young artists, they also spent their spare time painting and sketching their way across war-torn Europe. That artwork, most of which had been forgotten in filing cabinets or basement boxes for the past sixty years, is exquisite, which isn't surprising when you learn just who these soldiers were. Remarkably, some of them grew up to be nationally known figures such as fashion designer Bill Blass, artists Ellsworth Kelly and Arthur Singer, and photographer Art Kane. Bill Sayles of South Nyack shared a New York City studio with fellow Ghost Army veteran Arthur Shilstone after the war and had a long career as an art director, illustrator, and craft book producer. Another regional artist, Ned Harris of New City, became a renowned photographer and designer and eventually co-owned the New York design firm Wallack and Harris. Many others had distinguished lives in the arts and design fields.

"My father told us stories of moving inflatable tanks in the middle of the night, how they would drive around villages for hours and hours so it seemed like a lot of troops were moving in when it was only a couple hundred, of how Bill Blass resewed his uniform so it would fit better, all these bizarre stories," says Liz Sayles, an illustrator who lives in Valley Cottage. "They would sew patches on their uniforms to impersonate different divisions and then hang out in cafés, so spies would see them and think the 9th Army was in the area, when in fact they were nowhere near there." When filmmaker Rick Beyer stopped by to interview her father, "it dawned on me that this was a great story that others would be interested in, and it would make a great exhibit and art show," she says.

Beyer learned about the Ghost Army when he was introduced to a woman whose uncle was in the unit. "We met at a Starbucks, and she brought a binder filled with her uncle's drawings and paintings. I was stunned by it," Beyer remembers. The woman's uncle is John Jarvie, who became the art director for the in-house ad agency for Fairchild Publications, owner of *Women's Wear Daily.*

Not everyone was an artist, Beyer says. "The camouflage guys were engineers. They created tank tracks, spent shells and debris to paint the complete picture. They used sound effects in trucks along the road, so it seemed like a column of tanks was moving in. They used radio deception, copying real telegraph operators to create special effects like communications from phony headquarters. It really was a multimedia deception, a traveling show." His film, he says, is ultimately about the wonders of creativity.

Ned Harris was just eighteen, a student at Pratt, when he was drafted. "I was in a barracks-ful of artists and felt immediately at home," he says. He had forgotten about the watercolors he made, which he lugged through the war in a German grenade case and had never shown his family. "This exhibit and film are taking me back to another era in my life," he says. "It's a big surprise and very rewarding."

Last Stop, USA

More Than a Million World War II Vets Went to War from Camp Shanks, in Orangetown— and Forever Changed Rockland County

"In mid-August, the division assembled in regimental formation. A band played 'Over There' and the Red Cross girls cried as the men marched to the twenty trains waiting to take them off to war.... The trains headed north, toward Camp Shanks, 30 miles up the Hudson River from New York City."

The division mentioned here included E Company—Easy Company— of the 101st Airborne, on its way to D-day, as described in Stephen E. Ambrose's best seller *Band of Brothers*. The book and subsequent HBO series made Easy Company famous. But what was that Camp Shanks, thirty miles up the Hudson River from New York City?

From 1943 until the end of World War II, Camp Shanks was the largest army port of embarkation in the United States. It comprised 2,040 acres in Orangetown, Rockland County, and served as the staging ground for about 1.3 million troops, including 75 percent of those who took part in the invasion of Normandy. The GI's knew they were headed overseas from here, which is why they nicknamed the camp "Last Stop, USA."

The army selected Orangetown because it was served by two railroads and had quick access to nearby piers on the Hudson River that could handle large military ships, making it easy to get troops in from bases across the country, back out to New York, and on to Africa and Europe. It was also mostly farmland, which made it relatively easy to transform into an army base. So, on September 25, 1942, about three hundred residents were called to a meeting at the Orangeburg School (now the library) and told the US government was buying their land, which they could buy back at the same price at the end of the war. They had all of two weeks to get out. One hundred and thirty families lost their homes.

"I am sure many were upset, but we were at war," says Jerry Donnellan, director of the Rockland County Veterans Office and a volunteer at the Camp Shanks Museum. "By the end of '42 we weren't making much headway, and we were in pretty dire straits. There were worries of German submarines off the East Coast. They realized this was serious."

A New City in Three Months

As only the army can, it mobilized 17,000 workers to transform the fruit and vegetable farms into a city of 50,000 that included Quonset hut barracks, headquarters buildings, stores, chapels, a theater, a laundry, a bakery, and a hospital. "In three months, they built more than 2,500 buildings," says Donnellan. "You can't put a deck on your house in three months now."

Camp Shanks (named after the general who commanded New Jersey's Camp Merritt during World War I) opened in January 1943. Here soldiers would be "staged"—inspected for proper equipment and supplies and made ready for deployment. "After being trained all over the country, they came here to make sure their rifle worked, they had the proper boots, got their orders and were put into units," Donnellan says. There were seven staging areas, including one for the Women's Army Corps (WAC)—and one for African Americans. The military was still segregated, Donnellan says, and blacks were at times treated worse than prisoners of war, who also were housed at the camp. "The WAC area was near the POWs, but the blacks were kept all the way across the camp," he says.

The camp had its own baseball team, orchestra, and newspaper, whose staff included, at different times, famed cartoonists Bill Mauldin and Milton Caniff (later of *Terry and the Pirates* and *Steve Canyon* fame.) "And being so close to New York, it was easy for someone to put the arm on a celebrity and bring them up," Donnellan says, noting the camp hosted stars like Frank Sinatra, Jimmy Durante, Joe Louis, and Joe DiMaggio.

The GIs spent eight to twelve days here on average before shipping out. Some went off at the Piermont Pier, where harbor boats ferried them downriver to troop carriers in New York Harbor. Others went directly overseas on troop ships docked in Piermont. Camp Shanks processed about 40,000 soldiers per month this way. By war's end, 1,362,630 GIs had passed through. Another 1,200 Italian and 800 German prisoners of war lived here. When the war ended, a total of 290,000 POWs from other camps in the United States passed through Camp Shanks on their way back home. The last German left the camp on July 22, 1946. Camp Shanks then officially closed.

But its impact lives on. Though next to nothing of it remains, tiny, rural Rockland County was forever changed.

The Postwar Boom

Most of the original inhabitants left town, never to return. The now veterans returned home from the war, and more than half a million of them came back the way they left—up the Hudson and onto the Piermont Pier. They needed temporary housing, and Camp Shanks was converted into Shanks Village to serve that purpose. Many of the personnel who had staffed the camp—doctors, cooks, teachers, and the like—and their families stayed in the area. The vets, taking advantage of the GI Bill, started attending Columbia University, New York University, or City College. Rather than move to the city, they used GI Bill money to buy homes here and start families. The baby boom was on.

"Orangetown was no longer an agricultural community, it now was a bedroom community," says Mary Cardenas, Orangetown historian and director of the Orangetown Historical Museum and Archives. Within the next ten years, the Palisades Parkway and the Tappan Zee Bridge would obliterate any Shanks leftovers and accelerate the transformation. "But Camp Shanks and Shanks Village were the beginning of that switch," she says.

The village was dismantled in 1956, its remnants subsumed by suburban sprawl. For those who grew up in Rockland County just after the war, like Donnellan, Shanks was common knowledge. But twenty years ago, when he began formulating plans for a Shanks Museum, he realized that wasn't the case for younger residents. "For anyone who came along here after the mid-fifties, there was nothing left and no memory of it," he says. "The whole episode is like Brigadoon—it came out of the mist and went back just as quickly."

The War, Back Home

There are only two shrines to the memory of Camp Shanks and Shanks Village. The first is the Camp Shanks Monument, at Independence Avenue and Lowe Lane off Western Highway, in Tappan.

The Camp Shanks Museum, on South Greenbush Road near the intersection of Routes 303 and 340 in Orangeburg, opened in June 1994—the fiftieth anniversary of D-day. A recreated Quonset hut barracks has photos, uniforms, music, movie posters, and other artifacts of the era.

Favorite Son

*Beacon's James V. Forrestal Served FDR,
and the Nation, during World War II—Then
Died, Mysteriously, Four Years Later*

Robert Murphy, president of the Beacon Historical Society, once called him "Beacon's favorite son." Yet most Beaconites under retirement age would be hard-pressed to tell you why. Sure, there is an elementary school named after him. But unlike with schools named after, say, John F. Kennedy, only those who ask will know about the extraordinary life and mysterious death of James V. Forrestal, a civilian leader of the US military during World War II and, later, the nation's first secretary of defense.

James Vincent Forrestal was born on February 15, 1892, in what was then known as Matteawan. His father, also named James, an Irish immigrant, was a contractor who built a successful construction company that erected a hospital and commercial buildings in the 1890s. The father was also a loyal Democrat who served as Matteawan postmaster. Young James was known as Vincent, or Vince, to distinguish him from his father, Murphy says.

He was an excellent student and graduated from Matteawan High School at age sixteen. His abiding interest was journalism; he served as editor of the school's monthly publication, the *Orange and Black*, and then worked for two local newspapers, including the *Matteawan Journal*. Its editor, Morgan Hoyt, was a Democrat and early supporter and friend of Franklin Roosevelt, Murphy says. "In fact, because of Hoyt, FDR came to Beacon every election eve for the good luck that rubbed off of Hoyt." That may have been where the young Forrestal met FDR, who would later play an enormous role in his future.

At the tender age of nineteen, Forrestal was hired as city editor of the *Poughkeepsie News Press*, a predecessor of the *Poughkeepsie Journal*. But he left the paper to attend Dartmouth College the next year and transferred to Princeton for his sophomore year, where he edited the *Daily Princetonian*. He worked at the *News Press* over summer break, and on August 17, 1913, the cub reporter "had his shining moment," Murphy says. "Harry K. Thaw, notorious murderer of Stanford White, escaped from Matteawan State Prison. Forrestal scooped the story, put out a special edition of the paper, and acted as a liaison for the New York City papers trying to cover this national story. In later years, Hoyt said he would have made a great newspaperman if he had not gone into national service."

Voted "most likely to succeed" in his senior year, Forrestal left Princeton in 1915 without his degree, "apparently due to academic and financial difficulties, according to the US Navy," the *Poughkeepsie Journal* reported. And in 1916, Forrestal traded a career in journalism for one in finance, joining the investment banking firm of William A. Read and Co., which later become Dillon, Read.

The World at War

When the United States entered World War I in 1917, he enlisted in the US Navy. Commissioned an ensign in the Naval Reserve Flying Corps, Forrestal was discharged in December 1919 as a lieutenant. He returned to banking and in 1926 married a *Vogue* magazine writer named Josephine Stovall. Forrestal was as successful at banking as he was at reporting; he rose to president of the firm and made his fortune. He also worked for the Dutchess County Democratic Party, helping locals gain state and national office. One of those locals was his neighbor, FDR, who asked him to come to Washington as his special assistant in June 1940.

Later that year, he was appointed undersecretary of the navy. "He promulgated FDR's 'arsenal of democracy' program, adapting America's industry to wartime production for the navy," Murphy says. "He earned high praise" for his work, according to Murphy, and it was during this time, in 1943, that Forrestal returned to Beacon for "a rare visit." He presented something called the Army-Navy "E" Production Award to a rubber factory on Tioronda Avenue. He gave a heartfelt speech extolling the town and county as "representative of the amalgam of peoples which has given this nation extraordinary growth and world power within a century."

When Secretary of the Navy Frank Knox died in 1944, Forrestal was promoted to the then cabinet-level position. He served in that position until 1947, when President Harry Truman created the Department of Defense and nominated Forrestal as its first secretary. He had seemingly reached the pinnacle of an amazing career. He was still just fifty-five years old. And he would be dead in three years.

His political views were at times progressive, at times conservative. He was an advocate for racial integration of the military, which was implemented in 1949. He was also deeply fearful of Russian communism and an early supporter of Senator Joseph McCarthy. He argued against partition of Palestine to create the state of Israel, fearing backlash from the Arab nations that supplied the United States' oil. These views made him a target of scathing commentary from the Washington press, especially the influential columnist Drew Pearson, who called for his removal from the cabinet and labeled him "the most dangerous man in America."

Further scandal erupted after the election of 1948, when it was revealed that Forrestal had privately agreed to serve with New York Democrat Thomas Dewey when Dewey, as was expected, won the presidency. Dewey, however, famously did not defeat Truman, and when Pearson published the story, Forrestal was fired. He was distraught and fell into a deep depression that got him admitted, in April 1949, to the National Naval Medical Center in Bethesda, Maryland. Doctors covered his mental illness with a public diagnosis of "nervous and physical exhaustion." But he was given psychiatric treatments of the time, including insulin-induced shock therapy and barbiturates. On May 22, his body was found on the third-floor roof, a fatal distance from his sixteenth-floor hall kitchen.

A Casualty of War

Most likely, he jumped. But conspiracy theories of murder—by Communists, Zionists, or US agents—emerged almost immediately. None has been proved. "By all news accounts, prior to his resignation from Truman's cabinet, Forrestal appeared haggard and sick before his hospitalization," Murphy says. "Forrestal's Beacon friend Morg Hoyt, and his brother Henry and his family, all considered Forrestal a casualty of war—the Cold War—like any other wounded soldier." Murphy believes Forrestal took his own life suffering from severe mental illness. Forrestal is buried at Arlington National Cemetery.

Back home, James V. Forrestal Elementary School opened in 1953 on land that his older brother Henry and his wife donated to the Beacon Board of Education in 1951 in James's memory. On the national level, the first navy supercarrier, the USS *Forrestal*, was commissioned in 1954; it was decommissioned in 1993. And in 1969, the James V. Forrestal Building opened in Washington, DC, as a military office building that was called, for a time, the Little Pentagon. It is now the home of the US Department of Energy.

You're welcome, Beaconites. Now you know a bit about your favorite son.

Loomis's Secret Lab

*Alfred Lee Loomis, a Mysterious Wall Street Tycoon,
and His Team of Scientists Developed Radar
Technology That Helped Win World War II*

Tuxedo Park, the tony, grandly gated community in Orange County, wasn't named after the fancy dinner jacket. It was the other way around. Tuxedo comes from a Lenape word, *tucsedo* or *p'tuxseepu*, which means "crooked water" or "crooked river." The area was first used as a hunting grounds for the well-heeled in the late nineteenth century. They liked it so much, some of them decided to live there, creating one of the wealthiest addresses in the wealthy Gilded Age. When the gentlemen of the day adopted a new style of dinner jacket, fresh from Saville Row, at an annual ball, the jacket from that day forward took the name of the town. The place was so extended-pinky swank, it's where Emily Post wrote her famous *Blue Book of Etiquette.*

All of which is to set the tone for what happened here, in this rare air, in the 1920s and 1930s, when one of Tuxedo Park's own, a scion of money who made vastly more of it, was leading a secret life.

The man was Alfred Lee Loomis. His friends knew he was an amateur scientist who for years had funded a laboratory in the "Tower House" of his stately mansion. What his peerage peers did not know, however, was that, as war in Europe loomed, he was deeply involved in helping the United States play technological catch-up with Germany. He was in on the planning of the Manhattan Project, and his work, in conjunction with the world's greatest scientists and the federal government, led to the creation of radar, without which many believe the Allies may have been defeated. Yet the story of this secret lab and this eccentric genius was virtually forgotten until only recently.

Explosions Rattle the China

Jennet Conant remembers hearing stories about the lab as a little girl. Her grandfather, James B. Conant, was a noted chemist and president of Harvard. He was also a prominent member of the group of scientists, politicians, and academics who spearheaded the war effort. But he didn't talk much about it. "Every now and then, if other scientists came over for a drink and to reminisce, they would refer to this Wall Street tycoon who played this incredible role in the war," Conant says. "It was always with a little eye rolling. I could tell my grandfather felt ambivalence about him, because my grandfather was a buttoned-down scientist. This character both impressed him and annoyed him."

Later, as an accomplished journalist, she set out to document the story and in 2002 published *Tuxedo Park: A Wall Street Tycoon and the Secret Palace of Science That Changed the Course of World War II*. The story was so outrageous, even the modern-day scientists who were interviewed for a PBS *American Experience* episode based on the book did not believe it was true, she says. But it is.

Alfred Loomis was born with the bluest of blue blood in 1887. Phillips Academy, Yale *and* Harvard, hereditary member of the Society of the Cincinnati, married to a society gal, corporate lawyer, extended pinky. But his passion was science. During World War I he was a ballistics expert and invented a gadget to measure the muzzle velocity of artillery shells.

After that war he left the law and switched to finance, making gobs of money funding the electrification of the country. In 1927, he bought an empty, 18,000-square-foot Tudor mansion, built around 1900 for the financier Spencer Trask. A year later, Loomis foresaw economic troubles ahead and converted all his assets to gold. He thereby avoided the Crash of 1929, then bought up lots of distressed stock in its aftermath and made even more gobs of money.

With more cash than most major universities, he turned the mansion's tower into, arguably, the best-equipped lab in the nation. He flew in the world's leading scientists to collaborate, including—*quel scandale!*—Jews, like Albert Einstein, along with foreigners like Werner Heisenberg, Niels Bohr, Enrico Fermi, and other future members of the Physics Hall of Fame. Don't think the neighbors weren't watching through their imported French silk curtains. "Tuxedoites took note of the odd comings and goings at the big house on the hill, and the lab and visiting scientists soon became the subject of rumors: 'Strange outlanders with flowing hair and baggy trousers were settling down for weeks and months on end,'" Conant writes in her book.

"I suppose it's an unlikely sanctuary because Tuxedo Park was a residential community for the elite," says Johanna Yaun, Orange County Historian. (It should be noted, though, that later on, during the war years, "when many Jewish scientists were forced to flee their homes, Tuxedo Park became a sanctuary where they could live and continue their research under the patronage of Alfred Lee Loomis," Yaun adds.)

Loomis and his staff published important papers in the fledgling areas of spectronomy, electro-encephalography, precise time measurement, and even sleep study. Einstein himself called the place "a palace of science." Yet few knew what was really happening up in the tower. "Guests would become upset when the china rattled when bombs went off," Conant says.

Radar Love

While much of America remained stridently isolationist, Loomis knew that war was inevitable. And he knew that the United States was woefully behind in terms of technology. He devoted his attention to microwave radar, which he tested by loading equipment into a Tuxedo Park diaper truck, driving to a golf course, and aiming it at traffic.

President Franklin Roosevelt had created a science advisory board called the National Defense Research Committee (which included James Conant), and Loomis was tapped to head the microwave radar section. But he wasn't getting where he needed to be. Then the Germans blitzed England. Loomis had learned that the British had advanced technology, and in 1940 he attended a meeting in Washington, DC, at which the British, with Winston Churchill's blessing, turned over many of their trade secrets—including a key radar component, called a cavity magnetron, which was 1,000 times stronger than any he knew of and allowed radar equipment to be made small enough to fit into an airplane. Eureka!

This great advance, however, was the demise of his Tuxedo Park lab. Loomis was now in partnership with the federal government, which had more money than even he could raise. He packed up everything, found a building on the campus of the Massachusetts Institute of Technology, gathered together hundreds of scientists, including six future Nobel laureates, and spearheaded the MIT Radiation Laboratory, forever known as the Rad Lab.

He never set foot in his Tuxedo Park home again.

At MIT, the Rad Lab perfected radar technology that, among other achievements, helped sink German U-boats, guide and track parachute troops, and target land-based batteries and incoming Luftwaffe aircraft during the D-day invasion. After the war, those who worked at the Rad Lab liked to say that the atomic bomb ended the war, but radar won it.

After the war, Loomis dropped from public view. This was partly because, well, that's how he was raised. "He was high society, where you should only be mentioned in the press three times—your birth, your marriage, and your obituary," Conant says. It likely also had something to do with the fact that for years he had conducted an open affair with one of his lab assistants and divorced his first wife to marry her. (*Quel scandale part deux!*) They moved to Long Island, where they lived quietly until his death in 1975.

The Tuxedo Park house changed hands a few times, was turned into apartments in the 1950s, and is now owned by developer Michael Bruno of the Tuxedo Hudson Company. "It's a spectacular structure in excellent condition and the location is within Tuxedo Park," Bruno says. "Doesn't get much better than that." Only after he bought it and PBS came to film it did he learn the true history of the place. "I didn't know the windows were Tiffany," he says. "We could probably sell them for nearly what we paid for the entire building, but I would never do that!"

He and some family members live there, along with two tenants. "I'm currently living in Albert Einstein's old room," says Michael R. Coleman, director of community outreach for the Orange Media Group. His roommate is John Watson, a US naval officer and inventor. Though all the old equipment is long gone, the presence of Loomis's secret lab remains, Coleman says. "You can feel the energy here, whether you are spiritual or not," he says. "I don't really believe in that, but there is definitely an energy here."

Part 9:
Arts and Sciences

Storm Stories

The Storm King Art Center Celebrates the
Relationship between Earth, Sky, and Sculpture

Let me get this on the record up front: I am not an abstract art kind of guy. I'm way too literal. Show me a painting of three randomly colored stripes titled *The Birth of Man* or something equally air-quote *important*, and I roll my eyes. I don't see it. I don't get it. I am a Philistine.

And yet, there is one place, about an hour north of Manhattan, where I think I do get it. In fact, I get it while still in my car. After paying admission to this unusual place and driving toward the parking lot, my wife, Kimberly, daughter, Grace, and I pass a large, open meadow ringed with old-growth trees, beautifully natural, a perfect representation of the Catskill Mountains area in which it sits. And in the middle of the meadow is a huge, grey, steel ... thing, fifty feet tall, almost as wide. It has an arch in its center, as if to welcome you through, and it also has two long, outstretched arms, as if it is reaching up to the sky. As you pass it, your view changes—both of the sculpture (oh, that leg is sort of like a whale's fluke; ah, that arm kind of looks like a bird's wing now) and of the landscape (hey, you can see the mountains between those trees). It is heavy and grounded. It is light and uplifting. It seems to connect the earth and the sky. And you.

It is the perfect introduction to a magical world called Storm King Art Center.

The sculpture, by Alexander Calder, even has a name I can handle: *The Arch*. And though some of the more than one hundred post–World War II sculptures that live (and I use that verb thoughtfully) at the 507-acre art center do have eye-roll-worthy monikers, it doesn't seem to matter here.

Storm King is both art gallery and nature preserve, a theme park for aesthetes. Now in its fifty-first season, it celebrates modern art while placing it in a prehistoric setting. The earliest art, after all, was outdoors, from the cave paintings of Europe to the mysterious Easter Island stone heads to the Sphinx. Throughout recorded history, from ancient Greece and Egypt through the Renaissance, art has been an open, public conversation. Only relatively recently has it moved into museums. Storm King reminds us that, like eating, sleeping, and sex, art can be pretty great outdoors too.

Doing What Others Didn't Do

A little history. In the 1950s, Ralph Edward "Ted" Ogden and his son-in-law, H. Peter Stern, had a successful manufacturing business in the area. Ogden was friendly with a man named Vermont Hatch, who owned a beautiful, 1935 Normandy-style home and twenty-three acres in the well-named town of Mountainville, between the Schunnemunk and Storm King mountains. When Hatch died, Ogden bought the property with the intent of doing something there for the community. He and Stern founded the Storm King Art Center in 1960.

"Ted was very philanthropic, and he wanted a museum in the area," says his grandson and Stern's son, John P. Stern, now president and CEO of Storm King. Ogden's first thought was a showcase of Hudson River School art, and he held a few exhibits in the early 1960s. "But he wanted to have fun in his retirement, and to him, that meant doing what others didn't do," Stern says.

In 1967, Ogden visited the Adirondacks home of David Smith, a prominent abstract artist, two years after Smith had died in a car accident. Ogden saw Smith's large sculptures set against his bucolic mountain-home backdrop. "He was so moved by Smith's work, he bought thirteen pieces then and there," Stern says. "They really turned the vision of Storm King around and are still the core of our collection."

Ogden and the elder Stern began acquiring more land and art, including many commissioned, site-specific pieces, by the greatest abstract sculptors in the world: Calder, Claes Oldenburg, Andy Goldsworthy, Louise Nevelson, Isamu Noguchi, Nam June Paik, Richard Serra, Mark di Suvero, Maya Lin. Each piece is carefully situated by curator David R. Collens and, when commissioned, by the living artist to fully embrace the fields, hills, or woods in which it's placed.

Hatch's former home was turned into the Museum Center. It has galleries for smaller-scale exhibits, a gift shop, and offices. And it is, in itself, a bit of outdoor sculpture. The building was constructed in part of granite stones salvaged from Danskammer, an 1834 mansion that overlooked the Hudson River near Newburgh for almost one hundred years. Five of Danskammer's Ionic columns are now found freestanding—like the ruins of some millennia-old acropolis—on the front lawn.

Of Sky and Scale

The Museum Center was our first destination upon leaving the parking lot. To get there, we walked through the Meadows—Storm King is divided into geographically named sections—and passed two pieces called *Iliad* and *Adonai*. Why? No idea; the former looks like a big red jungle gym made from sewer pipes, the latter, like a kind of tan cannon. Both scream to be climbed upon, as Grace started to do, until we saw the signs asking patrons to stay off. (Other kids, we noted as proud and sanctimonious parents, were ignoring those signs.) Still, the physicality of the pieces is an important part of their power.

From there, we ascended Museum Hill, adorned with both large and small sculptures: tall spires that seem to mimic the trees, hilltop ovals, and blocks that look like welcoming rest stops, rounded shapes that merge into the far-off mountains.

Atop the hill we looked back down over the meadow and spotted, to me, one of the coolest pieces, David von Schlegell's *Untitled* (now *that's* a title I can appreciate). Three white picture-frame squares seem to hover over the grass. As you move, they frame different views—real-time landscape painting, kind of. Later, back in the meadow, we see the squares are supported on thin poles, which explains but in no way diminishes the illusion.

At the center, where we get our maps and bearings, pieces can be found in plain sight or hiding in the gardens. There are simply too many to describe, but each calls out for you in ways that art in a museum often doesn't. (They also make great photo ops—Grace stood in the middle of a Nevelson piece for one arresting shot.)

Back outside, and with a tiring child—prepare for lots of walking here— we took the tram to more distant pieces in the South Fields. Favorite vistas include the Alexander Calder hill, where five creature-like structures seem to wander the earth like abstract dinosaurs. Mark di Suvero's *Mother Peace* is a human-ish figure, arms outstretched to the mountains, with a small peace sign cut into one of its steel girders, letting the green trees or blue sky shine through, depending on where you stand. From afar, these massive pieces appear to own the land. Up close, their size and scale, their gravity, pull you near and then overwhelm.

And at the far end of the South Fields is, to Kimberly and me, the masterpiece, Maya Lin's *Wave Field*. The earth itself is the sculpture here. The famed architect of, among other things, the Vietnam Memorial in Washington, DC, designed a series of hills and vales that were bulldozed into place and left to grow native grasses and plants. From above, it is a green tide pulling and flowing for hundreds of yards. You stand on the hill above it, staring at the waves, as you would at the beach, and at the mountains and the trees and the clouds and the sky, and you feel, Oh, I see.

I get it now.

Cabin Fever

Just Twice a Year, Visitors Can Look into the Studio of America's Most Important but Least-Known Nature Writer

John Burroughs was no marketing genius. In 1895, when he built a little cabin in the woods in what is now the town of West Park, Burroughs, then America's preeminent nature writer, could have called it anything. He called it Slabsides.

Even he knew that was far from poetic. But he didn't care. As he wrote in his essay "Far and Near," "I was offered a tract of wild land, barely a mile from home, that contained a secluded nook and a few acres of level, fertile land shut off from the vain and noisy world by a wooded precipitous mountain . . . and built me a rustic house there, which I call 'Slabsides,' because its outer walls are covered with slabs. I might have given it a prettier name, but not one more fit, or more in keeping with the mood that brought me thither."

Had he chosen something more captivating—something along the lines of, say, Walden Pond—Burroughs might today be as well-known as Walden's Henry David Thoreau, the poster boy of American environmentalist writers. But Burroughs is barely remembered at all, which makes it all the more surprising to learn that, at the time of his death in 1921, this Hudson Valley icon was "perhaps the most famous writer in the country, if not the world."

So says Jeff Walker, an earth science professor at Vassar College and second vice president of the John Burroughs Association. "Burroughs wrote at a time when people were feeling trapped by the Industrial Revolution," Walker says. "They felt confined by the big cities. He wrote about nature in a way that was refreshing and approachable." And wildly successful.

Nature's Rhythms
John Burroughs was born on April 3, 1837, on his family's farm in Delaware County. The seventh of ten children, he was an avid reader, but his parents were barely literate and intellectually unsupportive. At seventeen, he

left home. For a few years he taught to earn money to continue his studies at, among other places, Cooperstown Seminary. While there, he first read the early naturalists, William Wordsworth, Ralph Waldo Emerson, and Thoreau. These writers rekindled his love of life on the farm and the rhythms of the plant and animal world, especially birds.

He published his first essay in a then new magazine called the *Atlantic Monthly* in 1860. He also continued to teach until 1864, when he got a job in Washington, DC, as a clerk at the treasury. He eventually became a federal bank examiner, but writing remained his passion. He even met Walt Whitman, who became his friend and encouraged him to pursue nature writing.

He did, publishing articles in the *Atlantic* and other popular magazines of the day, such as *Harper's* and *Scribner's*. In 1871, his essays were collected in book form and published under the title *Wake-Robin*. It was a hit. Though he continued to work in the government until the 1880s, he grew more famous—and financially successful—as a writer.

In 1874, Burroughs bought a nine-acre farm in West Park. He called his estate Riverby, and grew a variety of crops, his most successful being grapes. By 1895, he had enough money to purchase more land, and with his only child, Julian, built Slabsides as a writing cabin and studio to host visitors and students from Vassar.

Writer and Celebrity

"Life has a different flavor here. It is reduced to simpler terms; its complex equations all disappear," Burroughs wrote of Slabsides. That flavor inspired the writing that made him a celebrity. Slabsides became a destination for both anonymous nature lovers and turn-of-the century power brokers, including Theodore Roosevelt, John Muir, Thomas Edison, and Henry Ford, who reportedly gave him one of the first automobiles in the Hudson Valley.

"He took a train trip to Yosemite with President Roosevelt, and it was reported that there were more banners welcoming Burroughs than Roosevelt," Walker says. "A reporter from the *New York Times* wrote that Roosevelt was lucky to be spending time with Burroughs, not the other way around."

Burroughs was a quiet, noncombative gentleman who tried to please everyone, Walker says. "He commanded respect with his knowledge, and some argue that he was more influential in Roosevelt's starting the national park system than Muir, who was kind of obnoxious."

After Burroughs died in 1921, just short of his eighty-fourth birthday, Slabsides was presented to the newly formed John Burroughs Association. Over the years, the association raised funds to purchase additional acres, which now comprise the 170-acre John Burroughs Sanctuary. Slabsides was designated a National Historic Landmark in 1968.

The grounds are open year-round, but the cabin itself is only open twice a year. Preserved just it was when Burroughs occupied it, the cabin is made of slabs of lumber with the bark covering the exterior walls. Red cedar posts that Burroughs and his son set in place still hold the porch up. Inside, Burroughs's original furniture, much of which he made himself, also remains.

The "Nature Fakers" Controversy

Nature writing was all the rage at the turn of the last century—in more than one sense of the word. Two camps raged at each other during the four-year war of words now known as the Nature Fakers Controversy.

On one side were John Burroughs, John Muir, and other science-based writers and thinkers. On the other side were even more popular writers such as Ernest Thompson Seton, Charles G. D. Roberts, and William J. Long, who composed sentimental, highly anthropomorphic renderings of the animal world and passed them off as nonfiction.

By 1903, Burroughs had had enough. He published an article called "Real and Sham Natural History" in the *Atlantic Monthly* in which he called those works "yellow journalism of the woods." Singling out Seton's best-selling book *Wild Animals I Have Known*, Burroughs wrote, "Mr. Thompson Seton says in capital letters that his stories are true, and it is this emphatic assertion that makes the judicious grieve. True as romance, true in their artistic effects, true in their power to entertain the young reader, they certainly are but true as natural history they as certainly are not."

The War of the Naturalists, as the *New York Times* called it, was on.

As one example, he took on Seton's calling a crow's habitat a fortress and a college. "There is not a shadow of truth in it," Burroughs bellowed. "It is simply one of Mr. Thompson Seton's strokes of fancy. The crows do not train their young. They have no fortresses, or schools, or colleges, or examining boards, or diplomas, or medals of honor, or hospitals, or churches, or telephones, or postal deliveries, or anything of the sort. Indeed, the poorest backwoods hamlet has more of the appurtenances of civilization than the best organized crow or other wild animal community in the land!"

Even President Theodore Roosevelt got involved. He kept an eye on the debate and as a naturalist sided with his friend Burroughs. He even came up with the term "nature faker." In 1907 Roosevelt publicly came out against the sentimentalists: "As for the matter of giving these books to children for the purpose of teaching them the facts of natural history—why, it's an outrage."

And that, more or less, was the end of the Nature Fakers Controversy.

Backyard Naturalist

So why doesn't his reputation remain as well? Walker has two theories. "He published something almost every month the last decade of his life, so he was always in the public eye," he says. "But he wrote in popular magazines, so when he died, someone else took his place. His many book collections didn't continue his fame."

In addition, his contemporary, John Muir, wrote about more spectacular sites and raw wilderness. "Burroughs wrote more about backyard nature, so he can seem a bit tame," Walker says.

Still, Burroughs is worth reading—Walker teaches some of his work in his classes. "I find his style holds up pretty well. He does know how to write a good sentence," Walker says. "And I think his work is really important now, as more people live in cities than not in cities. Most people can't have the Muir kind of experience. The only nature they encounter is in their backyard."

And though he was lousy with names, no one wrote about backyard nature better than John Burroughs.

Puttin' on the Ritz

The Ritz Theater, in Newburgh, Once Shined
as Brightly as Anything on Broadway

The November 28, 1933, edition of the *Newburgh News* nearly succumbed to the vapors. "The Ritz Theatre, the most modern and luxurious in the Hudson Valley, will have its premiere tomorrow night at 7," it gushed. "Behind that simple declarative statement lies this miracle: Eugene Levy, Newburgh theatre owner, recently bought the old George Cohen Theatre on Broadway, and converted that playhouse of a gaudier era into an institution where cinematic and variety productions of the highest standard can be presented with amazing skill, and affording the fascinated beholder the ultimate in comfort and convenience."

My word! But then, that's what theaters meant to towns like Newburgh before television (never mind the Internet and, OMG, smartphones).

This particular theater actually had a more mundane start. It was built in 1883 as a factory, and for the next several decades it churned out such nonentertainment essentials as overalls, plumbing supplies, and cigars. In 1913, Newburgh businessman George Cohen opened Cohen's Opera House within the building, and, as an ad in the *Newburgh Daily Journal* (yes, there were competing newspapers! What a time it was!) put it, "The opening of Cohen's Opera House Monday night means much to the citizens of Newburgh.... Monday night we establish a standard for vaudeville in Newburgh. ... We want to impress upon you the fact that the show for Monday night is the best for the money that can be produced. And our prices are no higher than the same class of show is obtaining in New York City. Our standard will never be lower.... You have our personal word that you will always receive full measure for your money at Cohen's Opera House."

Vaudevillians continued to tread the stage into 1926, when the East-West Theater Company took up residence and changed the name to the State Theater. Then, in 1933, Eugene Levy, a local theater impresario with connections to the Paramount Theater in New York, bought, renovated, and renamed the theater, at which point it began its life as the Ritz. "It was a 'tryout house' for the Paramount," former Ritz executive director Tricia Haggerty Wenz told me when we talked in 2013. Performers would test their acts here before they opened in the city. "The old rumor is that there was a sign backstage at the Paramount that said, 'If you think this audience is tough, try Newburgh,'" Wenz said.

History Happened Here

In the 1930s and 1940s, some of the biggest stars of the day put on the Ritz. Ella Fitzgerald, Louis Prima, Mary Martin, Peggy Lee, Woody Herman, Dick Powell, Bill "Bojangles" Robinson, Eddy Duchin, Red Skelton, Xavier Cugat, the Inkspots, Les Brown . . . even a relatively unknown young crooner called Frank Sinatra, who walked onto the Ritz stage with Tommy Dorsey's band in 1940, just before his national popularity exploded. And on December 17, 1941, just ten days after Pearl Harbor, a B-movie actress named Lucille Ball made her stage debut, joined by her husband, Desi Arnaz.

"Nervous as a kitten, Miss Ball was like a schoolgirl with her first date as she prepared for her stage debut," the *Newburgh News* wrote the next day. "She wasn't quite sure she was going to be a success, but it turned out that she and her husband scored a tremendous hit with Newburgh's theatergoers. Their act was a bit like most vaudeville acts, but it was good. They did a piece of comedy, a little singing, a little dancing. The audience loved it."

Many credit this performance as the genesis of what would become *I Love Lucy*. Indeed, in 2006 *PARADE Magazine* presented the Ritz a "History Happened Here" Award, one of only ten sites chosen from a pool of over 2,000 applicants, for serving as the birthplace of the show. The performers who played there already knew of the Ritz's historical importance. The late Bill Yost, former artistic director of Eisenhower Hall at the US Military Academy, told Wenz a story once. "When Red Skelton played at Eisenhower Hall, he asked Bill to drive him by the Ritz in Newburgh," Wenz remembered. "Bill didn't even know it existed, but they sat in front of it and Skelton told him stories about how that was the first theater he ever played in."

Like all heydays, though, this one ended. First came World War II, and then television, and then urban flight. The stage was blocked off in 1959, and the Ritz became a movie theater with four screens. And then came I-84 and the Newburgh-Beacon Bridge, and downtown was for all practical purposes dead.

The Ritz closed in 1969, the stage was walled off from the house, and Cinemas I and II hung on until 1981. After what turned out to be its final screening, *Superman II*, vandals did $15,000 worth of damage, and the owner walked away, leaving "one more gap in a depopulating downtown commercial zone that some merchants feel will be a long time in recovering," wrote the *Saturday Record*. A former owner tried reopening in 1999 but drew only seven hundred customers in seventeen weeks and closed the Ritz for good.

Bringing People Downtown

Or so it seemed, until Wenz and Safe Harbors of the Hudson stepped up with other ideas. Wenz founded Safe Harbors in 2000 as a nonprofit organization that is, it proclaims, "committed to transforming lives and building communities through housing and the arts in the City of Newburgh." Wenz is a civic leader of the first order. She was chosen as one of Orange County's 40 under 40 Rising Stars, awarded Orange County's Social Justice Award, named a Woman of Achievement by the Girl Scouts Heart of the Hudson and the YWCA Orange County, and received a Women of Distinction Award from the New York State Senate. A native of New Jersey, she moved to the valley in 1997 (she now lives in Connecticut) and took Newburgh on as her project. "I discovered the old Newburgh Hotel in 1998, while I was working toward my master's in social work at NYU," she said. "I wanted people to come downtown again, and I knew we had to restore the theater and housing first so people would come stay in the hotel."

Safe Harbors bought the Ritz in 2002 and began raising the money needed to restore it. The original lobby was renovated first, along with the Cornerstone Residence next door. "We wanted to start building an audience right away," Wenz told me. "And so far we have presented amazing musicians here. This sounds totally made up but it's totally true—we've had Grammy winners, Tony winners, and one Academy Award winner."

The theater has continued to put on shows in the lobby while raising money to restore the main theater. In 2009, the late US congressman Maurice Hinchey secured $400,000 in restoration funding, and the late State Senator William Larkin snared another $250,000. In 2010, the Ritz received $200,000 in funding from the New York State Division of Housing and Community Renewal's Urban Initiatives Program. There is "clear, concise data," Wenz told me, that shows cultural activity is an engine for economic and social growth. "We shouldn't undervalue what the arts can do," she said. "They are a critical component for the vibrancy of communities."

In 2013, Lisa Silverstone replaced Wenz as executive director. Since then, the project has taken a new direction. Though a spiffy new marquee was added in 2014, a feasibility study revealed that recreating a proscenium-style theater didn't make sense. Creating a more flexible performing arts space that can accommodate music, movies, stage shows, TED-talk-like conferences and whatever else needs the room, did. As of 2019, the roof was being replaced, and Safe Harbors is looking for more money—a final cost could be around $10 million, Silverstone says—to build a new space in the old theater. With fingers tightly crossed, she hopes the project will be completed within five years.

Here's hoping Lucy, Old Blue Eyes and the other ghosts who once put on the Ritz can pull some strings from the Great White Way in the sky.

Thoroughly Modern Millay

Edna St. Vincent Millay Epitomized New York Bohemia,
yet Lived Much of Her Life in Rural Columbia County

If you've ever burned the candle at both ends, you know the poetry of Edna St. Vincent Millay. You also know a bit about her life and times from what "critics termed a frivolous but widely known poem," the *New York Times* said in her obituary. The poem, titled "First Fig," is short:

> *"My candle burns at both ends / It will not last the night; / But ah, my foes, and oh, my friends / It gives a lovely light!"*

Yet those twenty-five words convey the Jazz Age of the 1920s, in which the young embraced post–World War I life with a bohemian verve that wouldn't be seen again until the 1960s. Millay was at the center of the Greenwich Village scene, a flame-haired, musically voiced beauty with "a mouth like a valentine," one historian wrote. She also had an appetite for life: she smoked—a highly charged act for a woman at the time—she drank, and she took many lovers of both sexes and all marital statuses. Thoroughly modern Millay lived fast and died relatively young, at the age of fifty-eight, in 1950. All this even the most casual fan of poetry or literature likely knows.

Less known is that she died at her house in the Columbia County town of Austerlitz, near the Massachusetts border, where she had lived for almost half her life.

A Rock Star of Her Time
The writer Thomas Hardy once said that America had two great attractions: the skyscraper and the poetry of Edna St. Vincent Millay. Both made stunning and transformative entrances in the country's psyche. Born in Rockland, Maine, in 1892, Millay was raised with her two sisters by her single mother, Cora, who had kicked her husband out of the home in 1899. Cora was herself

a modern woman, and she taught her girls music, literature, and self-reliance. According to one account, Cora tried to bring up her daughters in "gay and courageous poverty."

A tomboy called Vincent by her family, Millay was just fourteen when she won her first poetry award and nineteen when her poem "Renascence," which she entered into a contest, earned acclaim, publication, and, soon after, a scholarship to Vassar College. There, she wrote poetry, got into theater, and, according to Poets.org, "developed intimate relationships with several women while in school."

She graduated in 1917 and moved to Greenwich Village. That year, she published her first book, *Renascence and Other Poems*. She also became a pre-war radical, befriending the Communist journalist John Reed and feminist Inez Milholland. She dabbled in theater and did "hack writing," according to the *Times*, for money. Her fortunes changed, however, with the publication in 1920 of her second volume of poetry, *A Few Figs from Thistles*, which includes "First Fig." She published two more volumes and a play in 1921. And in 1923, her work, which often explores such then taboo subjects as female sexuality and feminism, earned her the Pulitzer Prize.

That same year, she married Eugen Boissevain, the widower of her former lover Inez Milholland. "According to Millay's own accounts," Poets .org writes, "the couple acted liked two bachelors, remaining 'sexually open' throughout their twenty-six-year marriage." Boissevain managed her career, booking readings and public appearances, and Millay became famous. "She was a kind of rock star of her time," says Holly Peppe, literary executor at the Edna St. Vincent Millay Society in Austerlitz.

She was also tiring of city life and, like many an aging boho artist today, began scanning the *Times* classifieds for an upstate retreat. She found a run-down, nineteenth-century farmhouse and 435 acres, which the couple bought in 1925 for $9,000. They christened it Steepletop.

A Spokesperson for Personal Freedom

They soon purchased another three hundred acres across the street and spent the next twenty-five years there. At first, "it was like every other old house," Peppe says. "She wanted to redesign it to remind her of her old house in Maine." There were so many workmen around, Millay said, "I hardly know whether I am writing with a pen or a screwdriver."

They eventually built a writing cabin and a Sears Roebuck barn and had a working farm. The grounds featured several "outdoor room" gardens, an outdoor flagstone bar, a spring-fed swimming pool—where skinny-dipping was encouraged—and a badminton court. "They had legendary parties," Peppe says. "The outdoor bar was called the Ruins, and the joke was that the flowers were watered with gin. If you can be bohemian in the country, it was bohemian."

It was also, when the gin wasn't flowing, quiet and peaceful, which is what Millay needed to write. Her gregarious, larger-than-life husband, a master chef who encouraged formal dress at dinner, also took seriously his role "to keep things moving for her so she had time, space and peace of mind to write poetry," Peppe says. "Eugen was seen in town every day getting the mail, he was very social. Millay spent most of her time on the hill. She was always very private wherever she lived. She was not Dorothy Parker."

Millay continued to publish in the late 1920s through the 1940s, turning more toward political and social themes around events such as the Sacco and Vanzetti executions (she was even arrested at a demonstration in Boston), penning a 1940 *Times Magazine* piece against isolationism and a poem about a Nazi massacre in Czechoslovakia. ("The whole world holds in its arms today / The murdered village of Lidice / Like the murdered body of a little child / Innocent, happy, surprised at play.")

The 1940s were a tough time for her, Peppe says. She fell out of a moving car in 1936, which caused nerve damage to her arm and, to ease the pain, led to an addiction to morphine and alcohol. Several of her closest friends and family members died, including her mother. And in 1949, Boissevain developed lung cancer and died rather abruptly. She spent the last year of her life virtually alone at Steepletop, Peppe says, a recluse trying to work through her grief with her writing.

She also grew frailer, and on the morning of October 19, 1950, still in her nightgown and slippers, she fell down a flight of stairs. Her body was found later that evening by a caretaker who had come to fix her fire for the night. The *Times* reported that she died of a heart attack. She was fifty-eight years old. She is buried on the property, along with her husband, her mother Cora, her sister Norma, and her brother-in-law Charles Ellis.

Norma moved into the house in 1951 and became "keeper of the flame" until her death in 1986, says Peppe, who spent about a year living with Norma while working on her dissertation on Millay. For years, the house, which has been on the National Register of Historic Places since 1972, showcased all of Millay's furniture, books, and other possessions, many of which remained where they were on the day she died. Sadly, the financially strapped Millay Society announced that Steepletop would not open to the public in 2019.

Still, Millay's work is worth reading—or rereading, says Peppe. "For forty years, Robert Frost and Millay were the two best sellers in popular poetry," she says. Her literary legacy includes reversing gender roles in so-called love poetry and putting women in the lead. "But one of my goals is to promote that she was far more than a 'love poet,'" Peppe says. "She wrote about political injustice and social discrimination, in beautifully crafted poetry with profound messages. She expanded the content of poetry into the woman's realm, including women's sexuality, which was quite revolutionary. She was a spokesperson for personal freedom. That is why her poetry endures."

What Hath Morse Wrought?

Samuel Morse Invented the Telegraph in New York City, Then Fought to Own It from Poughkeepsie

There are many ways to reveal one's age. Not long ago, I was showing my daughter the scrapbook my mother kept of my earliest years. On the front page were several yellowing papers with the logo of Western Union across the top. "What are those?" she asked.

How old am I? I am so old that my birth was acknowledged by telegram. (No, they were not delivered by the Pony Express.)

I explained to her what they were and that the inventor of the telegraph, Samuel F. B. Morse, was as important and as famous in his day as Steve Jobs has been in ours. Both changed the way we communicate with one another, and communication is often the change agent of a generation. The telegraph, I told her, laughably quaint in an age of literally instant messaging, was in fact the smartphone of the mid-nineteenth century.

But there is much more to Morse, who used the wealth gained from his invention to buy Locust Grove, his home in Poughkeepsie, than the telegraph and the transmission code that bears his name. For starters, he was for much of his life better known for his first job: fine artist. Old as I am, I didn't know that Morse was one of the most accomplished painters of his time long before he began tinkering with electromagnetism.

Portrait of the Artist

Samuel Finley Breese Morse (April 27, 1791–April 2, 1872) was born in Charlestown, Massachusetts. He was already making a living as a painter when he graduated Phi Beta Kappa from Yale. His work earned him a three-year stay in England to study under the artist Benjamin West, and at the end of his apprenticeship, in 1811, he was admitted to the Royal Academy. He stayed in Europe until 1815, producing two of his best-known paintings, *Dying Hercules* and *Judgment of Jupiter*.

Back in America, he was commissioned to paint portraits of the likes of former presidents John Adams and James Monroe, the Marquis de Lafayette, and the wealthy patrons of Charleston, South Carolina. He also earned a commission to paint the House of Representatives for a touring exhibit called *The Halls of Congress*. He was one of the founders of the National Academy of Design and served as its president from 1826 to 1845 and again from 1861 to 1862. Not a bad first career—yet completely overshadowed by his second one.

That career was set in motion by tragedy. In 1825, while in Washington, DC, to paint Lafayette, he received a letter from his father: "Your dear wife is convalescent." A day later, he received another letter, telling him his wife was dead. By the time he got to his home, in New Haven, she had already been buried. Shaken by the fact that he had not known of his wife's illness and death until it was too late, he vowed to find a way to improve long-distance communication.

In 1832, he was sailing home from Europe when he met a man named Charles Thomas Jackson, who had studied electromagnetism. Morse visited Jackson and watched him work with an electromagnet. Intrigued, Morse put away his paintbrushes and began tinkering with a way to transmit electric signals over a wire. He wasn't alone, however. Two English inventors had created a telegraph before Morse and got a patent for one in 1837. Morse, who first demonstrated his version in 1838, earned his patent in 1840. By then, he knew of the English telegraph, but with $30,000 from the federal government, he set up a thirty-eight-mile experimental line between Washington, DC, and Baltimore. He first demoed his telegraph on May 1, 1844, when he sent news of the Whig Party's nomination of Henry Clay for US president from the party's convention in Baltimore to the Capitol Building. A few weeks later, on May 24, 1844, the line was officially opened with Morse's now famous words, "What hath God wrought," transmitted from the Supreme Court chamber in the basement of the US Capitol to the B&O Railroad's Mount Clare Station in Baltimore.

In May 1845 Morse formed the Magnetic Telegraph Company and began building telegraph lines from New York to Philadelphia, Boston, Buffalo, and beyond. And he got rich.

The House That the Telegraph Built

Until that time, Morse was, like most artists, saddled with the clichéd adjective "struggling." "Few artists get rich, most slog along," says Kenneth F. Snodgrass, executive director of Locust Grove Estate. "He liked to paint great historical themes, but there was no call for that. He did portraits, but it was hard to support a family on that. His great works are some of the best paintings created in the second quarter of the nineteenth century and are important in the history of American art, but they never sold for a lot of money." Indeed, after his wife's death, he mostly lived with friends and relatives and never had his own home until the telegraph took off.

He took some of that newfound wealth and bought an old farm in Poughkeepsie in 1847. The house was a fixer-upper, and he began fixing it up almost immediately, especially after he remarried in 1848. By 1852 he had turned what Snodgrass calls "a pretty plain, white box—Morse's line was that it had 'no pretensions to taste'"—into an ornate, Italianate home that "reflected his style as one of the best-known artists of his time. I call it the house that the telegraph built."

He hoped to create a working farm, but that never panned out. Morse had given up painting by now and concentrated full-time on his invention—more accurately, the fight to secure his claim as its rightful, legal inventor. "His initial idea was to live here year-round, but he was always traveling to deal with lawsuits," Snodgrass says. "He never spent a concentrated period of time at Locust Grove."

When he was at the house and not working on his company, he loved to get outdoors. In typical nineteenth-century tradition, he was a gentleman landscaper. "He was always tinkering with the gardens, and he would write letters to guide his workers on plantings, moving walls, and what to do with produce," Snodgrass says. His architect was the estimable Alexander Jackson Davis, but Morse had his own opinions and was not shy about sharing them. "I find the collaboration between them fascinating," Snodgrass says. "They bickered back and forth on how things should be laid out and designed, and that back-and-forth is really interesting, especially when the client has such extensive artistic credentials." Many of those letters survive, both at Locust Grove and at the Metropolitan Museum of Art in New York.

Locust Grove was primarily Morse's private getaway—his townhome in New York was for formal entertaining—but he was an involved citizen of Poughkeepsie. He sat on the founding board of trustees of Vassar College, served as an advisor for its museum, and was a friend of Matthew Vassar, whose home was just down the street. He was a donor to both the Children's Home in Poughkeepsie—to which he also had his farm's produce delivered—and the First Presbyterian Church. And he ran, unsuccessfully, to represent Poughkeepsie in the US House of Representatives in 1854. (His politics, it should be noted, were Trumpian: He was an anti-Catholic, anti-immigrant, pro-slavery, MAGA-type guy who also lost the 1836 race for mayor of New York as a member of the Nativist Party. Just reporting.)

The year before, Morse's patent case had been settled by the US Supreme Court, which ruled that his system was the first design to result in a practical telegraph. He died, on April 2, 1872, in New York City and is buried at Green-Wood Cemetery in Brooklyn. At the time of his death, his estate was valued at nearly $10 million in today's money. And though he could rightfully be called an artistic visionary, most of his paintings are still labeled, Snodgrass says, as "by the father of the telegraph."

The Irish Alps

*Jews Had the Borscht Belt, but the Irish Also
Once Claimed a Corner of the Catskills*

In September 2010, the main building at the Blackthorne Resort in East Durham burned to the ground. The resort lost its office, dining hall, and bar in the fire, but Kevin Ferguson gained an epiphany.

Ferguson is a journalist in Arlington, Massachusetts. He grew up in northern New Jersey. But much of his heart and soul resided in that lost building in the Catskills. As a child, he spent nearly every summer there among a clan of Irish immigrants and first-generation natives in what was known as the Irish Alps. What the Borscht Belt was to Jews, the area around East Durham was to the Irish.

But it was far less known, and Ferguson had wanted to write about this for years. The words never came. Then, pictures of the fire showed him a better way. He produced an independent film titled *The Irish Catskills: Dancing at the Crossroads*. It aired on PBS affiliate WMHT, in Troy, in March 2016.

"It was such a bizarre place," Ferguson says. "The town was completely transformed into an Irish town in summers. It's where my parents met, and where many Irish couples met, on the dance floor. It's where I learned to dance. It was charming and odd in so many ways and hard to describe in words, and the fire prompted me to go into film. It needs moving images and sound, because it is so imbued with music and dance. It's obvious, really."

"What County Are You From?"

When Ferguson's mother emigrated from County Cavan to America in 1950, her first address was a small boardinghouse in East Durham owned by her sister, called Mullan's Mountain Spring Farm. Ferguson says that Irish immigrants had been visiting the area, which was previously predominantly German, since the late 1800s. Many thought the landscape reminded them of the Olde Sod, what with its lush, soft, rolling green hills. In the 1930s and

1940s, with the Depression and then war in Europe, many Germans sold their boardinghouses and businesses to people of Irish descent, and the Irish Alps were truly born.

The towns of Leeds, South Cairo, Oak Hill, and East Durham offered boarding and sustenance at places with evocative names like the Shamrock House, the Weldon House, O'Neil's Cozy Corner and O'Neill's Tavern, Kelly's Brookside Inn, and McKenna's Irish House. In the summer, city dwellers looking to escape the heat and dirt headed upstate for the clean mountain air. As with the Borscht Belt, the Irish Alps hit their heyday after the war, from the 1950s through the early 1970s. In 1960 there were upward of forty Irish-run hotels or boardinghouses in the area, Ferguson says, filled each summer with Irish families singing, dancing, and playing music. "Leeds reminds me of a village in Ireland, with one main road, a few storefronts; it's only a block long, but in the day there was a street car," he says. "That's how much activity there was."

The union organizer Michael Quill played a big role in that. His New York transportation workers union, begun in the 1930s, helped a lot of Irish workers earn better pay and more time off. Many had been spending any free time at the Rockaways, a smorgasbord of Irish, Jewish, and Italian retreats. Now they could travel farther, for longer, and be with their own.

"It was an opportunity to be among themselves, without judgment," Ferguson says. "There was a lot of prejudice in New York and upstate, and like every ethnic group the Irish created their own community. You could go there, and the conversation had already started. You don't have to explain yourself. You don't ask, 'How are you?' You ask, 'What county are you from?'"

Ferguson's parents met in 1955. She was working at the hotel. "As family, you work," he says. "If you are remotely related, you work. Everybody pitched in." His father was an Irish American on vacation. They met on the dance floor, a tradition that was carried from Ireland to New York City and up to the Catskills. "Many marriages were made up there on the dance floor," he says. "It was a known thing." If new arrivals happened on the scene, the bandleader might announce their presence, what county they were from, and if any parent had a child who'd like to meet a nice Irish lad or lass. Ferguson says that almost any Irish couple of a certain age probably hooked up in this chaste, Old World–sanctioned way.

Every summer, Ferguson's mother would wait tables, his father would tend bar and sing, and other family members would chip in wherever needed. As a child Ferguson would help with small tasks like picking up trash. In his teens, in the mid-1970s, he worked six days a week, washing dishes, mowing lawns, painting fences, carrying luggage. "It was a lot of work," he says, "and a lot of play." In those free-range days, kids could roam about the woods and fields with nary a parent, helicopter or otherwise, in sight, while the community kept a watchful eye on everything.

"We Were Part of This Thing"

Ferguson stopped going upstate in the 1980s, when he went to college. By then, lots of others had stopped going as well. Discrimination had lessened, air travel had cheapened, other options had arisen, and, just as the Borscht Belt lost its Yiddish, the Irish Alps lost their Gaelic. Ferguson's old haunt became the Blackthorne, one of just a handful of resorts that still thrive as vacation spots but now for a much more diversified clientele. "The Blackthorne has a strong Irish following during Irish Arts Week and a few other weeks, but back in the day it was all Irish," he says. "Now they have a motorcycle rally and spaghetti wrestling. That wasn't happening when my aunt was alive."

Which is why he made his film—to record a bit of history that is in danger of slipping the bonds of memory. The Borscht Belt has been immortalized in countless movies, plays, and songs; why not so for the Irish Alps? "The Borscht Belt had better PR," he says. "We had no Jerry Lewis. The closest thing we had was, maybe, the Clancy Brothers."

Now, though, the recollections of those who made the area sing have some PR of their own. And Ferguson, in the process of making the documentary, says he learned more about his own history as well. "I danced as a kid, at *caelis*, it was just what you did. But I now see how important music and dance was," he says. "We all did it. We were part of this thing."

An Unlikely Artist

Robert S. Duncanson Was a Celebrated African American Painter of the Hudson River Valley School

There aren't many places with entire artistic movements carrying their names, but the Hudson River is one of them. The Hudson River School is world renowned, and most of us are familiar with the artists who dominated this movement: Thomas Cole, Frederic Church, Asher Durand, Albert Bierstadt.

But like any artistic movement, the Hudson River School inspired painters from elsewhere—in this case, painters from other parts of the country—to embrace majestic American landscape painting. One of the most celebrated and unlikely of these artists was an African American who never lived in the Hudson Valley. His name is Robert Seldon Duncanson.

Duncanson was born in 1821 in the Finger Lakes town of Fayette, New York. There are conflicting biographies, but Joseph D. Ketner II, the Foster Chair in Contemporary Art and Distinguished Curator-in-Residence at Emerson College in Boston, has done perhaps the most extensive research on the man and curated shows of his work. In a 2011 article for *Antiques Magazine*, Ketner says that Duncanson's parents were both, to use the term of the time, mulattos. His extended family came to New York from Virginia in the late eighteenth or early nineteenth century, "probably as a result of the manumission of some slaves in Virginia after the American Revolution," Ketner writes. The family moved onto land that the federal government had granted to Revolutionary War veterans, "which suggests that Duncanson's grandfather, Charles (c. 1744 –1828), may have earned his freedom in exchange for military service."

Census records list the family's members as "mulatto" and "free colored persons" who worked as carpenters, joiners, and painters. "The Duncansons participated in the growth of the black middle class at the turn of the nineteenth century, a time when African-American artisans were prevalent in the trades in the United States," Ketner writes, and Robert Duncanson apprenticed in both carpentry and house painting.

In 1841, he moved to Cincinnati, at the time a very progressive and socially dynamic city—it was known as the Athens of the West—that became a center for African American artists and abolitionists. Duncanson worked as a painter, both as a house painter and, as he advertised himself, as a "fancy painter." He had some success, and in 1842 three of his portraits were exhibited in Cincinnati. His life and work were forever changed, however, in 1848, when he went to an exhibit at Cincinnati's Western Art Union and saw Thomas Cole's Voyage of Life series. "The experience prompted him to focus on landscape as a metaphor for expressing American ideals," Ketner writes.

With no formal art training, he taught himself by copying Cole and Church directly to learn the style. "His work was an attempt to translate that style, which was considered to be 'American,'" Ketner says. As the still new nation was trying to define itself, landscape painting was one way it distinguished itself from the Old World. "He is trying to appropriate that by copying it, while also conveying the values of free African Americans," Ketner says.

Duncanson also set out to see America, taking "sketching trips" throughout the Midwest, into Canada, and down into the Hudson Valley, though it is not known if he ever met any of the painters who inspired him. He used those sketches to compose his paintings, some of which may include scenes from the region, though none are distinctly of the Hudson Valley.

Ketner writes that Duncanson emulated the romantic style and mission of Cole and Durand, "but he rarely created the kinds of dramatic and sublime views of the wilderness for which those artists are known, preferring instead more pastoral and picturesque scenes that he considered emblematic of the ideals of both the country at large and the free black community within it."

His career got its start through a large commission by a Cincinnati art patron who hired Duncanson to create a suite of landscape mural paintings for his mansion, which is now the Taft Museum of Art. The museum calls the murals "evidence of Duncanson's most ambitious artistic creations. . . . Together, the eight paintings constitute one of the largest existing pre–Civil War domestic mural decorations in the United States."

Duncanson himself wasn't a virulent abolitionist. His own son urged him to explore African American themes more overtly in his works. "I have no color on the brain; all I have on the brain is paint," Duncanson reportedly wrote to him. Though not on the front lines of the antislavery battle, he was involved with abolitionist societies and was celebrated in African American newspapers and by such figures as Frederick Douglass. And he did paint an abolitionist panel that traveled around the country. The panel, a six-hundred-yard-long abolitionist panorama called *Mammoth Pictorial Tour of the United States Comprising Views of the African Slave Trade*, was advertised as "painted by Negros."

The coming Civil War brought about the end of Cincinnati's black artistic community. "Racial tensions were running high in the city, and pro-slavery sentiment was directed at the free black population," Ketner writes. "Duncanson responded to the grave political climate by creating *Land of the Lotus Eaters*, his most ambitious easel painting." Ketner says that the painting, inspired by *The Odyssey*, "offered a plea for peace in a canvas where dark-skinned figures cross the river to white soldiers. The painting went on public display in the city as the war erupted."

Duncanson moved in 1863, at the height of the war, to Montreal and then in 1865 to the United Kingdom, which he toured with *The Land of the Lotus Eaters*. He was celebrated in both countries; the prestigious *London Art Journal* called him a master of landscape painting, and even the queen bought one of his works. After the war he returned to Cincinnati and painted many scenes of the Scottish landscape. But his health began to decline, both physically and psychologically. "He went insane," Ketner says, "thinking he was possessed of the spirit of a past artistic master—who was female, of all things. This is also part of what makes his story so interesting." Though there is no proof, he most likely suffered from lead poisoning, which many itinerant house painters acquired from mixing their own paints. He died in Detroit on December 21, 1872, at age fifty-one.

"He died at the perfect time," Ketner says, because his style of painting fell out of favor soon after. Though less known than the valley's homegrown artists, Duncanson nevertheless has left a worthy legacy. "In the West he was considered one of the most prominent painters," Ketner says. "Some of his paintings are every bit the equal to the work of Cole and Church, but his true value is in being a person of color trying to participate in the American Dream."

Local Boy Makes Good

Kingston's Jervis McEntee Was an Important but Lesser-Known Member of the Hudson River School of Artists

For a painter, Jervis McEntee was a fine writer.

Normally, that would be considered a backhanded compliment. In McEntee's case, however, it illustrates the fact that, though he was indeed a highly skilled and respected member of the Hudson River School's original class of landscape painters, his legacy is grounded in the journals he kept during his lifetime. Those journals paint a clearer and more lasting picture of the lives and times of the era than any of his canvases ever did.

In fact, even though he was a friend and peer of the Hudson River School's leading lights—Thomas Cole, Frederic Church, and Albert Bierstadt, among others—McEntee, a native of Kingston, had never received a major museum exhibition until 2015, when the Friends of Historic Kingston mounted *Jervis McEntee: Kingston's Artist of the Hudson River School*. A companion exhibition at the Samuel Dorsky Museum of Art, at the State University of New York–New Paltz, also ran that year.

"The art itself is beautiful and touching, and his family story is also quite compelling," says Ward Mintz, a museum administrator and FOHK board member. "He would not be forgotten as a painter, because his paintings are in major museums. The Met has his works. But he is more famous for the journals among a broad range of arts and cultural historians. This is a man everyone has turned to. The journals are absolutely critical to understanding his work, his attitude, his connection to other artists, art making, and the art business."

He also kept a lifelong residence in Kingston, Mintz says, and "his continued devotion to the area and to Ulster County, for us at FOHK, that was a very significant thing."

"J. McEntee . . . LANDSCAPE PAINTER . . . Studio at His Residence on the Hill . . . Rondout N.Y."

Jervis McEntee was born in Rondout, which later became part of Kingston, on July 14, 1828. His Scots-Irish grandparents had immigrated to the Utica area, and his father moved to Kingston to work on the D&H Canal, where he became chief engineer. Jervis was named after his father's mentor, John B. Jervis.

He was educated at the Clinton Liberal Institute in Clinton, near Utica, where he began his journaling. His writing, according to an essay penned by the FOHK exhibit's guest curator, Lowell Thing, "suggests a playful and self-confident young man with a special interest in writing, languages (Latin and French), and politics, but no evidence of any formal art training." He must have been interested in it, however, because in 1848 he asked Asher B. Durand, unsuccessfully, to be his tutor.

By 1850, he was already successful. He sold four paintings to the American Art-Union and had a painting accepted by the National Academy of Design, two of the nation's most prestigious art institutions. That winter, Frederic Church agreed to take him on as a student. McEntee rented a studio in the Art-Union Building, near Church's. But in 1851, he returned home to his parents' new, large homestead, the first on what would become West Chestnut Street in Kingston, and became a businessman. He also built an art studio on the property in 1854, which was designed by the estimable Calvert Vaux, who soon thereafter married his sister, Mary McEntee. (And soon after that, he designed Church's majestic Olana, Central Park in New York, and a few other noteworthy commissions.) McEntee married Gertrude Sawyer that year, and gradually they expanded the studio into a house. In 1855, he became a full-time artist, putting an ad in the Kingston newspaper announcing, "J. McEntee . . . LANDSCAPE PAINTER . . . Studio at his Residence on the Hill . . . Rondout N.Y."

He also kept a studio at the famed Tenth Street Studio Building in New York, where, as the only married couple, the McEntees became the center of a salon for the other artists and well-known writers and creative types of the day—including America's most famous actor, Edwin Booth, brother of John Wilkes Booth. After Lincoln's assassination, the McEntees openly supported Edwin against the public backlash (and may have offered a hiding place for him to escape scrutiny for a while). Booth so appreciated the help that, in later years, he occasionally gave them money when times were tough.

McEntee's other claim to fame—journaling—began in the early 1870s. He wrote about his artist friends and their daily lives, successes, failures, and challenges. He covered the social, political, and economic realities of the art world, including his own struggles with money, fame, and status. And he wrote about the decline of the Hudson River School's popularity in the face of impressionism, a movement he despised.

He also described the long walks he took from the family homestead. These walks afforded views that he would later draw or paint, and his surviving works show views that are recognizable today: the Hudson River, Hussey Hill, and scenes along the Rondout and Esopus Creeks close to uptown Kingston and Hurley.

The McEntees lived a gay life, even spending a year traveling to Europe, until Gertrude died, unexpectedly and young at age forty-four, in 1878. He was "devastated," Thing writes, but continued painting and traveling, to Mexico (with his good friend Church as a companion) and the American West, through the 1880s. In 1890, he grew ill, most likely from kidney disease, and died on January 16, 1891. He is buried in the family plot in Montrepose Cemetery in Kingston.

"I Look upon a Landscape as I Look upon a Human Being—Its Thoughts, Its Feelings, Its Moods, Are What Interest Me"

Why was McEntee less successful than his friends and peers? "We scratched our heads about this," Mintz says of the group that put the exhibit together. His paintings were certainly distinctive—moodier, less glorious, more introspective. At the time, the nation was looking for paintings that emphasized the grandeur of the American landscape and spirit. "Church is perfect for this, McEntee less so," Mintz says. "The majesty he presents is more intimate. I still think his landscapes are beautiful and make you want to experience the space, but it is a very different thing."

He also continually traveled between New York and Kingston, which put him at the forefront of another movement. "He was probably one of the first commuters," Mintz says. "He'd take a steamboat to New York to spend the week, then go back to Rondout on weekends. Sounds pretty familiar." But that may have dampened his sales and reputation. "The way people saw and bought your work was by going to your studio," Mintz says. If he wasn't there, he couldn't sell.

Whatever the cause, McEntee was troubled by it. "He complained a lot about money and not selling enough," Mintz says. He also disagreed with others' vision of his work: "Some people call my landscapes gloomy and disagreeable. They say I paint the sorrowful side of nature," he wrote in his journal. "But this is a mistake. . . . Nature is not sad to me but quiet, pensive, restful."

Take My Wife (to the Catskills) . . . Please!

A "Mountain Rat" Turned Academic Saves the Memory of a Bygone Era

As geography, the Catskills are a mountainous region of southeastern New York State. As synecdoche, they are a now vanished way of life. For your parents and grandparents, the Catskills from the 1920s through the 1970s were the Borscht Belt, the Jewish Alps, "Solomon" County, the summer place to schvitz.

A blurb on the home page of the Catskills Institute says it well: "New Yorkers hungry for mountain air, good food, and the American way of leisure came to the mountains by the thousands, and by the 1950s, more than a million people inhabited the summer world of bungalow colonies, summer camps, and small hotels. These institutions shaped American Jewish culture, enabling Jews to become more American while at the same time introducing the American public to immigrant Jewish culture."

The Catskills had been a resort area for Gentiles in the nineteenth century. As eastern European Jews immigrated in the early twentieth century, some became farmers in the area. And as their urban peers became more prosperous, they looked to do something they could never have imagined doing in the old country: take a vacation. They weren't welcome in most of what was still an anti-Semitic world, so the Jewish farmers began taking on boarders. Their boardinghouses morphed into small hotels and bungalow colonies, a cluster of small rental summer homes.

"Once Jews started to go in large numbers, they had their own built-in community," says Dr. Phil Brown, a professor of sociology and health sciences at Northeastern University and director of the Catskills Institute. "Farms, businesses, professionals, day schools, yeshivas. Yiddish was spoken, 95 percent were kosher. And they also liked being around their own people."

Club Med, Plus a Knish

The big resorts, like Grossinger's, Kutsher's, the Concord, and the Nevele, built on the previous incarnation's business model. "They were pioneers of the all-inclusive vacation," Brown says: three meals, snacks, entertainment, child care, sports facilities, everything you can get now at Club Med, plus a knish to die for.

Grossinger's Catskill Resort Hotel, in Ferndale, grew from a single-family house in which the owners rented rooms to a 1,200-acre, thirty-five-building resort—complete with its own its own airstrip and post office—that served 150,000 guests a year and became the first resort in the world to use artificial snow for skiing.

Kutsher's Hotel and Country Club, in Thompson, near Monticello, was the longest running of the Borscht Belt resorts. The four-hundred-room resort on 1,500 acres offered condos, two bungalow colonies, two summer camps, an eighteen-hole golf course, and a lakefront. It was also known as a sports mecca; legendary Boston Celtics coach Red Auerbach stayed there, and Hall of Famer Wilt Chamberlain worked as a bellhop there while in high school. Boxers Muhammad Ali, Floyd Patterson, and Leon Spinks all trained at Kutsher's.

The Concord, set on 2,000 acres in Kiamesha Lake, was the largest of the resorts with more than 1,500 guest rooms and a dining room that sat 3,000.

The entertainment was first-rate. Musicians like Duke Ellington, Louis Armstrong, and Dean Martin and comics Rodney Dangerfield, Henny Youngman, Woody Allen, and Jerry Seinfeld all toured the hotels.

But things change. Anti-Semitism declined, so Jews could go other places. The next generation had no interest in vacationing at the same places they had been dragged to as children, and as intermarriage took hold, neither did their *Goyishe* spouses. Their parents got old and moved to Boca Raton or Scottsdale, "where it felt like a permanent vacation," Brown says. And the hotels and bungalows, most of which were never great profit centers to begin with, fell into decay. The old bungalow colonies, meanwhile, were often usurped by Hassidic Jews.

A Capsule of Jewish Culture

And then, things changed again. Brown had lived and worked at his parents' hotel, Brown's Hotel Royal in White Lake, and at other hotels in the 1950s and early 1960s, "every year from Memorial Day through the Jewish holidays." His parents' deaths "shook a foundation: Where do I come from?" he asked. "I thought in earnest about doing research." He was not alone. He formed the Catskills Institute in 1995 to promote research into and education about the significance of the Catskill Mountains for Jewish-American life. During his thirteen years of running a conference on the Catskills, "I was always surprised how many people we could find who would come to talk," he says, "academic and nonacademic researchers, entertainers, filmmakers, a never-ending string of speakers."

In the process, he has begun to answer his foundational question. "I got a much fuller view of the place and also a glimpse of things many years before my own memory, and that helped me figure out that a lot of my formative life was there," he said. "It was a prototype of life, not all good or bad, where you learned to hustle to make a living and apply those lessons to make a life and build a career. I learned more about Jewish culture and history and began to see its place in the larger American Jewish context. It was not just a summer place, but a capsule of many parts of Jewish culture."

Brown has compiled some of his research on a webpage at web .northeastern.edu/philbrown/centers-and-institutes/catskills-institute. The Catskills Institute Archive is the world's largest repository of material on the Jewish experience in the Catskills. It includes reminiscences, literary texts, photos, menus, rate cards, postcards, memorabilia, business records, interviews, lists of books and movies, and both published and unpublished memoirs, poetry, and short stories.

If you never spent a minute there, the archive offers you the smallest sense of what the Catskills were back then. If you spent a week, or a month, or a summer, or your entire childhood there, you'll be transported back in time.

Part 10:
Modern Times

A Mixed Legacy

Letchworth Village Was Both a Model for Compassionate Care and a Symbol of Institutional Abuse—and It Helped Make Geraldo Rivera a Household Name

Ileana Eckert is now the superintendent of the North Rockland Central School District, but during high school and college, in the 1970s, she worked a part-time job at Letchworth Village, in Thiells. This community-within-the-community had housed mentally and physically disabled children and adults since 1911. It was one of the biggest employers in the area and at one time had a worldwide reputation as one of the most progressive centers of its kind. Eckert worked in the cafeteria and remembers a loving, compassionate environment. "The people I knew were so caring," she says, "and the patients I saw every day felt happy and secure."

Yet, in 1972, then local newsman Geraldo Rivera reported in his career-making and Peabody Award–wining documentary, *Willowbrook: The Last Great Disgrace*, that residents at a similar facility on Staten Island called Willowbrook and at Letchworth Village were living in overcrowded, dirty, and neglectful conditions. Such disturbing reports about Letchworth had actually begun as early as the 1930s and 1940s, but the Rivera documentary played a big part in the reforms enacted in how the disabled are cared for in this country, and Letchworth Village was slowly emptied of patients until it closed in 1996.

This sad end contrasts sharply with the institution's much heralded beginnings and early years and with the recollections of most who worked there. "People spent their whole careers there, and I think they have fond memories," Eckert says. "It was pretty stable here, nestled in a caring community. The residents were like town characters, people knew who they were and embraced them." She calls the Rivera report "a shame. I am sure some of the reports were accurate—who knows what goes on behind closed doors—but

I did not see any abuse or neglect. I saw patients hugging attendants. I never saw anyone mean or nasty. I think it should be remembered as a place where people with disabilities felt safe and were cared for."

"Beautifully Planned and Built"

That was certainly the intention of William Pryor Letchworth. A successful nineteenth-century businessman (his estate near Rochester is now the stunning Letchworth State Park), Letchworth retired at age fifty, in 1873, to devote his life to his Quaker ideals of philanthropy and the welfare of the less fortunate, especially disabled children. Appointed president of the New York State Board of Charities in 1878, he pushed for a new, progressive model of care that was a radical departure from the high-rise asylums and decrepit almshouses of the time: a self-contained and self-sustaining village of small cottages on a working farm that would allow the residents a more humane and productive lifestyle, under the care of the leading researchers and physicians of the day.

The state approved his plan in 1907 and secured property in Thiells in 1909. Letchworth died before the village was completed but lived long enough to know it would bear his name. The first residents were admitted on July 10, 1911. They were grouped into three then medically accepted but now cringe-worthy types of "feeble-mindedness": "idiot," "imbecile," and "moron," based on IQ. Under the direction of Superintendant Dr. Charles Sherman Little, a psychiatrist, the village grew to comprise more than 130 buildings on 2,000 acres and was designed to care for 3,000 patients. According to their abilities, they helped farm, plow, care for animals, cook, sew, and clean and were provided vocational training in carpentry, shoe repair, welding, and other useful skills. The village had its own power plant and recreational facilities. The neoclassic fieldstone buildings were patterned after Monticello and afforded abundant sunlight. The power and phone lines were buried. "This facility was beautifully planned and built," says Corinne McGeorge, an amateur historian and exhibit maker.

Dr. Little and his staff conducted research into the causes of, as it was known in his time (cringe), "mental retardation," and offered courses to doctors visiting from throughout the United States and Europe. Much of the financial support came from Mary Harriman, the wife of railroad tycoon E. H. Harriman, who joined its board in 1913 and funded researchers and doctors, as well as a building now named after Dr. Little's chief researcher, Dr. George Jervis.

At its peak, the village employed about 10,000 locals. "Almost every family in North Rockland had someone working up there, and many in the same family worked in various buildings," McGeorge says. "It was the top facility of its kind in the whole country. But it became a victim of its own success."

"We Failed Them"

Letchworth Village reached its 3,000-patient limit in 1935. It had hoped to be able to discharge patients as fast as new ones arrived, but that hope failed to materialize. New arrivals from places like Bellevue Hospital in New York soon overcrowded the facilities and overwhelmed the staff. Despite pleas for more funding, "Albany then was what Albany is now, and nothing much changed," McGeorge says.

In the 1940s, a photojournalist named Irving Haberman released photographs of naked and dirty residents sleeping on floor mattresses. By the 1950s, 4,000 patients were on-site, with over 5,000 by the late 1960s. Nevertheless, the vast majority of the doctors and staff stayed devoted to their patients, who continued to farm and make toys to sell at Christmas time. And the institution remained an important research facility, even helping in the fight against polio. The immunologist Hilary Koprowski created the first polio vaccine, and after Kaprowski tried it on himself in 1948, Dr. Jervis asked Koprowski to try it on Letchworth patients. (The rules for human testing were clearly less stringent back then.) The vaccine was administered to a total of twenty children; seventeen developed antibodies to the virus, none developed any complications, and within a few years this vaccine (and others, like the ones developed by Albert Sabin and Jonas Salk) tamed this terrible disease.

In the wake of the Rivera report, though, the state began the long, slow process of deinstitutionalization. It moved residents to group homes, phased down admissions, and finally closed Letchworth Village in 1996, when the last resident left. The towns of Haverstraw and Stony Point purchased the land and used it to build the Rotella and Patriot Hills golf courses. Some of the buildings were converted into the Fieldstone Secondary School, Willow Grove Middle School, and Stony Point Justice Court and Cooperative Extension. Indeed, McGeorge became interested in the site's history as she drove to her grandchildren's events at Fieldstone. "The buildings are magnificent," she says. But other buildings remain empty and derelict. The contrast illustrates the mixed legacy of this well-intentioned and ambitious but doomed institution.

"Letchworth did not fail," McGeorge says. "We failed them. If the state had used common sense and provided money to hire sufficient staff and transferred out those who could not be helped, then Letchworth could have continued to provide the service it was doing, in magnificent fashion."

New York's Main Street

The Opening of the Thruway in the Mid-1950s
Forever Changed Life in the Hudson Valley

In March 1954, the citizens of Sleepy Hollow were especially sleepy. So sleepy, in fact, that a writer in the *New York World-Telegram* suggested that "residents of this historic community think maybe the name will have to be changed to Insomnia Hollow." The reason: construction of the "$600,000,000 State Thruway bridge across the three-mile Tappan Zee of the Hudson."

Crews were operating pile drivers twenty-four hours a day to make up for time lost to bad weather, the article reports. Police switchboards were swamped with complaints. Some people claimed their beds shook. And no rest for the weary was in sight: "Burt Sanders, project manager, said he was very sorry but the nocturnal pounding will have to continue for the next eight weeks."

Sleep loss may have been one of the earliest consequences of the New York State Thruway, but it was hardly the only one. The new road, dubbed "the Main Street of New York State" in early promotional material, changed how people in the Hudson Valley and throughout the state lived, worked, and played. It also predicted similar changes across the United States, as it in large part inspired the nascent interstate highway system that transformed the country in the late 1950s and 1960s. That same promotional flyer even predicts that because the thruway was "arousing national interest," it would inevitably become "one of America's top tourist attractions."

OK, so no one would mistake the thruway for Mount Rushmore. But you can forgive the enthusiasm. In the 1950s, superhighways were a concrete symbol, literally, of America's newfound, postwar power. They signaled the triumph of the automobile as the country's preeminent mode of transportation and mythological totem. And they forever altered life everywhere they flowed. Starting here.

The Thruway Giveth

The Hudson River Valley has always been the Northeast's center of transportation, from native trails through the shipping and railroad routes that connected the port of New York to the rest of America. "It was river transportation first, including the Erie Canal; then the railroads came in the 1870s, especially the east shore line," says Tom Lewis, emeritus professor of English at Skidmore College and author of *The Hudson: A History* and *Divided Highways: Building the Interstate Highways, Transforming American Life.*

Though automobiles drove onto the scene in the early 1900s, there was only one river-crossing bridge south of Albany, the Bear Mountain Bridge, until 1924. The valley's many disparate communities were connected by "ribbons of roads up the east and west side of the river," Lewis says, routes 9 and 9W, for example. There was no easy way to get from the city to upstate New York and beyond. Towns had been built on the railroad model, near the stations, because "you can't get more than a couple miles from there without horse and carriage," Lewis says. "The thruway gave the opportunity for the first time to move swiftly from the exits into the valley, to penetrate into the area as never before. People could drive up and down the river, cross at the new bridges, because it was easy to do."

The most striking example is that sleep-shattering new bridge across the Tappan Zee. "It changed the culture of Rockland County," Lewis says. The bridge opened in 1955, and in the next two decades Rockland's population density nearly tripled, from 500 to 1,300 people per square mile, he says, "because now it was accessible to New York City. The thruway gradually made it possible to link what were disparate communities."

It also linked business. "The real catalyst for getting IBM to move to Kingston was the thruway," says Roger Panetta, visiting professor of history at Fordham University and author of *The Tappan Zee Bridge and the Forging of the Rockland Suburb.* The company had a large training center in Manhattan and a "smattering" of centers throughout the state, he says. They were planning to move at about the same time the thruway was proposed. "Trucking networks were on their mind, and in their planning documents they talked about the thruway, how they could move their heavy products to the city easily, and Kingston was right off the thruway," Panetta says. "I know their planners were thinking about that; it was very much on their mind."

It was on the mind of many business executives. "Where it went brought lots of development, which Governor [Thomas] Dewey anticipated. He said this would be the new Erie Canal for New York State," says Bruce Dearstyne, author of *The Spirit of New York: Defining Events in the Empire State's History.* "That's hard to measure, but he was probably close to right. On the other hand . . ."

The Thruway Taketh Away

There is always another hand with all large-scale endeavors. The thruway is no exception, and it brought with it unintended and sometimes deleterious consequences. The towns and cities that the thruway bypassed did not fare well, Dearstyne says. Some disappeared. Others are stuck in time. "They were villages, as they are now, and many have not changed a lot since the 1950s. The people and development went elsewhere," he says. Route 9W still goes where it always went, but with less traffic, "land values did not boom like they did near the thruway."

Geoffrey Stein, senior historian emeritus with the New York State Museum, remembers "the decline of restaurants, filling stations and motels" on the roads he was most familiar with. "The abandoned buildings were many," he says. "The State Museum staff once talked about acquiring a tourist camp cabin for preservation at the museum, but it may be too late."

The environment, of course, also took a hit. "So much of the thruway cuts through quite lovely territory, but it divided the community from the land," Lewis says. "That is especially true with a city like Albany, and I would put New Paltz in that category as well." He says that a Rensselaer Polytechnic Institute–trained civil engineer once told him that building a highway through wetlands was considered a "two-fer. You didn't have to pay for the land. You had complete control over the land. Aquatic life doesn't talk back," he says. "That was very much the thinking at the time."

Today, highways are an anathema. There are too many cars. Too many suburbs. Not enough mass transit. Things change, attitudes change. So the thruway has to be understood in context. "The car was king in the 1950s," Dearstyne says. And so was New York State. "This is an example of New York greatness. Having a big vision costs a lot but will help us stay number one, which we were in those days. I think New York is arguably the most significant state in the nation, maybe until the present. It is inclined to be on the leading edge, be bold about things like the Erie Canal, the thruway. Where we went, other states followed. For the most part this is a pretty positive story."

Get your motor running. Head out on the highway.

Leaving Albany

Ode to a City Neighborhood

Patty and Smitty are leaving Albany. Their kids are grown, and Smitty is tired of fixing things in their lovely, old house in their lovely, old neighborhood. When their furnace died this spring, he had had enough. They are building a new house in a new development. Their nearly twenty-five-year tenure on the block is ending. So the block threw another party, this one to say farewell.

It was organized by four families, and about two-dozen couples chipped in to cover the costs of food, drink, and party favors. The rain stopped just in time to set up the tables and chairs on the driveway that Mark and Ron, who hosted, share with Joe and Kathy, who also contributed their fridge and stove.

After drinks and dinner, Kathleen transformed an empty bottle of Riesling—Patty's favorite—into the talking stick and started the toasts and roasts. Even though Patty and Smitty aren't much older than most of their neighbors, they have always been the block's de facto parents. Patty, a nurse, was on call 24/7 for any medical question or treatment. Smitty would always lend a helping hand. And, of course, they were front and center at the many parties this remarkable block has held during their time here.

This is the kind of neighborhood that people in the suburbs lament. Here, everyone does know his or her neighbor, not just by name but also by family history, by temperament, by character, even by eccentricity and annoying habit. While they all float in at least one, and more likely all three, of Albany's strongest currents—Irish, Catholic, Democrat—they celebrate their differences as well and, despite them, navigate life's whitewater together. Those three shared currents and the various unique tributaries merge here, on this block, into a deep and soothing confluence of family, community, and fun.

So the toasts and roasts covered how Patty and Smitty were solid shoulders during difficult times and enthusiastic cheerleaders during happy times. Paul told a funny one about how Patty came over at three in the morning when Leslie went into labor. Nearly everyone had a story about Patty ministering to an ill or injured child. Sharon told how thrilled she and Sean were to finally do a favor for them, when Smitty asked Sean to restore their son's crashed computer, only to find a box of Omaha steaks delivered soon after. "Patty got one up on us again—the bitch!" Sharon laughed. Jennie remembered the dessert contest, which Patty won by suggesting the kids serve as judges, then whipping up a box of store-bought brownie mix with frosting and sprinkles, which of course the kids preferred to all the fancier entries. "I wore my daughter's tiara the rest of the day!" Patty boasted.

Kathleen presented Patty and Smitty with the block's going-away gift, an oil painting of their old house to hang in their new home, and said how everyone would miss them and envy their new windows, which don't have cracks in them and are easy to open and shut. Patty cried, as she always does, and told everyone how lucky she and Smitty were to have such great friends who were all such an important part of their lives and who helped them raise three great children.

Then it was back to partying. Laura, Molly, and Caroline, who were hired to serve and clear, rolled their teenage eyes as the grown-ups laughed too much and drank too much and, as they always do, had more fun than parents should have in public. They bit their teenage lips as Beth and Sharon and Sean and both Pauls, as they always do, sang too loudly and danced too vigorously to ancient songs from the 1970s and 1980s. But the teenagers also learned, as all the neighborhood kids have learned at block parties throughout their lives, how a community comes together, how families support and celebrate one another, how a neighborhood should be.

As things wound down, Patty reminded everyone that they'd be back for future parties—Karl and Bridget's biennial Thanksgiving dessert party, whoever throws this year's Christmas party, maybe another Mardi Gras bash at Mark and Ron's (though the last one got way out of hand). Then Smitty invited everyone to visit them in their new home. They aren't moving to Alaska, after all, just to Watervliet. It's only seven miles away; Francis Phelan would have walked there in *Ironweed*. But it's not Albany. Nobody at the party knew exactly where their new home was. Nobody had ever been to that particular area before. And, as Mike pointed out, there was another problem they would face, leaving Albany: Republicans live there. Everyone laughed—even the Republicans.

Get Your Beer Here

*Hudson Valley Brewers Fill Our Cups with Some of the
Freshest, Tastiest Beers in the Country—Bar None*

"Beer is proof that God loves us and wants us to be happy."
—Benjamin Franklin

It's 11 a.m. on a Tuesday, and the early lunch crowd shuffles in to Brown's Brewing Company on River Street in Troy. A man sits at the bar, reading his paper, drinking coffee. If he looked up, he'd notice another man, clearly visible through the plate glass window behind the bar, who is standing rubber-booted and hip deep in a seven-hundred-gallon stainless steel tank with a shovel and a hose. This man is Rob Rafferty, a brewery assistant, and his current job is to clean the vat of mash, a gloppy porridge that is left over from the first step in what will be Brown's Pale Ale.

Scenes like this are familiar to beer connoisseurs up and down the Hudson Valley. Dozens of small, local craft breweries and brewpubs dot the landscape from Troy and Albany to Westchester County and nearly every town in between. Some, like Brown's, have been around more than two decades, nearly from the big bang of the US craft beer explosion. Others are just getting their sudsy feet wet. They serve English-style beers, Belgian-style beers, German-style beers, beers made of wheat and barley and rye, beers flavored with chocolate and pumpkin and maple syrup, extra-hoppy India pale ales and extra-fruity cranberry white ales, Wassails in winter and hefeweizens in summer and whatever else fancies the brewer that day.

What they don't make is thin, pale, tasteless, American-style beer. ("Why is American beer served cold?" the old beermaker's joke goes. "So you can tell it from urine.") And while thin, pale, tasteless, American-style beer still accounts for about 96 percent of all beer sales in this country, the remaining 4 percent who drink craft beers—a number that likely skews a bit higher in regions like the Hudson Valley—do so with a passion and devotion that can sometimes border on the religious. They complain when a personal favorite is dropped from the rotation. They pester while awaiting a seasonal style. They expect to see brewers like Rafferty mucking about with shovels and hoses in the background.

As more than one of the Hudson Valley's humble brewers pointed out, "We don't own our beers. Our customers own our beers."

"Beer brings enjoyment to the world!"
—King Gambrinus of Brabent, the patron saint of brewers

America was once a nation of brewers. According to an article in the *New Yorker*, a highly reliable source, there were about 4,000 regional breweries in 1873.

One of those was the C. H. Evans Brewing Company. In 1860, Cornelius Evans bought a Hudson-based brewery, which had opened for business in 1786, and produced award-winning ales for another sixty years. Then came Prohibition, which killed off Evans and most local brewers nationwide. The rest were snuffed out by the rise of mass production following Prohibition's repeal. That also put our native beer's variety, freshness, and flavor on the verge of extinction. By 1965, there was just one craft brewer left standing, Anchor Brewing, in San Francisco.

Now, thanks to changing laws and changing palates, there are more than 1,500 breweries nationwide, the highest number in a century. One of those is, once again, C. H. Evans. C. H. Evans IV, Cornelius's great-great-grandson, revived his family business as C. H. Evans Brewing at the Albany Pump Station ten years ago. Neil, as he is known, never heard much about his family's brewing history until his twenties, when he got to know a great uncle, the last survivor of the Hudson brewing days. "It totally fascinated me," he says, "but I never thought I could do anything about it."

Then, in the 1980s, the brewery laws changed. "There were now some tax benefits to opening a small brewery," Evans says. That's when the craft brew boom really got going. As defined by the Brewers Association, a craft brewery produces less than 2 million barrels a year. (A barrel contains two kegs, to give you a recognizable, frat-party reference.) A microbrewery produces less than 15,000. A brewpub serves at least a quarter of its beer in house. Hudson Valley brewers are at the small end of microbrewing; Brown's, for example, topped off just 2,100 barrels in 2009. "What we brew in a year, the big breweries spill in a day," co-owner Kelly Brown says.

By the 1980s several craft breweries were pretty well established on the West Coast. And in the late 1980s they drew Kelly and her then boyfriend, Garret (Garry) Brown, on a cross-country trek that led to Brown's Brewing.

"Garry was a photojournalist, and I was a flight attendant," says Kelly. "He introduced me to craft beer. I had never had one—I tried the tasteless yellow stuff in college and didn't like it. Once I tried real beer, I was hooked. And he had this idea to start our own brewery."

Like most nascent brewers, they first tried home brewing. "We made beer for our wedding in 1990. We called it Wedding Feast Ale. It was completely awful," Kelly laughs. Undaunted, they teamed up with a partner, bought an abandoned warehouse on the Troy waterfront, spent three years rehabbing it themselves, and launched Brown and Moran's in 1993. (Jim Moran left the business a few years later.) It wasn't long before others in the Hudson Valley—like Neil Evans—followed their lead.

In 1996, after a successful career in the casino and food service industries, Evans began pondering his family heritage. If he was going to start brewing again, he needed to get his hands hoppy. Like the Browns, he tried home brewing. "Then I knew that was what I wanted to do," he says. He hoped to open again in Hudson, but the demographics weren't right. He found an abandoned water pump station in downtown Albany, remodeled it, hired a professional brewer named George De Piro ("I knew I wasn't good enough," he admits), opened in 1999, and has been winning beer-making awards ever since.

"When I first pitched the idea, everyone said I was nuts," Evans says. "It took a couple years, but those doubting Thomases came to me and said, wow, you were right. That was fun."

But financial I-told-you-so's weren't his motivation. "I was a successful businessman prior to this," he says. "I did this out of passion."

"Without question, the greatest invention in the history of mankind is beer. Oh, I grant you that the wheel was also a fine invention, but the wheel does not go nearly as well with pizza."

—Dave Barry

Garry and Kelly Brown originally planned to open just a brewery and tasting room but were convinced that they needed food to entice an uneducated beer populace. Joey LoBianco, who co-owns Hyde Park Brewing in Hyde Park, which opened in the mid-1990s, and Skytop Steakhouse and Brewery in Kingston, came from the opposite direction.

"I was already in the restaurant business, and an old friend from the CIA was looking for a new idea," LoBianco says. "He put this concept of brewing in the restaurant to us. He said it was going on in California and he thought it would sweep the East Coast next. He was right."

Rick Rauch, co-owner and managing partner of the Gilded Otter in New Paltz, who opened his pub in 1998, also added beer to food rather than vice versa. "A restaurant is just a restaurant, and there are many theme restaurants out there. We needed a gimmick to ensure success. People see the tanks and all the bells and whistles. It was a good gimmick at the time, and it's proven to be a lasting gimmick." Still, 95 percent of his customers come for the food, he says. "The brewery is our cherry on top of the sundae."

For others, though, beer is the ice cream, hot fudge, and whipped cream.

"He was a wise man who invented beer."

—Plato

According to another highly reliable source (well, Wikipedia), beer is the world's oldest and most widely consumed alcoholic beverage. It trails only water and tea as the most popular drink on earth. Its origins are prehistoric, and when humans first began writing, they often wrote about beer. The Code of Hammurabi, circa 1790 BC, was in part a liquor licensing authority; it included laws regulating ancient Babylonian brewpubs. In its Draconian eye-for-an-eye style, rule 108, for example, says that female barkeeps who overcharge should be drowned.

Flash-forward 3,800 years, and we write about the valley's newer brewpubs. Tim and Amber Adams opened Cave Mountain Brewing just over a year ago in Windham. It's the first brewery ever in Greene County, Tim claims. A restaurant chef since 1991, he says, "I always wanted to open a fish fry or barbecue place. But then I started home brewing six years ago. My first batch was five gallons of pale ale. I followed the instructions to a T, and it came out incredible, just mind-blowingly delicious." He had been called to the church of beer.

Cave Mountain is small, making just one barrel at a time. Out of that one barrel he can supply six mainstay taps with blond ale, Irish red ale, English nut-brown ale, German hefeweizen, Centennial IPA, and oatmeal stout, as well as six seasonal brews like cranberry white, spiced winter ale, blueberry wheat, and Oktoberfest. But he's done so well he is planning to open an off-site brewery and try regional distribution.

"My wife and I had no idea we would be this popular," he says. "We thought it would be us two and a couple waitresses, but after two weeks we were a lot busier than we ever imagined." He doesn't have time to cook or brew anymore. "I now manage—I'm a consultant for the brewery and kitchen," he says, leaving the beer to his head brewer, Chris Tilley.

Though Adams is also a chef, he fully credits his success to his beer. Cave Mountain recently was named best brewery at the Hunter Mountain Microbrew and Wine Festival, beating out other local brewers and larger producers like Sam Adams and Sierra Nevada. Talking to him, a relative newbie, you sense his wonder at his new calling. "The word 'brewery,'" he says, "is a magical thing."

"This is grain, which any fool can eat, but for which the Lord intended a more divine means of consumption . . . Beer!"
—Friar Tuck, *Robin Hood, Prince of Thieves*

Stomp some grapes and put them in a barrel, and they will turn into something like wine on their own devices. Beer, however, requires a guiding hand. In fact, there is some archeological argument about whether humans first cultivated wheat in order to make bread or beer.

"For grain to turn into an ale or lager, it has to be malted, cooked, strained, cooked, strained, fermented in a barrel, and sometimes again in a bottle," Burkhard Bilger wrote in the *New Yorker*. That alchemy of biology, chemistry, and mechanical engineering (see sidebar) can be so captivating, it causes otherwise sane men and women to utterly change their lives. Indeed, the best way to become a brewer, one learns by talking to them, is to be something else first. Along with photographer, flight attendant, and casino executive, some Hudson Valley brewer once held the title of biochemist, health-care manager, state worker, and knockabout.

Tommy Keegan, proprietor of Keegan Ales in Kingston, studied biochemistry at San Francisco State and worked in a lab. He was home-brewing on the side and found a master's program in brewing science at the University of California–Davis. "That seemed like too much fun to pass up," he says.

He then moved back to his native Long Island and got a job as a biology lab manager at the State University of New York–Stony Brook. When a Long Island brewery called Blue Point offered him a job, he took it. But with a mortgage and a second child on the way, he thought he needed a "real job." He almost took a position with a pharmacy company. Then he learned about a defunct brewery in Kingston and moved in, in 2003. He made three beers—he makes many more today—and his first batches won medals at a beer festival. Life in the lab was never an option again.

John Eccles, head brewer at Hyde Park and Skytop, was in hospital management until his late thirties. But, like all the others, he home-brewed and was hooked. "I ingratiated myself with the late, great brewmaster Jay Misson at Mountain Valley brewpub in Suffern, which is no long there," he says. "I left the hospital at three, got to the pub at four, and Jay gave me the worst possible jobs to get rid of me—scrubbing the tanks, pulling the grain, going into the cellars on hands and knees scrubbing the gunk. That would dissuade most people, but I really wanted to do this. I worked for free almost three years just to learn, then became a brewer when they expanded."

Darren Currier, the Gilded Otter's brewmaster, worked in air-pollution control for the Vermont Department of Environmental Conservation. Home brewing got the better of him as well. "I had bought a home-brewing kit for my father, who loved beer, but he was too busy to use it," Currier says. "I found it as a freshman in college [at SUNY New Paltz], tried it, and I loved it from the first batch." He left the DEC to attend the Siebel Institute for Brewing in Chicago and took over the Gilded Otter soon after it first opened.

> *WOODY: What's going on, Mr. Peterson?*
> *NORM: The question is, what's going in Mr. Peterson? A beer please, Woody.*
> —
> *SAM: What'd you like, Normie?*
> *NORM: A reason to live. Give me another beer.*
> —
> *WOODY: Hey, Mr. Peterson, Jack Frost nipping at your nose?*
> *NORM: Yep, now let's get Joe Beer nipping at my liver.*
> —Cheers

Cheers was born just before the craft beer revolution; if it were to be remade now, no doubt Sam's pub would brew its own. A Coach's nutty ale, perhaps, or a Carla's bitter, or a Normie's Irish stout. Cheers wasn't a brewpub, but it certainly was a pub, and that is the real strength and sustenance of all these brewing establishments. The beer is great, to be sure. But they are even more special in that they truly are places where everybody knows your name.

"It's all about relationship building," says Amy Acer, who runs Defiant Brewing in Pearl River with her husband, Neill. "There are no TVs here. We are like an old English pub where you come to talk to your neighbors."

Beer 101

Good, fresh beer typically contains just four or five ingredients: water, malt, hops, yeast, and sometimes flavoring agents, which can be any carbohydrate or sugar such as grain (rye, wheat), fruit, honey, chocolate, or even maple syrup.

In step one, ground malt, which is germinated and roasted barley, steeps in hot water for about an hour. This converts the malt's starches into sugars. The sweet liquid, called wort, is pumped to a boiling tank. The leftover gruel is called mash, and many brewers send it to local farms as animal feed.

Next, the wort is boiled for up to two hours to sterilize and purify the liquid. Hops, the flower clusters of the humulus plant, are added during the boil. Hops come in many different varieties and are used to add flavor, aroma, and bitterness—the hoppier a brew, the stronger the bite.

After boiling, the wort is allowed to settle a while to remove sediment. Then it's pumped through a heat exchanger to cool it rapidly and then piped into a fermentation tank. Here, the brewer adds the yeast, which feeds on the wort's sugars, producing alcohol and carbon dioxide. Like hops, yeast comes in many varieties and determines what type of beer will result: lager, ale, porter, Belgian-style, German-style, what have you.

After anywhere from three to eight weeks or so, depending on the brew, the yeast has consumed all the sugar and goes dormant. It settles to the bottom of the tank and is removed and reused. The rest is beer.

More to the point, it's craft beer. What makes craft beer taste better than Bud or Coors or Miller? As with any foodstuff, it's the ingredients. Large, industrial brewers typically substitute cheaper grains like corn and rice for the more expensive malt. Some even add corn syrup. That results in lighter-colored, lightly flavored beer. And once you've had a craft beer, you will never drink it again.

Including the ones who may have inspired the very beer you're drinking. When Tommy Keegan draws a pint of his Hurricane Kitty IPA, Hurricane Kitty herself—Keegan's grandmother—may be knocking back a pint next to you. "When she walks in the band yells, 'Hurricane Kitty's in the house,'" Keegan laughs. "The rugby players ask her to autograph a bottle. She has Alzheimer's and doesn't remember it later, but she loves it." (Sadly, Katherine "Hurricane Kitty" Keegan passed away March 8, 2012.)

Pubs, after all, are fun places to be. The libations they serve are fun to drink. The people who make and serve them have fun doing it. That's not to say it's always easy. Success brings its own frustrations. "I spend more time thinking about workers comp than I do about beer these days," says Keegan. Many brewers complain that they can't experiment with new recipes too much for fear of losing customers who expect their favorites. Brown's expansion plans—they built a new brewery in Hoosick, which opened in 2011—have Peter Martin, once a one-man brew crew, juggling more and more responsibilities.

Still, when asked why he likes his job, Martin hesitates for just a second, as if it's the dumbest, most self-evident question he's ever heard. Then he smiles, shrugs, and offers the obvious answer:

"Because it's beer."

WOODY: What's the story, Mr. Peterson?
NORM: The Bobbsey twins go to the brewery. Let's cut to the happy ending.

Just Breathe

A Capital District Art Project Shines Light on Darkness Visible

Full dark, midnight dark, though the dashboard blinks that it is just 6:19 p.m. Rain, light and persistent, spatters the windshield as we drive through the forgotten streets of Albany's blighted South End. Block after block lined with derelict houses, abandoned and empty, padlocks on doors, plywood over windows, weeds reaching through cracked steps, many marked by an ominous red X, warning even the bravest to stay away, should they burn, crumble, or fall. We feel anxious, disoriented, strangers in our own land, as if the world we know and knew has been painted black.

We drive down streets we never knew existed—Alexander, Elizabeth, Tuenis, Broad—and streets we know to avoid. Our neighbors uptown, out in the suburbs, are settling into Wednesday night dinner, but my wife, daughter, and I are spending a few moments on the last night of November looking for light. There is little to find. Then, 48 Elizabeth Street, where windows glow startlingly bright. The light then dims, then brightens again, in rhythm to our own slow, human breath. In, out. Bright, dim. Death comes alive with breathing light.

Another house breathes with light on Delaware Street, and more on Fourth and Second avenues and Stephen Street and other forsaken streets of the Capital District. They are part of *Breathing Lights*, the art installation that brought attention to these empty patches of Albany, Troy, and Schenectady this past fall. The project was one of four winners of the Bloomberg Philanthropies Public Art Challenge, which encouraged city mayors and artists to create art that speaks to community and civic engagement.

There is little civic engagement here. Only a few houses are inhabited. On a shaky porch, a business transaction takes place. These are the only souls we see during our half-hour tour of this Love Canal, this Chernobyl within our own borders.

And yet, life stirs, if only in fits and starts. A string of Christmas lights on this door, a plastic Santa on that stoop. A handful of Habitat for Humanity homes stand clean and new and proud among the wreckage. There's a functioning church. Three land bank lots are being turned into a community garden. Harriet Tubman Democratic High School offers alternative education; a park and playground offer recreation. The tour notes from *Breathing Lights* breathe with optimism:

> *Notice a new house on Osborn Street being built by a retired couple from Clifton Park on a land bank vacant lot.*
>
> *Notice the circular mosaic on the side of the land bank building adjacent to the vacant lot.*
>
> *Notice the nearly intact streetscape and family scale buildings on this block. This block was historically a family street.*
>
> *Notice the circular mosaic on the land bank building across the street.*
>
> *The buildings themselves are difficult, but this would be a good block to invest in.*

We finally spill onto South Pearl Street, drive past a bodega and a chicken restaurant and the DMV, then back to Madison Avenue and back uptown. The rain comes down harder now, the urban glow of streetlamps and neon signs and headlights broken and distorted through the rain drops, full *film noir*. We are all quiet, reflective. "It's unbelievable," my wife says. And yet it's where we live. Our city, our country, is not what we thought it was. There is darkness we did not know, right next to us, threatening, threatening. *Breathing Lights*, it seems, offers the slimmest glimmer of hope. Just breathe. Breathe in the light. It's not much. It's everything.

Part 11:
Cornucopia

The Worst Woman on Earth

Serial Killer Lizzie Halliday Terrorized
Sullivan County in the 1890s

If you should be reading this around the time of Halloween, the world's creepiest holiday, you are in luck. We now take you back to one of our creepiest decades: the 1890s. Back then people read such creepy new works as *Dracula*, *The War of the Worlds*, *Heart of Darkness*, and *The Picture of Dorian Gray*. They lived through the Gilded Age of creepy wealth and creepier corruption. And they were terrorized by sensational, horrifyingly creepy crimes. Lizzie Borden took up her axe in 1892. Jack the Ripper continued to haunt London with a string of murders begun in the late 1880s. But nothing and no one was creepier than Sullivan County's own serial killer, Lizzie Brown Halliday.

In fact, while Borden was acquitted and Jack never identified, Halliday was known to have killed five people, convicted of one murder, and believed to have offed many others. She was sentenced to die in the electric chair. That sentence was commuted, and she spent the last twenty-four years of her life in the Matteawan Hospital for the Criminally Insane, where she killed her last victim, a prison nurse.

She was front-page news all over the world and for a time was suspected of being the actual Jack the Ripper. Yet her story was almost forgotten. "I don't think anyone was aware of the case until I wrote about it," says John Conway, Sullivan County historian and history professor at the State University of New York–Sullivan, who published articles about her in 2007. "It is a fascinating story, and the most fascinating thing is that there was such a broad geographic area and so many potential victims, no one is really quite sure how many people she killed."

So dim the lights, light some candles, play some creepy music, and read about Lizzie Halliday, dubbed by the *New York Times* "the worst woman on earth."

A Criminal Prodigy

Eliza Margaret McNally was born in Ireland in 1864 and immigrated to the United States in 1867. She was a criminal prodigy—"Apparently her murderous tendencies started fairly early," Conway says—and you may need a scorecard to track her heinous exploits. Her first husband, Charles Hopkins, also known as Ketspool Brown, died two years after their marriage, in 1879. She then married Artemus Brewer, who died less than a year later. The *Times*, reporting on her trial in 1894, hinted, "Whether these men died natural deaths or were murdered, is not known."

Her next "venture," as the *Times* put it, was Hiram Parkinson. He fled within a year, so she promptly married another man, George Smith, who was a friend of Artemus Brewer. "In a few months she tried to kill Smith by giving him a cup of poisoned tea. Failing in her design, she fled to Bellows Falls, Vermont, taking with her every portable article in the house," the *Times* wrote.

In Vermont, she married Charles Playstel (that's three living husbands, if you're keeping score at home) but disappeared after about two weeks. She reappeared in Philadelphia, where she took lodging with a family called the McQuillans, who had lived near the McNally family back in Ireland. There, she opened a shop, only to burn it down to collect the insurance money. That resulted in her first stint in prison, where she served two years in Philadelphia's Eastern Penitentiary for the crime.

Her crime spree continued after her release in Newburgh, where she met an aging Civil War veteran and widower with two sons from Sullivan County named Paul Halliday. She married him too. "Their married life does not seem to have been pleasant," the *Times* reported ("in what must rank as one of the greatest journalistic understatements of all time," Conway pointed out in his writings), because she stole a team of horses to elope with a neighbor—who then left her. She was arrested, pled insanity, and entered an asylum.

In 1893, Paul Halliday sprang her from the asylum. That August, she burned his house and barn and a mill. One of Halliday's sons died in the fires, and Paul was nowhere to be found. The neighbors did not believe her story that he was traveling, so they poked around. They found two dead bodies under a haystack. Margaret and Sarah McQuillan, the wife and daughter of the man with whom she had lived in Philadelphia, had both been bound and shot. Lizzie Halliday was arrested, and a few days later, her husband's body was found hidden under the floor of his house. He too had been tied up and shot.

While in Sullivan County Jail awaiting her trial, she refused to eat, tried to strangle a sheriff's wife, set her bedclothes on fire, tried to hang herself, and cut her throat and arms with broken glass. "For the last three months it has been necessary to keep her chained to the floor," the *Times* wrote.

"Without Parallel in the Annals of Crime"

Halliday was on the front pages of many New York City newspapers, and the story was picked up around the country. Conway uncovered the following in the *New York World*: "From its circumstances, origin, conception and execution; its unique characteristics, the abnormal personalities and peculiar localities it involves, and, above all, in the strangeness and mystery of its great central figure, it is unprecedented and almost without parallel in the annals of crime."

She was even put forward as Jack the Ripper. Sullivan County sheriff Harrison Beecher, in what Conway believes was a reach for publicity, told the press, "Recent investigations show that Mrs. Halliday is in all probability connected with the famous Whitechapel murders." He had no evidence to support his claim, and when asked directly if she had been that killer, Halliday reportedly replied, "Do you think I am an elephant? That was done by a man."

At her trial, in Sullivan County Oyer and Terminal Court on June 17, 1894, Halliday was convicted of the murder of Sarah McQuillan and sentenced to death. When that sentence was commuted after she was judged insane, she lived out the rest of her life in the Matteawan Hospital for the Criminally Insane. Hardly a model prisoner, she tried to escape several times and attacked many prison workers—most viciously, nurse Nellie Wickes, whom she stabbed with scissors more than two hundred times and who became Halliday's final victim in 1906. Halliday herself died in Matteawan on June 18, 1918.

Some at the time believed that she was not really insane, only acting so. Conway doesn't buy that. "There were attempts to diagnose her condition and somehow tie that to her motivation, but I don't know how successful they were," he says. "She seemed just flat-out crazy." Her connection to the Whitechapel murders has similarly been dismissed. In the end, why she committed her grisly crimes remain unknowable. "What stands out to me," Conway says, "is that, for all we do know, there are so many unanswered questions that could help explain her actions."

We'll just have to be content with knowing that Sullivan County was once home to the worst woman on earth. Happy Halloween.

The Speed of the Wind

Ice Yachting Took Hold in the Hudson Valley More Than Two Hundred Years Ago

"In the old days it was custom to race over a long course, the most popular being from Poughkeepsie to New-Hamburg and back, nine miles each way. Of recent years, the custom has been changed, and the yachts now keep in sight of a given point. It is an inspiring sight to see a fleet of twenty or more ice yachts, with their white sails sparkling in the frosty air, circling around each other with the speed of the wind. No railroad train can keep up with an ice yacht when the conditions are favorable."
—*New York Times*, March 7, 1896

One Saturday afternoon in February 1982, John Sperr, of Rhinebeck, was skiing with friends in Barrytown and saw a sight that changed his life. "I skied down to the river, where there was a fleet of old boats sailing on a glorious, twenty-mile sheet of ice," he says. "The boats looked so beautiful as they did their graceful dance across the ice. I felt compelled to come back." He did come back the next day and got his first ride on an ice yacht. "I was hooked," Sperr says, and he soon was introduced to a group called the Hudson River Ice Yacht Club, which had formed nearly a century earlier, in 1885, to organize a sport that had actually been a Hudson Valley institution for a century before that.

Ice yachting started in Europe, but by 1790 it had become quite popular in these parts, especially around Poughkeepsie, which by the mid-1800s had become the ice yachting center of the country. The term "yacht" is somewhat misleading; in the early days, this was a sport of the masses, not the wealthy. By the eighteenth century, smaller boats had opened sailing up to the general public, who used them both for work—fishing, transportation—and for leisure. One historian called early ice boats "primitive vessels" that were "more or less square boxes with three runners attached. Two of these were directly mounted to the box, the third one was flexible and could act as a rudder." This particular type of boat, Sperr says, was first built by Oliver Booth of Poughkeepsie in 1790. "It is generally credited with starting the recreational iceboat movement in the United States," he says.

By the 1850s the boats became more sophisticated, with the now familiar triangular frame, jib, and mainsail. Around this time ice yacht clubs formed in Newburgh, New Hamburg, Poughkeepsie, and Hyde Park. The members of the various clubs raced for awards such as the "Challenge Pennant of America" and the "Captain William Drake Flag." They also liked to race against the trains that had just started running up and down the river; in 1871 the *Icicle* beat the Chicago Express on its run from Poughkeepsie to Ossining.

That's because, the money came in. In 1869 Commodore John E. Roosevelt, FDR's uncle, built the *Icicle*, the largest and fastest ice yacht to date. Ten years later H. Relyea of Catskill built an even faster vessel, which he christened the *Robert Scott*. According to a history written by the Chelsea Yacht Club, "He replaced the heavy framework of timbers and wooden side-rails with a single long center timber, and steel guy wires to keep it square with the runner-plank. He also reduced the size of the jib and brought the sail's center of effort further forward, where it was resisted by the main runners, instead of partially by the rudder as before. The reduction in weight and improvement in control was a real breakthrough, and with very few exceptions, all iceboats built along the Hudson were 'Scott' boats or 'wire boats,' as distinguished from the earlier 'side-rail' or 'wishbone' type." After Relyea "soundly" beat Roosevelt in a race, the commodore ordered a new *Icicle* built like the *Robert Scott*.

In 1892, one of the era's biggest races, the Ice Yacht Challenge Pennant of America, was inaugurated by the Orange Lake Ice Yacht Club of New Hamburg. A man named Archibald Rogers, a neighbor of Commodore Roosevelt, and his boat *Jack Frost* raced against the *Icicle*, *Robert Scott*, and other boats until 1902. This period was the high–ice water mark of Hudson River ice yachting. The 1890 Chelsea Yacht Ice Club had forty-two members and fourteen yachts registered, and the 1903 club listed sixty-nine members and nineteen boats. But interest waned in the Hudson Valley during and after World War I, while the sport grew quickly in the upper Midwest.

It came back in vogue around here in the 1960s, thanks in large part to Raymond Ruge, a Cornwall architect and member of the Chelsea Yacht Club. The *New York Times* reported, "When he died in 1985, Ray had transformed the sport from a millionaire's hobby to a recreation for local townspeople."

Cold Comforts

"Sailing on ice is much different than sailing on water," Sperr says. "The elements of wind and temperature are much more demanding." Ice creates far less friction and resistance on the boat's runners than water does on a hull, and as a result the wind works more efficiently to power movement. "The speed is much greater in an iceboat, so the decisions about when to tack or how to steer clear of other boats come quickly and have larger consequences," he says. And changing winds present unpredictable challenges. With a sudden gust, a docile ride "can quickly become a real beast to control, demanding considerable physical strength, as well as skill and experience, to get it safely home."

As for the temperature, well, it's winter. "You have to prepare for the cold," Sperr says. "Many people do not enjoy being outdoors in twenty-degree temperatures for ten hours." For those who do though, the heat of competition keeps them warm. Most iceboat races are conducted with two marks: the upwind and downwind mark, Sperr says. "On the Hudson River, a surveyor would be hired to accurately stake out a course, with the marks five miles apart on the north and south reaches of the river."

Despite the high speeds and numb fingers, Sperr doesn't consider ice yachting particularly risky. "I think the average age of the top sailors in the DN World Championships is almost forty years old. [The DN is the largest iceboat class.] Same for the A-Skeeters, the fastest iceboats in the world," he says. "Serious injury in organized competition is very rare. While they are very competitive on the racecourse, most ice boaters are very concerned about safety."

What they are not concerned about is money. Unlike water-based yacht races, ice yachting wins you only bragging rights and maybe a trophy. "It is a hobby," Sperr says. "There are no multi-million-dollar sponsors such as Oracle, Red Bull, or Emirates as in America's Cup racing. Still, it is more competitive than normal sailing, where the person with the larger checkbook generally wins."

Take Me to the River

Competitive, yes, but agreeably so. "Ice boaters in general are a very social and congenial bunch," Sperr says. The bigger boats can require a crew of four to eight people to carry them out on the ice and get them sail-worthy. "Our group likes to make our sailing outings a festive social occasion," he says. "There's always a pot of soup on the stove, several bottles of good wine and all manner of other tasty treats being shared by sailors and spectators to celebrate a perfect winter's day on the ice."

Sadly, those types of days are harder to come by. The ice-sailing season has always been short, and the warm winters we have experienced recently have made it shorter still. "Ice seems to be forming up later in the season and with less regularity," he notes. "We also seem to be having less snow. Lots of snow helps the formation of ice on the Hudson River. The ice also goes out sooner. South Tivoli Bay is filling with sediment and has had a very difficult time making a decent sheet of ice in recent years."

The last two winters were near-total busts. In 2011–2012, there was no sailing on the Hudson River or Tivoli Bay due to lack of ice. Last winter offered periods of thin ice, gale winds, rain, and snow. "People who put boats on were only able to experience about four hours of actual sailing," Sperr laments. "The season is so short that many people do not find the investment of time and energy worthwhile."

The most passionate sailors, however, find it more than worthwhile. They buy smaller boats, which can be transported on the roof of a car to track down ice wherever it may form, from Pennsylvania to Maine. Or they just wait here for that elusive but transcendent perfect winter day. "There is something incredibly seductive," Sperr says, "about gliding across the ice of Tivoli Bay with just the soft rush of the wind in your face, the creak of the rigging, and the clatter of the runners on the ice."

Mysteries of the Hudson Valley

Buried Treasure, Unsolved Crimes, Missing Persons, UFOs—the Valley's Seen It All

The Hudson Valley has always been a land of mystery. Even Washington Irving knew as much: "A drowsy, dreamy influence seems to hang over the land, and to pervade the very atmosphere," he writes in "The Legend of Sleepy Hollow." "Some say that the place was bewitched," he reports, and its people "are given to all kinds of marvelous beliefs, are subject to trances and visions, and frequently see strange sights, and hear music and voices in the air. The whole neighborhood abounds with local tales, haunted spots, and twilight superstitions; stars shoot and meteors glare oftener across the valley than in any other part of the country, and the nightmare, with her whole ninefold, seems to make it the favorite scene of her gambols."

The nightmare with her ninefold have continued to gambol in this scene ever since. Herewith, we examine just a few of the many unexplained events that have bewitched, bothered, and bewildered the valley and now ride alongside Irving's cranium-deficient equestrian into local legend.

The Missing Cadet

On January 14, 1950, second-year cadet Richard Colvin Cox left his dormitory at the US Military Academy in West Point to meet a friend for dinner. He was never seen again. Was he murdered? Was he abducted by the Soviets as part of some Cold War espionage plot? Those were just some of the theories that "explained" his disappearance.

What is known is that Cox was born in Ohio and later joined the army in 1946. He was stationed near the new postwar border between East and West Germany as an intelligence officer. According to the 1999 book *Oblivion: The Mystery of West Point Cadet Richard Cox*, by Henry Maihafer, Cox served with another army official who was mysteriously known as "George."

In 1947, Cox received his appointment to West Point. On Saturday, January 7, 1950, a man phoned Cox's classmate Peter Hains looking for Cox. The caller's "tone was rough and patronizing, almost insulting," Hains told Maihafer. "Well, look, when he comes in, tell him to come on down here to the hotel," the caller said. "Just tell him George called—he'll know who I am. We knew each other in Germany. I'm just up here for a little while, and tell him I'd like to get him a bite to eat."

Cox got the message and met George in Grant Hall. The two men went to George's car, which was parked on the West Point campus, and drank whiskey; later Cox forged his time log so that it would appear that he had attended the 6:30 p.m. cadet supper formation, which he had missed—a violation of the Cadet Honor Code that could have gotten him expelled. George made a second visit to Cox the next day, and on January 14, he came by again. The two left the grounds, and Cox vanished. His disappearance was big news for a time, until Cox was declared legally dead in 1957.

A retired schoolteacher named Marshall Jacobs dug into the mystery in the mid-1980s, poring over files acquired through the Freedom of Information Act and interviewing Cox's family, friends, and classmates; CIA, FBI, and CID agents; and West Point and army officials. He then collaborated with Maihafer on the book. The end result: "Jacobs decided he had learned all he was going to," Maihafer writes, "and he accepted the fact that neither he nor anyone else would ever know the full story."

Cox is the only West Point cadet who ever disappeared without being found dead or alive.

A Grave Finding?

In July 2000, the *Times Herald-Record* of Middletown published an astonishing story on its front page. Two amateur historians, Roger A. King of Monroe and Robert Brennan of Pine Bush, claimed to have found the grave of the son of Thomas Jefferson and his slave and mistress, Sally Hemings.

The two sleuths said they had discovered two pieces of a tombstone, one of which read, "Son of Thomas Jefferson and Sally Hemings," in the Orange County hamlet of Southfields. At a news conference held at the Red Apple Restaurant, on Route 17 in Southfields, they told the gathered media, including a reporter from the *New York Times*, that they believed Hemings gave birth in 1809 to her eighth child, a son that she had with Thomas Jefferson. The boy, named Thomas Jr., was brought north to New York, out of slavery, by Elizabeth Monroe, wife of soon-to-be-president James Monroe and friend of Hemings's.

"Mr. King and Mr. Brennan presented as evidence two sisters who claimed to be descendants of the newly discovered Thomas Jefferson Jr.," the *Times* reported. "They recalled how one of their uncles had researched the family tree—then stopped, mysteriously. There were rumors in the family, the women said, that he had discovered the connection between Jefferson and his mistress, and the uncle did not want to know more."

Some of the reporters then trekked to the John Coffey Jr. Cemetery in Southfields, "a small, lumpy knoll with stones in various stages of disrepair. There, they saw the stone that read 'In memory of Thomas Jefferson who died April 25, 1855 Age 46 Yrs & 12 Ds.'

But, writes the *Times*, "the piece of stone identifying him as a son of Jefferson and Hemings was nowhere to be found. The same was true of Mr. King, who was, it turned out, one of the few people around claiming to have actually seen the second half of the gravestone."

According to the *Times*, King had given rubbings of the stone to Brennan and to Chris Sonne, the historian for the town of Tuxedo—neither of whom had actually seen the stone with his own eyes. After King skipped town, Sonne said, "I have every reason to believe [the missing stone] to exist, because you can't fake an etching, but I am really somewhat mystified."

Two esteemed Jefferson scholars interviewed by the *Times*, however, were in no way mystified. They both strongly doubted that this Thomas Jefferson was the son of *that* Thomas Jefferson.

Kipsy, the Hudson River Monster

Loch Ness has Nessie. The Himalayas have the Yeti. Most of North America has Bigfoot. The Hudson River, not to be outdone, has Kipsy.

Of course, to paraphrase Bill Clinton, that depends on what your definition of "has" is.

All these alleged monsters are known as cryptids, creatures of dubious existence, from the Greek *krypto*, as in cryptic. In 2006, river goers claimed to have seen an enormous manatee, more commonly found around Florida, swimming near the Chelsea Piers in Manhattan and on up into Westchester County waters.

Not as interesting as a sea monster, to be sure, but you play the cryptid you're dealt.

The Newburgh-Beacon Bridge Killing

"Somebody knows what happened."

That's what Joanne Leone, a senior investigator with the state police in Wappinger, told the *Poughkeepsie Journal* in 2002—five years after the mysterious murder of Richard Aderson in Fishkill.

Aderson, an assistant superintendent in the Orange County school district of Valley Central, was shot dead on February 5, 1997. He was driving to his home in LaGrange after work when he got into a fender bender just west of the Newburgh-Beacon Bridge. The two cars pulled over onto the shoulder near Exit 12 on I-84 eastbound in Fishkill. Aderson and the other driver got into an argument. Aderson called 911, which recorded a gunshot. The shooter fled east on I-84. Aderson died en route to St. Luke's Hospital in Newburgh. The forty-seven-year-old left behind a wife and three young children.

According to the *Journal*, Aderson was able to describe his assailant and the car he was driving, a late-model green Jeep Cherokee–type vehicle, possibly with New Hampshire license plates. The New York State Police described the suspect as a white male, about six feet tall and then between forty-five and fifty years old. Despite this information and even a segment on TV's *Unsolved Mysteries*, no suspect has ever been identified.

"We're hoping someone will come forward with the information we need," Leone said in 2002. "There's someone this has got to be bothering."

Missing since 2001

On January 24, 2001, at around 11:30 p.m., Anthony Urciuoli Jr., thirty-one, told his parents, Anthony and Sandra, that a friend had paged him and invited him for a game of pool. The next morning, Sandra looked into her son's room. It was empty. "Sandy woke me up and said, 'Tony never came home,'" Anthony told the *Poughkeepsie Journal*. "We still don't know why." Urciuoli has been missing ever since.

The next day a family member found Tony's car in a parking lot at Spratt Park. His wallet was locked inside. There were no signs of a struggle, and no forensic evidence shed light on what had happened or where he had gone. And the police have never been able to trace the page he received the night he disappeared.

Detectives don't know if he was abducted, murdered, or simply ran away. "There's no concrete evidence either way," town detective Michael O'Dell said in 2004. His parents insist it was not plausible for him to leave without warning, and his coworkers at the Dutchess Diner on Route 9, where Tony worked as a waiter for several years, said he was a hardworking, trouble-free employee.

His parents appeared on Montel Williams's TV show with psychic Sylvia Browne in a desperate search for information. They have offered substantial rewards and hired private detectives. They have held vigils in Spratt Park to keep their son's case on everyone's minds.

So far, however, nothing has led them to Tony.

Dutch Schultz's Treasure

His real name was Arthur Flegenheimer, which wouldn't scare a kitten. So he became Dutch Schultz, one of the biggest and baddest gangsters of Prohibition-era America. As for most of his peers, his career choice was lucrative but short-lived. His legend, however, lives on to this day in the village of Phoenicia, where, or so it is believed, Schultz buried a specially constructed metal safe containing diamonds, gold, and millions of dollars in cash—in $1,000 bills—and bonds. Schultz, who once said, "If I had kept the name Flegenheimer, nobody would have heard of me," has managed to keep his name alive in the Hudson Valley to this day.

In the 1930s, Schultz was being pursued by New York's federal prosecutor, Thomas E. Dewey, for tax evasion. According to the book *Dutch Schultz and His Lost Catskills' Treasure*, by John Conway, Schultz "had seen many of his contemporaries put away for various terms in prison, only to come out without a dime and with their former territories taken over by rival thugs, and he was determined to avoid a similar fate. So it was that he ordered his henchmen to gather up the millions he had hoarded over the years and stash it away for the proverbial rainy day."

Schultz eventually beat the tax charges but decided that Dewey needed to be eliminated. He proposed as much to the syndicate of mob bosses, who voted against it. Schultz was furious and vowed to do it anyway. "That fit of temper was enough to convince [Lucky] Luciano and [Meyer] Lansky that Schultz was even more unstable than they had initially believed, and coupled with their own desire to take over the Dutchman's profitable rackets, sealed Schultz's fate," Conway writes. "The Syndicate would eliminate Schultz and his gang before they could eliminate Dewey." Which they did, at the Palace Chop House in Newark, in 1935.

As he lay in his hospital bed, delirious and dying, he rambled incoherently, reportedly mentioning Phoenicia, Liberty bonds in a box, and mysterious woods whose owner will "never know what's hidden in 'em." Those ramblings were recorded by a police stenographer and published.

Soon, there were as many versions of the legend of the buried treasure as there were stories of the Dutchman himself.... Several versions of the treasure tale place the location of the burial ground somewhere along Route 28 between the roadway and the Esopus Creek. Some place it along the railroad tracks leading into Phoenicia. One of the most popular stories is that Schultz and [bodyguard] Lulu Rosenkranz carried a steel safe containing the loot to Phoenicia on an April night in 1933 and buried it in a grove of pine trees near the Esopus, with the obligatory "X" marking the specific tree under which the digging was done.

The Stone Chambers of Putnam County

Are they simply colonial root cellars or Native American dwellings? Or are they evidence of European visitors before Columbus? The answer, of course, depends on whom you ask about the hundreds of stone chambers that dot the Putnam County landscape.

The chambers, which come small and rectangular, large and square, round- and flat-topped, can also be found in Dutchess and Westchester counties and in Connecticut and Vermont. But Putnam County contains the mother lode of stone chambers with no known origin. "Locals have long considered these structures the handiwork of 18th-century farmers who they say built them to store meat, dairy products, and vegetables on farms that have since gone back to forest," the *Times* reported in 2001. More imaginative sorts have "spawned a proliferation of theories about explorers (ancient Celts or Irish monks, Libyan sailors, Iberian adventurers or Phoenician traders) being lured by Putnam's rich iron reserves, and hypothetical uses of the chambers: Viking dwellings, Celtic cathedrals, Indian burial tombs, runaway slave hideouts and witches' hovels." What about aliens from outer space? That has been posited as well.

Many face east to southeast, which leads believers to speculate they were positioned for solstice/religious reasons, while skeptics think the builders simply wanted morning light to do their work. On the other hand, why would early farmers go to so much trouble hauling enormous rocks when there was plenty of wood around to build with?

As with any mystery, neither side wants to give ground on this debate. Stop by one of them—on Cherry Lane, Hosner Mountain Road, Route 301, the Ninham fire tower road, Peekskill Hollow Road, and numerous other locations—and see for yourself. Root cellar or alien landing zone: we report, you decide.

The 1930 Germond Family Murders

On the day before Thanksgiving 1930, a still unknown assailant committed what the Poughkeepsie *Eagle-News* called "Dutchess County's most brutal crime."

"While the Stanfordville countryside slept fitfully in barricaded homes last night, police looked outside Dutchess County for slayer [*sic*] who sometime Wednesday evening, wiped out the simple farm family of James Husted Germond, father, mother, son and daughter," the *Eagle-News* reported the following Saturday.

Germond, forty-seven, who ran a small milk farm during the Depression, and his family—wife, Mabel, forty-seven; daughter, Bernice, eighteen; and son, Raymond, ten—were stabbed a total of twenty-three times with a knife. Their bodies were found the next day, Thanksgiving, after a colleague came by to see why Germond had failed to make milk deliveries.

The first suspect was an "unidentified foreigner" named Florentino Chase, a suspicious fellow who had been seen in the area that day but "fled in a hired auto" to catch a train out of New York City that evening. Other suspects were questioned but never charged. The knife was found a day or two later, but any evidence attached to it—blood, fingerprints—had been destroyed. Evidence at the farm had also been compromised by the thousands of curious people who wandered through the house and grounds in the days following the murders.

Rewards of up to $25,000 were offered for information. In 1933, a neighbor, Arthur Curry, who apparently had a beef with Germond over money or land, was charged with the murders. But evidence was lacking, and the charges were dismissed. The case went cold. In a 2013 private investigation into the murders, a forensics analyst named Vincent P. Cookingham concluded that Curry was the most likely culprit. He also claimed, "This was one of the worse handled [*sic*] cases that I have ever looked into."

The Murdered Landlord

As in any well-constructed whodunit, many people may have wanted L. Richard Rosenberg dead.

Rosenberg, fifty-six, was a real estate and construction magnate with holdings in Dutchess, Orange, and Ulster counties; he had built or renovated nearly 3,000 apartments, and one person told the *Poughkeepsie Journal*, "If you lived in Chelsea, then Rosenberg was probably your landlord."

The landlord was murdered November 9, 1995. He was shot once in the upper torso after leaving his office in the Chelsea Ridge Apartments and died of internal bleeding. There were rumors that he had also been stabbed numerous times, his throat had been cut, and he had actually been shot three times.

"Mr. Rosenberg had enemies in many places," the *Times* reported. "He often spoke out against unions and tenants' groups. Contractors say he tried to renegotiate deals after their work had been done. He sued people and towns often—for rent, to change zoning laws, to fight those fighting his developments. The Dutchess County Clerk's office in Poughkeepsie lists more than sixty cases in which he is listed as the plaintiff (in twenty-two more he is the defendant) dating to 1987. These do not include the few dozen cases where Mr. Rosenberg sued individuals, towns and corporations under one of his corporate names." A contractor who worked for him called Rosenberg "the worst guy to do a job for."

Others called him abrasive, rough, a loner, and a yeller. A former employee told the *Times*, "I always thought if he wasn't giving people heart attacks, he was going to have one."

The UFO Outbreak of the 1980s

In the 1980s, thousands of people throughout the Hudson Valley claimed they saw an unidentified flying object. One of them was my brother.

Rob Levine was working at the Culinary Institute of America in the summer of 1986, after he had graduated from there. Driving home after closing the St. Andrews Café for the night, he saw what he first thought was a low-flying airplane or helicopter. "Then all of a sudden it was much closer," he says. "Then it was further away. The size seemed to vary, and there were colored lights moving around it, like on a blimp."

He pulled over and watched for he doesn't know how long. "I looked up and down the river valley, staring at this," he says. "It seemed to get bigger and smaller, closer and farther, in the blink of an eye. The lights were moving in a V or triangle shape, and colors would change into shapes that looked like unknown letters, like it was trying to communicate something—to who I don't know. And there was no sound whatsoever. There was light coming from it, but it appeared to go from the ground up instead of from the object down. I was, like, this isn't a helicopter."

When he first told me this story, I thought he had dipped a bit too heavily into the cooking sherry at work that night. But could more than 5,000 others—including police officers, professionals, and other highly reputable sources—also have been drinking the same potion in order to report essentially the same thing between 1982 and 1986, making these sightings one of the biggest clusters of UFO reports in history? On March 24, 1983, alone, there were more than three hundred reports, all describing a V-shaped craft adorned with colored lights that hovered slowly and silently in the sky. And these are just the reported sightings; countless others undoubtedly saw something and questioned their own eyes—or sanity.

Like my brother, who, oddly, didn't tell his wife, Amy, or anyone else what he saw that night and then essentially forgot it until he heard an episode of *The Geraldo Rivera Show* several months later. "They were talking about this, and I jumped off the couch and yelled, 'Oh, my god! I saw that!' It came rushing back like a movie flashback. Amy thought I was crazy."

He has since read everything he can find about this and other unexplained flying phenomena. His conclusion: "No conclusion. I can't say for sure it was a spaceship, but it was like no aircraft I ever experienced. I believe in life off planet, so 51 percent of me says it was a UFO, and 49 percent says I'll never know. I hope I live long enough to find out."

So do many others, regarding this and every other mystery of the Hudson Valley.

"I Own a Island!"

*Tiny Iona Island: Native American Fishing Spot,
Dutch Homestead, Failed Vineyard, Amusement
Park, Navy Depot, Nature Preserve*

On a rainy weekend in May, a few dozen hardy and curious hikers gathered at the kiosk by the railroad station near Route 9W in Bear Mountain State Park. There they met Donald "Doc" Bayne, an environmental educator and historian at Sterling Forest State Park. Bayne was about to lead them onto a spot of land in the Hudson River that has intrigued him since he was a teenager.

"I always wondered, What is Iona Island?" says Bayne. "I mean, what is it? I drove out there onto the causeway when I was seventeen—and got thrown out."

Bayne surely isn't the only local to wonder about Iona, which, when the tide is in, is actually a small archipelago of three islands near Doodletown. But he now knows as much as anyone about its colorful history and leads occasional hikes for like-minded naturalists through the otherwise closed-to-the-public preserve.

That history begins at least 3,500 years ago, when Native Americans spent the summers here fishing. "There were seven-pound oysters back then," Bayne says. Native rock shelters still dot what came to be called Rock Island, which joined Salisbury and Round Islands, tidal marshes, and mud flats to make up the bedrock spit of land.

On August 14, 1683, members of the Van Cortlandt family purchased the land from the natives. Dutch ancestors lived there for nearly two hundred years, during which time Salisbury Island was also known as Weygant's Island (for a local family named Weygant or Weiant.) In 1849, a man named John Beveridge bought it for his son-in-law, Dr. E. W. Grant. "When he got the land, he told people, 'I own a island,'" Bayne says. "That's how it got the name."

Grant used the land to grow a type of grape he called Iona grapes. "Turns out they weren't very good grapes," Bayne says. Grant also planted fruit trees and supplied the Union army with produce during the Civil War. That didn't work out so well either, and in 1868 his creditors foreclosed on him. The next year the island was sold to a group of investors and turned into a summer resort. Grant's mansion became a hotel, and the investors gradually added a carousel, a dance floor, and a pavilion. Steamships—up to twenty-five a day, some carrying as many as 2,500 people—came up from New York and New Jersey and deposited weekenders. And in 1882, the West Shore railroad opened, bringing even more visitors. "It was said that during its height you couldn't walk ten feet without stepping on a blanket," Bayne says.

The fun ended in 1899 when the owners sold out to the US Navy, which needed an ammunitions depot. "It supplied most of the munitions for both World War I and II," Bayne says. After the wars, the navy built other depots, and Iona became a storage facility for the Defense Department in the 1950s.

The fun almost returned in the 1960s, when the state bought it as part of the Palisades Interstate Park Commission. Governor Nelson Rockefeller envisioned new boat docks, man-made beaches, and swimming areas. The old buildings were torn down and the island cleaned up. "Then Rocky left office and there was no money," Bayne says.

To naturalists like Bayne, that may have been the best thing to happen to the island and its wetlands since the natives sold it to the patroons. In 1974, Pete Seeger held a concert for Clearwater on the island, and that same year it became a registered National Natural Landmark. It was closed to the public in the 1980s and today looks much like it did before the Europeans arrived. It has become a prime spot for bald eagles to nest, and dozens of other species draw birders and their binoculars from all over. Native animals and plants have returned as well. "It's being reborn, going back to what it was," Bayne says.

And to keep it that way, conservationists are constantly tracking plant and animal species and investigating ways to control invasive plants. What they learn will help those stewarding other protected areas to preserve their natural environments.

"It's really cool," says Bayne, who spotted deer, fox, and "all kinds of birds" during his May excursions. "It's a great thing that the park is doing all this research, and keeping people off the island is important for that reason. It's really a gorgeous place, and people always ask me, 'Why can't we go there?' But after they see it, they understand."

The Old Man and the Rink

The Hudson Valley Loves Hockey, but Playing It When You're Fifty Requires Its Own Grace under Pressure

He is an old man who plays hockey in an old man's hockey league called the Capital District Masters, and he hasn't won a game in many weeks. He knows his luck must change. So he loads his tattered bag of equipment and his banged-up hockey stick into his ten-year-old wagon and drives through the dark and the snow and the ice to Hudson Valley Community College.

He enters the rink. The stands are filled. Young people cheer their college team. "They once cheered us like this," he says to his hockey stick. (The old man talks to inanimate objects often these days.) He enters the locker room. There are other old men like him, grey and soft and round-bellied and far removed from their time. The old man, after all, has been playing hockey since Lyndon Johnson was president.

"Is it a bad sign when you're already winded just putting on your skates?" someone laughs.

"Funny how your feet get farther away every year," another observes.

The old man removes his bifocals and puts on his sports glasses. They are thick and black, and the other old men hoot. "You look like one of the Hanson brothers," one says. "Actually, in high school I *did* look like a Hanson—long, wild hair and all," the old man says. His hair is neither long nor wild now. He looks around the room. But at least I *have* hair, he mutters softly.

He does not, however, have a protective cup. The old man is forgetful. He tells no one. That would be dangerous, because these old men are still boys at heart.

The old man emerges from the locker room. The arena is now empty and silent, save for the rumbling of the Zamboni. The young people have gone. He steps onto the ice and lies down. He must stretch his body's muscles to make them pliant. He doesn't remember having to stretch back when Lyndon Johnson was president or when he looked like a Hanson brother. "But one must do what one must do," he thinks, flat on his back, trying to straighten a balky hamstring. An errant puck clunks him in the helmet.

And then the game begins, and a magical transformation occurs. The old man is suddenly strong and swift and sure. On skates, he is somehow freed from gravity's relentless pull, skimming and skittering across the ice, the sweat flowing, the frigid air filling his lungs, and he remembers why he is here, to be a young lion again, playing with other young lions. "The great Gretzky would understand," he thinks. The old man feels something like grace.

Until he collides with his own teammate and crashes heavily to the ice, losing the puck to an opponent, who takes it and scores against his team. "You are a worthy adversary, Red Team," he mutters. "But tonight we must vanquish you." The old man seeks redemption. Soon, he steals the puck from a foe and shoots and scores. It is good, he thinks.

But not good enough. His Blue Team loses, again.

It is midnight, which is late for the old man, who normally goes to bed by 9 p.m. on a school night. The bruises are starting to show their purples and blacks and yellows. The locker room fills with the sounds of laughter and ripping tape and rending Velcro. Beers are passed around, and aches and pains and indignities are compared. "My knee's a mess." "Can someone untie my skates for me?" "Dammit, I forgot a towel again."

The showers, those that work, are tepid. Muscles tighten, then tighten more as the old man drags himself and his tattered equipment through the cold air to his cold car and drives through the dark and the snow back home. He enters quietly so as not to wake his family and sets his hockey stick against the wall. It immediately crashes to the floor, waking his family.

"Sorry," he whispers. He crawls into bed, exhausted but content. Happy, in fact. This is the best night of his week, even in defeat. What would the great DiMaggio think about that? The old man doesn't care. He tells his pillow an old joke. (He talks to inanimate objects often these days.)

"Do you know why the great DiMaggio played baseball?"

"Because he couldn't play hockey."

Senior Moment

Celebrating (?) a Rite of Passage

"There's good news and some very disturbing news," my wife, Kimberly, says.

We were planning a family trip to Saratoga to have breakfast at the track, play the ponies, and visit the Thoroughbred Racing Museum and Hall of Fame. Kimberly and our daughter, Grace, have been looking into the details.

"The good news," Kimberly says, "is you get a discount to the museum."

"What's the disturbing news?" I ask.

"You're a senior citizen!" Grace gleefully announces.

"At fifty-five?" I ask. Kimberly, also a bit more gleefully than seems appropriate, says, "Yup. The museum gives senior discounts starting at age fifty-five."

"Just breathe, Dad," Grace says.

I breathe. Deeply.

My first reaction: righteous indignation. I ain't no senior citizen, I sniff. I don't fit the profile. "Senior citizen," Wikipedia says, "is a common polite designation for an elderly person in both UK and US English, and it implies or means that the person is retired." *Elderly*? I have a daughter in middle school, for cryin' out loud. *Retired*? I'm in the prime of my working years and retirement is still just a pipe dream. *Polite*? Don't condescend to me, mister. I'm in excellent physical shape, mostly. Sure, my lower back sometimes feels as if rigor mortis has already set in. I have more forehead than I once did. And, yes, on occasion I forget my neighbor's name or where I put my cell phone, or what we had for dinner last night . . . chicken, I think . . . no, we had chicken on Tuesday . . . I wonder if Tuesday Weld is still alive . . . What was I saying?

No matter. The point is this. Wikipedia (see how young I am? I use the Interwebs!) also says the common age for this designation is sixty-five, not fifty-five. I'm not sixty-five, pal—not that there's anything wrong with that—and I have been smugly ignoring the AARP mailings for years. Our collective vision of "senior" is all messed up. No one retires in his fifties anymore, except government workers, and few people are elderly in their sixth decade. Fifty is the new thirty, right?

On the other hand, I'd have to be senile to turn down free money, also right? I'll take their discount if they want to give it to me. In fact, maybe I should reframe this whole deal. Just because someone says I'm a senior doesn't mean I'm a senior. I've been called lots of things that I am not. (Never mind what.) Perhaps this is an opportunity to exploit. The game is afoot.

Where else can I cash in on my newfound seniorhood? The *Senior Citizen Journal* ("Your Partner in Productive Aging") lists many restaurants that cater to me and my allegedly over-the-hill peers. Sadly, I would never eat at any of them. Sorry, Arby's. (Ben & Jerry, however, I'll see you when I'm sixty.) Likewise retail stores. Wait, here's one: Regal Cinemas. They dominate the Albany market. I give them a call to confirm; no, they only discount sixty-somethings. The Spectrum, my theater of choice, starts at sixty-five. Age-ists.

There must be something ... The Albany Tennis Club gives me $25 off membership, but I don't play tennis. I qualify to move to some retirement communities, but my wife couldn't join me for another decade. Hmmm . . . no.

I need some help, fellow geezers. Where in the Hudson Valley can an elderly brother get a *what-what*? In the meantime, I'll just take my $2 discount from the Thoroughbred Racing Museum and treat myself to one of them fancy coffee drinks the kids seem to like.

Now, where did I put my wallet . . .

Weathering Heights

Others Ran, Biked, Skated, and Strolled across the Walkway over the Hudson—Could I?

I didn't used to be a wuss. And I am not sure exactly when I became a wuss. But now, a wuss is what I am. And my wussiness reared its wussy head about fifty yards into my family's initial foray on the Walkway over the Hudson. Hello, my name is David, and I am an acrophobe. I am afraid of heights.

I am not fearful by nature. Really. I have no other phobias. I'll eat just about anything, go just about anywhere. Snakes? No problem. Bugs? Don't love 'em, but happy to kill spiders when my wife asks. Germs? Please—I play hockey, and have you ever been in a hockey locker room?

But about twenty-five years ago, out of the blue, I suddenly got—I believe the technical term is "creeped out"—when driving over a bridge. Looking down from a balcony or rooftop shivered me timbers. I couldn't get within ten feet of a cliff edge. I never had this problem as a kid. I remember thinking, Where the hell did *this* come from? And I still think that every time I feel its wussy presence.

It's not always a logical phobia (which I suppose is an oxymoron, isn't it?). I am fine in airplanes but not so much in cars. Inside the penthouse, I'm all "Look at that view!" Out on the terrace, I am Jell-O in a moving subway.

My family, of course, is well aware of my predicament. "Are you gonna be OK with this," my wife, Kimberly, asked when she saw me slide to the absolute center of the walkway.

"*Imfine*," I barked, in one syllable. Since I was clearly not fine, my daughter, Grace, then asked me, every three minutes or so, "Are you OK daddy?" "Are you OK daddy?" "Are you OK daddy?"

I am going to push through this, I told them. It's not a petrified-stuck-to-the-ground-unable-to-move fear. I just feel a bit queasy. My anxiety needle ticks up a couple of notches, like when the cop car pulls in behind you and follows you for a few moments before he tears off after the other guy.

I am going to make it across, I told myself.

But man, it's *really* high up here . . .

Meanwhile, a grand parade passed me in each direction. Some were on foot—runners, walkers, limpers. Some were on wheels—bikers, skateboarders, rollerbladers, babies in strollers, seniors in wheelchairs. Dogs could do it. Cats could do it. (Yes, someone had a cat on a leash.) All of them seemed completely oblivious to the fact that they were one hundred plus feet above a turbulent river and could . . . could . . .

"Could what, exactly?" I asked myself. Reasoning with a phobia is like arguing with a Fox News fan, but I tried anyway. "Could the bridge collapse?" Short of a major earthquake or terrorist attack, no, it couldn't. "Could you fall off?" Short of the previous two events or you downing a fifth of bourbon, no, you couldn't. "What else you got, 'fraidy cat?" I challenged myself. I knew I had nothing to fear but my fear itself.

Then, just then, a tiny boy, not more than four or five, zipped past me on a tricycle. His head was down, his legs were pumping furiously, he was having the kind of pure fun only a tyke on a trike can have. And he was one hundred plus feet above a turbulent river.

"I said, what else you got, wuss?"

I got nothing.

So I made it to the other side of the river and walked back with my family. I still hewed to the center rivets mostly. But I did edge toward the edge to read the informational placards on each side of the bridge. And by the end, I had found a steady state, a walking rhythm that let me actually enjoy where I was. It really is quite beautiful up there.

Conclusion:
Glory Days

Twenty-Five (Heck, Twenty-Six) Important Events in Hudson Valley History

A Random, Subjective, and Highly Arguable List

11,847 BP (before present time): The Last Ice Age Ends

Okay, this date may be off by a year or two—or a millennium or two. But on some warm summer day 12,000 years ago, give or take, the last icy bits of the great Laurentide ice sheet melted away, leaving behind the wet, rocky, inhospitable land that now constitutes the Hudson Valley. The Laurentide sheet was part of the mile-thick Wisconsin Glacier that stretched, at its maximum about 22,000 years ago, from southeastern Alberta, Canada, across the Great Lakes and over New England. New York City and Long Island sat under the southernmost edge of the glacier and wouldn't look like they do without all the rocks, sediment, and water left behind as it retreated. It's why Cortlandt is hilly and Port Chester is flat, why so-called kettle ponds like Thompson Pond, in Pine Plains, are so cold and deep, and why Long Island exists at all. (You'll learn where to find other remnants of the Ice Age by reading Ice Capades, on page 9.)

1609: Henry Hudson Sails Upriver

This was the Hudson Valley's big bang—for white Europeans, anyway. For many centuries, the *Mahicannituck*, the waters that are never still, were traveled and fished by the *Muhheconneok*, the people of these waters. The elders spoke of strange ships sailing nearby in earlier times (1524 and 1525 on Western calendars), but on September 3, 1609, a ship sailed up the river, into the headlands and 150 miles north, before being turned back by narrow passage and sailing away twenty days later. Over those twenty days the native peoples traded furs with the visitors (and killed one of them with an arrow to the neck). The people could not know that their sacred river would soon bear the name of this man, Henry Hudson, and that Hudson's people and their followers would, within two hundred years, force them from their home forever. (The story as told from the Mahicannituck point of view begins on page 12.)

1657: The Stockade District Established in Kingston

While most of these United States are fully British in history and temperament, the Hudson Valley remains, both at its deepest roots and in more visible ways, Dutch. As early as 1617 or 1618, Fort Nassau had been built near Albany—years before the Pilgrims set sail for the New World. It was succeeded in 1624 by Fort Orange, from where the Dutch colonized the rest of the valley while the Brits were still trying to figure out how to survive in Plymouth. And one of their first and most successful settlements was Wiltwijck, now known as the Stockade District of Kingston.

Wiltwijck sat on a high plain near the effluence of Rondout Creek that was chosen for its defensive advantages. Dutch colonial governor Peter Stuyvesant supervised the construction of the stockade and ordered all settlers to move to the village.

One of just three original Dutch settlements in New York still surrounded by the outline of its stockade, the district remains home to many historic buildings from the seventeenth, eighteenth, and nineteenth centuries, and those structures help trace the history of the Dutch-to-English transition. Indeed, the intersection of Crown and John streets, with colonial-era Dutch stone houses on all four corners, is the only intersection in the country that Stuyvesant himself might still recognize. One doubts, however, that he would recognize Stuyvesant Plaza, up in the outskirts of Fort Orange.

1664: The Dutch Lose Control of New Netherland to the English

This book is in English, not Dutch, because Peter Stuyvesant handed over the keys to New Amsterdam with barely a *strijd*. (That means "struggle," which you'd know if he had mounted one.)

He did this because, quite frankly, he was tired of the headaches. Though legend has it that Peter Minuit bought the land, in 1626, from the native tribe for a bunch of whatever the Dutch word for *tchotchkes* is, Stuyvesant was charged with making the business—and it was, more than anything, a business—run. But continual war with the native peoples up and down the valley made him an unpopular leader. On August 27, 1664, four English frigates sailed into New Amsterdam's harbor and demanded New Netherland's surrender. Stuyvesant wanted to resist the English, but his subjects did not and refused to support him. On September 6 Stuyvesant sent a team of lawyers—proving that nothing has really changed in 350-plus years—to sign the official articles of capitulation.

In June 1665, New Amsterdam was reincorporated under English law as New York City, named after the Duke of York, later King James II. It has remained so, except for a brief return to Dutch rule in 1673–1674, ever since.

But while people now call places like Albany and Kingston home, many others live in Catskill and Yonkers and countless other Dutch-inflected towns and villages from Guilderland to the Bronx. We eat waffles and cookies, play golf, await presents from Santa Claus, and root for the Yankees and Knickerbockers all because the Dutch got here first. Their short but significant reign in North America left no greater legacy than in the Hudson Valley.

1776: The Battle of White Plains

During the run-up to the War for Independence, both Loyalists and revolutionaries occupied what became Westchester County, and after the Continental Army's defeat at the Battle of Long Island, George Washington and his men retreated into the hills around White Plains. British general William Howe's troops advanced from New Rochelle and Scarsdale and, on October 28, engaged Washington at Chatterton Hill (also known as Battle Hill). British and Hessian soldiers charged up the hill from the Bronx River, drove the American troops from the hilltop, and forced them to escape to New Jersey. The loss devastated the area; in 1780, war chronicler Dr. James Thacher described "a country in ruins. A large proportion of the proprietors having abandoned their farms, the few that remain find it impossible to harvest their produce. Banditti, consisting of lawless villains . . . devote themselves to the most cruel pillage and robbery among the defenseless inhabitants between the lines."

1779: The Battle of Stony Point

Saratoga and Yorktown are better known, but the small battle of Stony Point, on July 16, 1779, was critical to America's victory in the Revolutionary War. Here, George Washington displayed his brilliant military mind, boosted his army's morale, gained control of the Hudson River, and secured West Point, all necessary for his later success.

Under Washington's leadership, Brigadier General "Mad" Anthony Wayne's light infantry corps attacked a British redoubt at midnight. They captured the site's fortifications and soldiers in just twenty minutes. The British were so demoralized, Stony Point was the last significant battle in the northern theater. (For more on the battle, flip to "Point Well Taken," page 48.)

The Stony Point Lighthouse, which was built in 1826 and is the oldest lighthouse on the Hudson River, houses a museum with exhibits about the battle, along with reenactments highlighting eighteenth-century military life, cannon and musket firings, cooking demonstrations, children's activities, and blacksmithing demonstrations.

1782: General George Washington Sets Up Shop in Newburgh

Washington really did sleep here. From April 1782 to August 1783, in fact, he lived here while leading the evolution of the revolution, from colonial uprising to the establishment of a new nation.

Following the British surrender at Yorktown in 1781, Washington made his headquarters in the 1750 Jonathan Hasbrouck House, located in Newburgh, overlooking the Hudson River. It was a relatively safe location and near West Point, both important considerations. He moved in on Sunday, March 31, 1782, while the remaining 7,000 troops of the Continental Army were encamped near what is today Vails Gate, a few miles to the southwest.

This was a critical year in the nation's history, and he was the de facto leader of the country. While at Hasbrouck House, Washington rejected the so-called Newburgh Letter, which proposed that the government should be a monarchy and he its king. He ended the Newburgh conspiracy, preventing military control of the neo-nation. He created and awarded the Badge of Military Merit, forerunner of the Purple Heart. He circulated a letter to state governors that influenced the writing of the Constitution. And on April 19, 1783, Washington issued the Proclamation of Peace, which formally ended the war.

The house, which was Washington's longest-serving headquarters during the war, was designated a state historic site in 1961. It is also the oldest house in the city of Newburgh and the first property acquired and preserved by any US state for historic reasons. It is still a popular attraction for tourists and history buffs.

1802: US Military Academy at West Point Founded

Washington considered West Point to be the most important strategic position in America—and who's to argue with the man who wouldn't be king? He personally chose Thaddeus Kościuszko, one of the heroes at the Battles of Saratoga, to design the fortifications for West Point in 1778. After securing the area during the Battle of Stony Point, Washington moved his headquarters there in 1779.

Continental soldiers then built forts, batteries, and redoubts and extended a 150-ton iron chain across the Hudson to control river traffic. The site was so critical, Benedict Arnold tried to sell the plans for it to the British. He rather famously failed. West Point is, in fact, the oldest continuously occupied military post in America.

Many of the war's leaders, including Washington, Henry Knox, Alexander Hamilton, and John Adams, lobbied to create a homegrown institution devoted to the arts and sciences of warfare. In 1802, President Thomas Jefferson signed legislation establishing the US Military Academy at West Point. Its graduates have led our country into battle ever since, including against one another: both Ulysses S. Grant and Robert E. Lee were alumni, no doubt making for an awkward college reunion.

The location may be of less strategic military value in the twenty-first century, but the mission and spirit of West Point remain critical for our defense. And it's one of the Hudson Valley's most visited tourist attractions.

1807: Robert Fulton's *Clermont* Sails up the Hudson River

Advances in transportation have changed history throughout history, from the first humans to tame and ride horses to the jumbo jets that whisk us around the world in just hours. One such transformative leap occurred on August 17, 1807, when a large, noisy, smoky apparition sailed up the Hudson River.

As one eyewitness later recounted, "A knot of villagers was gathered on a high bluff just opposite Poughkeepsie, on the west bank of the Hudson, attracted by the appearance of a strange, dark-looking craft, which was slowly making its way up the river. Some imagined it to be a sea-monster, while others did not hesitate to express their belief that it was a sign of the approaching judgment."

Neither monster nor apocalypse, Fulton's steamship did push the world into the future. The *Clermont* was not the first steamboat to be built, but it was the first to become a practical vessel and to anchor a commercially successful company. And that changed travel and commerce forever. By the mid-1850s there were as many as 1,200 boats sailing in New Orleans alone, and the steamship was transportation's state of the art until the railroads came along.

Not bad, considering the sea-monster took thirty-two hours, including an overnight stop, to sail from New York City to Albany, at an average speed of five miles per hour. Even Amtrak is faster than that. Usually.

1820: "The Legend of Sleepy Hollow" Published

"From the listless repose of the place, and the peculiar character of its inhabitants, who are descendants from the original Dutch settlers, this sequestered glen has long been known by the name of Sleepy Hollow. . . . A drowsy, dreamy influence seems to hang over the land, and to pervade the very atmosphere." So wrote one Diedrich Knickerbocker in the sixth installment of the serial *The Sketch Book of Geoffrey Crayon, Gent.* Both Knickerbocker and Crayon, of course, are pseudonyms for Washington Irving, who almost singlehandedly created America's first and most abiding myths, anchored in Westchester County. The Headless Horseman, by the way, may have been inspired by a real-life Hessian soldier who lost his head to cannon fire during the Battle of White Plains.

1825: Hudson River School of Art Established by Thomas Cole

You know you've made it when the US Post Office puts you on a stamp, and in 2014 that honor befell the painters of the Hudson River School of Art. Widely considered the first uniquely American style of art, the Hudson River School was unofficially opened in the fall of 1825, when a twenty-four-year-old English immigrant and largely self-taught artist named Thomas Cole took a steamboat up the Hudson River, got off at Catskill, and hiked into the Catskill Mountains to make some pencil sketches.

Back home at his father's apartment on Greenwich Street in New York City, he turned those sketches into three large oil paintings, which he put, as the *New York Evening Post* reported on November 22, 1825, "in the hands of Mr. Colman, a picture dealer in the city, for sale, hoping to obtain twenty dollars apiece for them." An artist and collector named John Trumbull soon came by. "On casting his eyes upon one of the pictures by Mr. Cole, he exclaimed, 'where did these come from!' and continued gazing, almost incapable of understanding the answer." He bought one of them for $25, telling the owner to keep the change and adding, "What I now purchase for 25 dollars I would not part with for 25 guineas. I am delighted, and at the same time mortified. This youth has done at once, and without instruction, what I can not do after fifty years of practice."

What Cole had done was channel the nascent, purely American literary movement of transcendentalism and its reverence for nature into images of the Hudson Valley. As the Thomas Cole Historic Site puts it, "His vision of wild and untouched scenery with majestic mountains and tangled forests stood in stark contrast to the gentle landscape images that had come before."

Cole was instantly famous and attracted the attention of both New York's cultural elite and other landscape artists, including Asher Durand, Frederic Church, Sanford Gifford, Jasper Cropsey, and others. Those artists produced images of the valley that captivated the world—as they still do, even on postage stamps.

1842: The Croton Dam and Aqueduct Open

The cholera epidemic of 1832 killed about 4,000 people in New York City and forced city leaders to realize that, as its population neared 1 million, the city needed more clean water. The best source for that was the Croton River. Work began in 1837—and with it, Westchester County was changed forever. On the plus side, the project and other reservoir systems that followed brought new workers, mostly Irish and Italian immigrants, who settled in Westchester. However, later reservoirs created at the end of the nineteenth century, "destroyed or forced the moving of some of the villages that the railroad helped create—Purdys and Katonah, to name just two," says Susan Thompson, town of North Salem historian. Indeed, as city surveyors mapped the dam and aqueduct, about two hundred property owners whose land would be flooded or otherwise disrupted filed complaints in area courts. The city ended up paying them a total of $250,000—for land worth $60,000. When the aqueduct was fully opened on June 27, water flowed into the Yorkville Receiving Reservoir at today's Central Park, witnessed by Governor William Seward and a crowd of 20,000 residents. On July 4, the water made it to the reservoir at 42nd Street and Fifth Avenue, where the main branch of the New York Public Library now stands. That night, about 25,000 residents visited the new reservoir, where they imbibed Croton Cocktails: Westchester water with a twist of lemon.

1844: The New York & Harlem Railroad Opens Service to White Plains

"The arrival of the trains was probably the most important change that Westchester has ever seen," says Bronxville Village historian Eloise Morgan. "Small villages like North Salem's Purdys and Croton Falls came into being and grew up around the railroad stations. To be able to move goods and people by rail changed everything." The dairy farms were early beneficiaries, now that milk could be shipped to the city in one day. But more lasting change came as city residents ventured into the country, liked what they saw, and stayed, turning a rural county into a suburb and farmers into commuters. This railroad, which took its first passengers on December 1, 1844, was soon joined by others like the Hudson and New Haven lines. Thus began the era of mass transit between the city and Westchester, the rest of the valley, and, indeed, the nation.

1882: The Birth of FDR

The Roosevelt name is as iconic as it gets in US history. It's also the most important name in Hudson Valley history, save only—perhaps—for the guy who had that valley named after him.

Do we really need to say more about the man who dominated the first half of the twentieth century, who both guided and transformed the country through not one but two momentous events during four terms as president—often from his sleepy hometown of Hyde Park, New York? In fact, we do—see "The Picnic That Won the War," on page 186.

1888: A Few Friends Play a Round of Golf

Golfers in the Hudson Valley, and in fact all of America, can thank a Scotsman named John Reid and his buddies, who on February 22, 1888, wandered onto a Yonkers pasture and knocked a few balls around a three-hole "course" they designed. They came back again and enlisted an old apple tree to serve as their clubhouse, where they could hang their jackets, and their nineteenth hole, where they enjoyed their flasks of Scotch. Later that year, this auspicious adventure led to the formation of the St. Andrews Golf Club of Yonkers (John Reid, president), the oldest continuously operating golf club in the United States. The USGA and the PGA of America were established in Westchester County, the first national amateur and professional open championships were played here, and one David Mulligan lent his name to the practice that has saved hackers strokes for decades here (and everywhere golfers cheat). The sport was not played here first—that probably happened in South Carolina in the 1730s—but Westchester is universally recognized as the birthplace of modern golf in America.

1923: First Section of Appalachian Trail Opens in Bear Mountain State Park

Hikers had been talking about creating a "super trail" for some time when, in 1921, a man named Benton MacKaye wrote an article called "An Appalachian Trail: A Project in Regional Planning," published in the *Journal of the American Institute of Architects*. He proposed a series of work, study, and farming camps connected by a hiking trail along the ridges of the Appalachian

Mountains, from the highest point in the north (Mount Washington in New Hampshire) to the highest in the south (Mount Mitchell in North Carolina).

A small crew took up the torch and built the first stretch of that trail, from Bear Mountain west through Harriman State Park to Arden. On October 7, 1923, it opened. And almost a century later, hikers continue to pass over these trails on the now 2,174-mile trek from Springer Mountain in Georgia to Mount Katahdin in Maine.

1924: Catskill Aqueduct System Completed

Progress often creates both winners and losers. In 1924, the aqueduct project, which took seventeen years and cost $177 million (about $2.5 billion today) was completed. New York City won. Many small Catskill towns lost—flooded out of existence by the dams and reservoirs created to quench the thirst of the rapidly growing metropolis to their south.

1925: The Bronx River Parkway Opens

It began as an environmental project to turn the polluted Bronx River into a park connecting Bronx Park and the Kensico reservoir. But when chief engineer Jay Downer led the addition of a roadway, which opened to traffic on November 5, 1925, it created the nation's first public parkway designed explicitly for automobile use and became, according to the Westchester County Archives, "a pioneering example of modern motorway development. It combined beauty, safety, and efficiency by reducing the number of dangerous intersections, limiting access from surrounding streets and businesses, and surrounding motorists in a broad swath of landscaped greenery." It also allowed easier access to parts of the county not near the railroad and influenced the development of the other north-south parkways that helped populate the county. "You say Robert Moses? I say Jay Downer first!" says Patrick Raftery, Westchester County Historical Society librarian.

1955: Tappan Zee Bridge Opens

The postwar boom brought Westchester numerous benefits—but traffic was not one of them. Existing bridges and tunnels couldn't keep pace, and by 1950 the Port Authority of New York and New Jersey was considering building a new bridge across the Hudson near Dobbs Ferry. But Governor Thomas E. Dewey wanted a bridge that would link the soon to be born New York State and New England thruways. To do that—and to ensure tolls went into thruway, not Port Authority, coffers—he had to bypass the Port Authority's jurisdiction. Political haggling finally placed the new bridge as near to the city as possible, but outside the twenty-five-mile Port Authority radius—which happens to be the second-widest crossing point in the river, making it more expensive to span. Politics—it was ever thus. Nevertheless, construction began in March 1952, under the design of one Emil Praeger, who had helped design floating caissons for the invasion of Normandy. Traffic first poured over the bridge on December 15, though it wasn't officially named the Tappen Zee Bridge until February 28, 1956. It became an important section of New York's Main Street, which you can read about on page 244.

1963: Newburgh-Beacon Bridge Opens

Just as Fulton's *Clermont* revolutionized transportation and changed the valley's fortunes, so too did the Newburgh-Beacon Bridge, which opened to traffic on November 2, 1963, as a two-lane span.

One day later, 220 years of ferry service, which had served George Washington and both John and Samuel Adams during the Revolutionary War and convinced Washington to set up headquarters nearby before the Battle of Yorktown and to use the site to oversee British withdrawal following Cornwallis's surrender, ended. The last two remaining ferries, the Dutchess and the Orange, met at mid-river at 5 p.m., signaled a final salute, and gave way to the cars that could now pass rapidly over the Hudson—opening up travel to New England as never before—for just $2.

1972: The Culinary Institute of America Moves to the Hudson Valley

This CIA began operation in New Haven in 1946 as the New Haven Restaurant Institute. Its first class: fifty GIs returning from World War II. In 1951, it changed its name to the Culinary Institute of America, and in 1972 it moved to Hyde Park and took over the turn-of-the-century brick edifice that had been the Jesuit seminary St. Andrew-on-Hudson. In doing so, it also launched the valley's transformation into Napa East.

The CIA and its justly famous student-run restaurants are among Dutchess County's top tourist destinations, with more than 250,000 visitors annually. More importantly, the school has married the region's enviable agricultural riches to its culinary mastery, fostering a Hudson Valley farm-to-table movement that rivals the West Coast's in national acclaim.

And many CIA graduates have stayed in the region, giving valley residents a selection of food and beverage options that make the rest of the country's mouths water with envy.

1981: The Scenic Hudson Decision Is Rendered

In January 1963, Consolidated Edison applied to the Federal Power Commission for a license to build a power station at the base of Storm King Mountain, a mile-wide reservoir behind the mountain, and fifteen miles of transmission lines across Putnam and Westchester counties. Little did the utility know that, in doing so, it had launched the modern environmental movement in the area—and, arguably, the nation.

That fall the Scenic Hudson Preservation Conference was formed to stop the project, protect the water supply, and preserve the natural beauty of the area. The battle escalated, but Scenic Hudson, armed with thousands of supporters both locally and nationally and not a few powerful lawyers, refused to back down. After a seventeen-year legal battle in both New York State and federal courtrooms, the two sides settled in December 1980. Con Ed agreed to drop its plans for Storm King, reduce fish kills at Indian Point and other power plants along the Hudson River, and establish a research fund for the Hudson River ecosystem. On July 23, 1981, the Federal Energy Regulatory Commission approved Con Ed's surrender of the Storm King license. "Surrender" indeed.

The effects locally were considerable, but the repercussions for the American conscience were even greater. The Scenic Hudson battle established environmental law as a new and important legal specialty. Better still, it proved that citizens *can* fight the power. And win.

1993: IBM Announces Layoffs

"2,700 fired."

That was the headline in the *Poughkeepsie Journal* on March 31, 1993, the day after IBM announced that, for the first time in its history, it was laying workers off. The mid–Hudson Valley was very much a company town, and Big Blue, the biggest computer maker in the world, was that company. Even though IBM had been downsizing—to use that horribly anodyne term—for years, this was a crushing blow.

IBM settled in the valley in 1941, making aircraft cannons for World War II. It segued into office equipment and, by the mid-1960s, mainframe computers. As *Business Week* wrote in 1995,

> For four decades, IBM thrived—and the Hudson Valley boomed. Kids got high-paying manufacturing work out of high school. Developers devoured the dairy farms around Poughkeepsie, building offices for IBM and housing for the engineers and managers flooding in. Home prices soared, as

did wages. 'Beemers,' as the locals called them, populated local zoning boards and ran charities; their money fueled a vibrant retail sector. And the companies that supplied IBM with parts, engineering services, food, and landscaping slipped into comfortably monogamous relationships with their big benefactor. All of which made the crash, when it arrived, that much more cataclysmic.

Cataclysmic it was. Unemployment tripled, support businesses failed, housing prices collapsed. Approaching thirty years later, the valley is in better shape. But it is not in the same shape. The scars left from Big Blue's departure remain deep and long-lasting.

2009: Walkway over the Hudson Opens

A big bandage over the wounds left by IBM's departure appeared on October 3, 2009, when the Walkway over the Hudson opened as the world's largest pedestrian park on what had once been the world's longest bridge.

The former Poughkeepsie-Highland Railroad Bridge, which began carrying trains across the Hudson in 1889, was the first bridge to cross the river between New York and Albany, and it connected the valley with the rest of the country. It closed in 1974. In a sense, the walkway has helped connect the valley to the world once again. In just ten years it has become perhaps the most popular and important tourist destination here.

The reason for that is, quite literally, easy to see. From its soaring perch, you sense the incomparable beauty of the river and the magnetic power of the valley that captivated its namesake, precisely four hundred years earlier, the beauty and the power that has been pulling humans here since the Ice Age ended. Even acrophobes make the effort; see "Weathering Heights," page 282.

2012: Hurricane Sandy Strikes

On October 29, the most devastating left turn in the area's history brings Hurricane Sandy off the Atlantic Ocean and over Brigantine, New Jersey. By the time its tropical rains, storm surge, and hurricane-force winds subside, Sandy has impacted the entire eastern seaboard, becoming the second-costliest US hurricane since 1900, after Katrina. No place is harder-hit than New York City and its lower Hudson Valley suburbs. The governor's office estimated the storm cost the county and its residents nearly half a billion dollars. Rye Playland's damages totaled $12 million; part of the log flume ride was still floating in the Long Island Sound weeks later. The Tennis Club of Hastings lost its courts and deck. Seaside Johnnies in Rye had eight feet of water in the basement, and the Pier Restaurant and Tiki Bar's freezer was "blown to smithereens, so we had a couple thousand pounds of shrimp strewn across the sea walk area," co-owner John Ambrose said. Like everyone else in the county, though, Ambrose persevered. "We gathered a crew of people to put Humpty Dumpty back together again."

2015: *Hamilton: An American Musical* Opens

Hamilton-mania was launched on August 6, 2015, and Hudson Valley historians have been happily overworked ever since. Historical tourism became a thing, and Alexander Hamilton's deep Hudson Valley roots, especially in Albany—check out that story, on page 44—blossomed into a must-see destination for both history and theater nerds from around the world. When the road show came to Proctor's Theater, in Schenectady, in the summer of 2019, Hamilton, the Schuyler sisters, and the rest of the *dramatis personae* swept up the capital region—especially the Schuyler Mansion, where he lived, and the Albany Institute of History and Art, of which he was an early supporter—into a frenzy of Revolutionary love and hip-hop.

Index

Knickerbocker Ice Company, 150
Knox, Frank, 199
Knox, Gen. Henry, 95
Koprowski, Hilary, 242
Kościuszko, Thaddeus, 52, 54, 289
Kościuszko Uprising, 55
Kregier, Capt. Martin, 27
Kutsher's Hotel and Country Club, 236
Kykuit, estate, 147

L

Lafayette, Marquis de, 45, 54, 56, 90, 92, 121, 223
Lake Albany, 10
Lakeville Iron Trail, 70
Landa, Keith, 5
Lang, Allynne, 86
Last Stop, USA. *See* Camp Shanks
Late Woodland Period, 13
Laurentide Ice Sheet, 10
Lawes, Lewis, 168
Lee, Mother Ann, 141
Leeds, New York, 227
Legend of Sleepy Hollow, The, 291
Lenape, tribe, 13, 15, 26, 28, 201
Lenik, Edward, 67
Leone, Joanne, 270
Letchworth Village, 240, 242
Letchworth, William Pryor, 241
Levine, Rob, 274
Levy, Asser, 31
Levy, Eugene, 214
Lewis, Tom, 245
Liberty, New York, 32
Liberty Street Negro Presbyterian Church, 24
Licameli, Frank, 94
Liederkranz, cheese, 161, 162
Lin, Maya, 207, 208
Lincoln, Abraham, 101, 104, 107, 117
Little, Dr. Charles Sherman, 241
LoBioanco, Joey, 251
Locust Grove Estate, 223
Longfellow, Henry Wadsworth, 131
Long, William J., 212
Loomis, Alfred Lee, 201, 203, 204
Louis XIV, 35
Louis XVI, 56
Luciano, Lucky, 167

Luddington, Sybil, 128
Ludington, Col. Henry, 72
Lundberg, James P., 96
Lyndhurst, estate, 147

M

Mabee, Carlton, 114
MacAulay, Lorraine, 90
MacCracken, Henry Noble, 122
MacFarlan, Daniel, 103
Machin, Thomas, 51
Macy Pavilion, 183
Madam Brett Homestead, 89
Madison, James, 97, 108
Magnetic Telegraph Company, 223
magnetite, 67
Mahicannituck River, 12, 26
Maihafer, Henry, 267
Malaria, 132
Mamaroneck, New York, 32
Manchester, Connecticut, 6
Mandracchia, James, 40
Manhattan Project, the, 201
Mann, Steven, 170
Marshall, Thurgood, 25
Martin, Peter, 256
mastodon, 8
Matteawan Hospital for the Criminally Insane, 262
McEntee, Jervis, 232, 233
McGeorge, Corrine, 241
McGill, Joseph, 21
McNally, Eliza Margaret. *See* Halliday, Lizzie Brown
McVickar, John, 124
Meachum, Father Joseph, 142
Mehling, Carl, 4
Melville, Herman, 83
Mesozoic Era, 2, 3
microwave radar, 203
Milholland, Inez, 219
Mill Street Synagogue, 32
Millay, Edna St. Vincent, 218, 219, 220, 221
Mills Mansion. *See* Staatsburgh State Historic Site
Mills, Ogden Livingston, 184
Mintz, Ward, 232
missing persons, 267

Sterling Iron and Railway Company, 68
Sterling Iron Works, 53
Sterling Mountain Railway Company, 69
Stern, H. Peter, 207
Stern, John P., 207
Steuben Memorial Historic Site, 57
Steuben, New York, 57
Stockade District, 287
Stockbridge, Massachusetts, 17
Stockbridge-Munsee Mohican nation, 17
stone chambers, Putnam County, 272
Stony Point Battlefield, 48
Stony Point, New York, 50, 242
Storm King Art Center, 206
Stovall, Josephine, 199
Stowe, Harriet Beecher, 117
Stroudsburg, Pennsylvania, 8
Suckley, Daisy, 188
Suffern, New York, 32
Sullivan County, 260, 261, 262
Sullivan, Ned, 109
Sunnyside, estate, 146, 147
Sutton, Willie, 167
Swallow, steamboat, 86
Swartekill, estate, 115
Sylvis, William H., 93
Synagogue of Shearith Israel, 32
synapsids, 4
Syndicate, the, 271
Sypher, Sallie, 129

T
Tadeusz Kościuszko. *See* Kościuszko, Thaddeus
Taft, Dr. Charles Sabin, 105
Tappan Zee Bridge, 146, 197, 294
Tappen, Christopher, 51
Tarrytown, New York, 32
Tayler, Judge John, 47
telegraph, 132, 194, 222, 223, 224, 225
Teller, Alice Schenck, 90
Teller Mansion, 90
Tewksbury, Donald G., 127
Thacher State Park, 8
Thatcher, Dr. James, 288
Thaw, Harry K., 199
Therapods, 5
Thiells, New York, 240, 241
Thing, Lowell, 233

Thomas Ellison House, 45
Thompson, Susan, 292
Thruway, the, 244, 245, 246
Tilley, Chris, 253
Tilly Foster Mine, 68
Titus, Johanna, 9
Titus, Robert, 9
Tode, Adolphe, 161
Town & Country, 131
Townsend, Peter, 53, 68, 69
Townsend II, Peter, 69
Treaty of Ghent, 97
Triassic period, 3, 4
Trombini brothers, the, 171
Troy, New York, 92, 97, 103, 249
Truman, Harry S., 199
Truth, Sojourner, 24, 114, 115, 116, 117
Tuxedo Park, 201, 203
Tzu, Sun, 71

U
UFO, 274, 275
Ulrich, Laurel Thatcher, 89
Ulster County, 23, 26, 27, 63, 114, 116, 117, 128, 134, 135, 157, 159, 182, 183, 232
Ulster, New York, 23
Uncle Sam, 98
Underground Railroad, 24, 82
Underhill, John, 16
Union Church of Pocantico Hills, 147
United States Military Academy at West Point, 61
Urcioli, Anthony, 270
U.S. Base Hospital 38. *See* Westchester Medical Center
U.S. Colored Infantry's 20th Regiment, 24
US Military Academy, 55, 94, 97, 215, 267, 289

V
Valley Forge, Pennsylvania, 57
Van Bergen Overmantel, 21
Vanderbilt, Alva, 185
Vanderbilt, Frederick William, 148
Vanderbilt Mansion National Historic Site, 9, 10
Vanderbilt National Historic Site, 148
Vanderbilt, William Henry, 148

About the Author

PHOTO BY GRACE LEVINE

David Levine is a freelance writer and editor. He is the author, coauthor, or ghostwriter of six sports books, including *Life on the Rim* and *In the Land of Giants*. He writes about everything from history and business to beer and whiskey as a contributing writer for *Hudson Valley*, *Westchester*, and *914INC.* magazines. He has written about health and medicine, law, business, and sports for many publications, including the *New York Times*, *Sports Illustrated*, *U.S. News and World Report*, *American Heritage*, *Governing*, *New York Daily News Sunday Magazine*, and dozens of other publications, and his work has been selected for two editions of *Best Sports Stories*. He lives in Albany, New York, with his wife, Kimberly, daughter, Grace, and diabetic dog, Sadie.